KU-592-931

Captain Scott's Invaluable Assistant
EDGAR EVANS

ISOBEL
WILLIAMS

The
History
Press

This book is dedicated to Gary Gregor whose knowledge about Edgar Evans and whose enthusiasm for the work has been a constant source of encouragement

Front cover photograph: Edgar Evans dressed for exploration. (Courtesy of Scott Polar Research Institute – SPRI)

First published 2012
Reprinted 2012

The History Press
The Mill, Brimscombe Port
Stroud, Gloucestershire, GL5 2QG
www.thehistorypress.co.uk

© Isobel Williams, 2012

The right of Isobel Williams to be identified as the Author
of this work has been asserted in accordance with the
Copyrights, Designs and Patents Act 1988.

All rights reserved. No part of this book may be reprinted
or reproduced or utilised in any form or by any electronic,
mechanical or other means, now known or hereafter invented,
including photocopying and recording, or in any information
storage or retrieval system, without the permission in writing
from the Publishers.

British Library Cataloguing in Publication Data.
A catalogue record for this book is available from the British Library.

ISBN 978 0 7524 5845 8

Typesetting and origination by The History Press
Printed in Great Britain

Captain Scott's Invaluable Assistant

Contents

Acknowledgements

Dr David Wilson, the great-nephew of Dr Edward Wilson, Scott's confidant and friend, has been a remarkable source of friendship, encouragement and advice throughout the work. My colleagues, Dr John Millard, Dr Howell Lloyd and Dr Aileen Adams, have diligently read the work and offered helpful comments, as has Mrs Jackie McDowell.

Professor Stuart Malin has patiently guided me through the intricacies of longitude and latitude. Lieutenant Commander Brian Witts, Curator of HMS *Excellent* Museum, Portsmouth, assisted me with details of the field gun run competition at Olympia. I am greatly indebted to these colleagues and friends. I accept responsibility for any misunderstandings or omissions.

The assistance of the staff at the Scott Polar Research Institute, The Naval Museum at Portsmouth and the Swansea Library has been greatly appreciated; all have been unfailingly courteous, helpful and enthusiastic.

Alison Stockton and James Oram, a Classics Undergraduate at Durham University, have patiently proofread the work and I am grateful for their help.

I have to thank Professor Julian Dowdeswell, Director of the Scott Polar Institute, for permission to publish extracts from those manuscripts over which the Institute has rights, also the Debenham, Shackleton, Skelton and Scott families for kind permission to quote from family papers. The Auckland Institute and Museum of New Zealand have allowed me to quote from Charles Ford's journals as have the Dundee Art Galleries and Museums in relation to James Duncan's papers. Mr John Evans, Edgar's grandson, has allowed me to quote from Edgar's sledging journal. Every reasonable effort has been made to trace copyright holders; any omissions or mistakes will be inserted into subsequent editions of this work.

Finally, my thanks must go to my husband, Dr David Williams, whose assistance and help made this work possible.

Introduction

Saturday 17 February 1912, Antarctica.

A man crawls helplessly on the icy snow, his clothes are torn open, his skis are off, his gloves and boots lie discarded on the snow, bandages trail from his frostbitten fingers.

He dimly sees four images coming towards him, but in his confusion he cannot work out what is happening. When his companions arrive he can hardly speak. He can barely stand and after a hopeless attempt at walking he falls back onto the snow. Three of his exhausted rescuers plod back wearily to the camp for a sledge.

They lay him on the sledge and struggle to pull him over the snowy waste. On the way he loses consciousness. He is never to be aware of his surroundings again. In the tent, as his companions watch, his breathing becomes irregular and shallow; he dies quietly at 10 p.m.[1]

So ended the life of Edgar Evans, the 'Welsh Giant' from Middleton in South Wales, a man who contributed hugely to Antarctic exploration, a Petty Officer who had built a relationship with his leader, Robert Falcon Scott, that transcended the barriers of class, rank and education. Theirs was a loyalty that had been built over long periods of interdependence as they endured the horrors of prolonged man-hauling at sub-zero temperatures in Antarctica.

Scott wrote that Edgar was a 'giant worker with a truly remarkable head piece',[2] that Edgar was 'hard and sound' on a trek and had an 'inexhaustible supply of anecdotes'.[3] He chose Edgar as one of the five to go to the Pole.

Edgar died on the return, overcome by circumstances so awful that his four companions were soon to join him in icy tombs in Antarctica.

This is Edgar Evans' story.

Notes

1 Ed. King, H.G.R., Edward Wilson *Diary of the Terra Nova Expedition to the Antarctic 1910–1912*, Blandford Press, London, 1972, p. 243.
2 Ed. Jones, M. *Robert Falcon Scott Journals Scott's Last Expedition*, Oxford University Press, Oxford, 2005, p. 369.
3 Ibid., p. 303.

1

The Gower Peninsula: Early Life

Edgar Evans came from the Gower Peninsula in South Wales. Jutting into the Bristol Channel and open to the Atlantic gales, Gower is a place of outstanding natural beauty, a location that attracts visitors to its shores year after year. It boasts other famous attractions: in one of its coastal caves, the Paviland Cave, the oldest human skeleton in the British Isles was discovered – the 'Red Lady of Paviland'[1] (actually male remains) is tens of thousands of years old.

It would have been a remarkable astrologer who foretold fame for Edgar Evans when he was born on 7 March 1876 in Middleton Hall Cottage, Middleton – a village in Rhossili and one of the remote parishes on the peninsula. Edgar's mother, Sarah, had moved to Middleton Cottage, her sister's home, for her confinement.

This was a modest family. Their roots were firmly in Gower. Evans' paternal grandfather, Thomas, and three previous generations of his family, came from the peninsula. Thomas was employed in a local limestone quarry (limestone was shipped across the Bristol Channel to fertilise the fields of north Devon). Thomas' son, Charles (1839–1907), the father of Edgar Evans, was one of the famous 'Cape Horners', hardy seamen who sailed from Europe around Cape Horn to the west coast of America, a journey that could last six months.

The 'Cape Horn' trade grew because Swansea was then the world centre for smelting copper, essential in industry, construction and ship-building (the copper covering on ships' hulls prevented the wood from rotting and made the vessels faster).

There were copper works in Swansea from as early as 1717. Approximately 2 tons of coal was necessary to smelt 1 ton of copper, and since South Wales was rich in coal, copper was brought to Swansea rather than coal being taken to the copper sources. When British ore was worked out, copper mines further afield were sought and Cuba and South American countries, particularly Chile, were used. These voyages to South America, in coal-carrying sailing ships, were hazardous undertakings. Life at sea was brutal and unforgiving. Off the Horn, with 'winds at full-gale strength, waves as high as the maintops, sometimes hail and then snow coming down thick, clouds so low they enfold the mastheads, spume and sky indistinguishable',[2] forward progress was often impossible, some days the ship was set back by miles. Sometimes the voyage lasted four months, often much longer and many men died on the 'widow-making' passage. Added to the physical horrors of the crossing was the ever-lurking possibility of spontaneous combustion of the coal, likely to be disastrous in wooden ships and more probable if the coal was damp. After managing to survive the voyage, the sailors still had to contend with the perils of disease in South American ports. And then, having endured all that, the sailors faced the daunting prospect of the return journey. Years later, one of Edgar's companions in the Antarctic wrote that only those who had had the experience could realise what it meant: handling frozen sails in the dark, short handed … and 'so cold that the chocks (fittings for securing the ropes) have to be thawed with hot water before a rope will run through them'.[3]

But Charles Evans pursued this trade until he was in his mid-30s, well after the time he married and had children. In 1862, when he was 23, Charles, described as 'Mariner, son of Thomas Evans, Quarryman', married Sarah Beynon in St Mary's church, in the village of Rhossili. Rhossili is one of the many villages dotted over Gower. It had 294 residents[4] and was connected to its closest neighbour by just a muddy lane. Sarah was a local girl, the daughter of William Beynon, the licensee of the Ship Inn in Middleton, and his wife, Ann. She was 22 at the time of her marriage and her family had held the licence for the Ship Inn for most of the nineteenth century.

The ceremony was performed by the Reverend John Ponsonby Lucas BA, MA, an Oxford graduate, who ministered to several of the local villages. St Mary's, with its beautiful Norman doorway, remains an active, functioning church. For many years a plaque in the aisle wall has proudly commemorated the life of Charles and Sarah's famous son, Edgar.

As was usual in Victorian households, the couple produced a large family – there were eight known children. Birth control was unknown in working class communities in the late 1800s, and a high birth rate was a type of insurance policy against an unsupported old age. Four of the children are listed in the 1871 census: Charles, 7; John, 4 (both described as scholars); Mary-Ann, 2; and Annie Jane aged 1. The gap of three years between Charles and John suggests an infant death. In 1874, another son, Arthur, was born, followed, in 1876, by Edgar. A seventh child, George, was born in 1878 and a sister, Eliza Jane, in 1879. In fact Sarah Evans gave birth to more than the eight children; in 1913, after Edgar's death, she was interviewed by a local reporter, and exhibiting stoicism difficult to imagine nowadays, she said that she had buried nine of her twelve children, three having died from consumption.[5]

Mrs Sarah Evans registered the birth of her fourth son in the sub-district of Gower Western on 13 April 1876. The 7 March was recorded as the birth date and Mrs Evans, unable to write (as was common, even six years after compulsory education was introduced),[6] recorded her mark with a cross.

Interestingly, when Edgar entered the navy in April 1891, his Certificate of Service states that his date of birth was 9 March. Probably, once the error was officially recorded, the Boy, 2nd Class, then aged 15 years and 37 (or 39) days, thought it more prudent to go along with the official record than to challenge it, and he never corrected the date, although he is likely to have been aware of his registered birth date. Years later, in 1911, he wrote in his diary on 9 March, when he was on a sortie, that it was the 'first time he has spent his birthday sledging'.[7]

Edgar was born into a small, tight-knit community. In the pre-First World War era, many people stayed within a few miles of their birthplace for the whole of their lives, and there was a huge interconnection of families through marriage. Sarah Evans had family links with many people in her village as well as brothers and sisters, some of whom were still living at the Ship Inn. So Edgar was born into a ready-made network of uncles, aunts, grandparents and cousins, as well as the immediate family crowded into his family's cottage, which housed up to four of his older brothers and sisters as well as the babies, George and Eliza Jane. In addition, his father added to the crush on his intermittent visits home.

He learnt to speak in English as Welsh was hardly ever heard on that part of the peninsula. There must have been some incomers in Gower over the years because the villagers spoke in the 'Gower Dialect'. This dialect, now virtually forgotten, had evolved through the influence of settlers from south-west England.

As a little lad he kept well out of the way of the local dignitaries; when the doctor visited on horseback or, occasionally, driving his horse and trap which carried the brightly coloured bottles of medicine that could be prescribed for virtually every ailment (since many of the residents could not read they were thought to be particularly impressed by the colours), Edgar took care to avoid him. Likewise, the Rector was an important local man. The Evans family were definitely 'Church' rather than 'Chapel' (the place of worship for the local Methodists). It is surprising nowadays to read of the chasm that existed between the two in some parts of the country (reminiscent of the Catholic/Protestant divide in Northern Ireland), but in Gower the division was only a pale and peaceful reflection of those clashes. When the Reverend John Ponsonby Lucas had married Edgar's parents, he gave a girl a lift in his pony and trap, a journey of about an hour, but he was forbidden to speak to her because he was of the established Church whilst she was a Nonconformist.

By the 1881 census the family had moved to Pitton, the next small hamlet east of Rhossili. As was usual, only the people actually in the house on the day the census was recorded were counted, and Mrs Evans, 'Mariners Wife', registered her four younger children, now including Edgar, aged 5, as 'scholar' at the village school at Middleton. Forster's Elementary Education Act of 1870 had stipulated that all children between the ages of 5 and 12 were obliged to attend school. The thrust behind this act was the fear that Britain's status in the world could be threatened by the lack of an efficient national education system. It was a move by no means universally welcomed; there were fears that education would make members of the labouring classes, such as the Evans family, 'think' and so become dissatisfied with their lot. The Church also had doubts; its support for the biblical story of creation (which implies, amongst other things, that we are born to the station that we are meant to remain in) resulted in reservations. Also, the Church was already the recipient of state money for educating the poor and was reluctant to relinquish this. But once the Act was law, children were educated perforce. Edgar would be at Standard 1. He learnt his letters from an elementary reading book by copying a line of writing, in 'good, round, upward writing', and later wrote a few common words from dictation. He did simple addition and subtraction (of not more than four figures), as well as learning his multiplication tables (up to 6). Strict instruction was given on how to hold a pen – in the right hand with the thumb nearly underneath and three fingers flat out on the top; if his teacher saw him with one of his fingers bent he would have been rewarded by a rap on the knuckles.[8] Edgar certainly benefited from the education he was given before he left school at the age of 12. His writing in later years was clear and his prose concise. The only thing that seems to have escaped his attention is punctuation; sentences flow effortlessly and sometimes confusingly, one into another.

In 1883, when his father Charles was 44, the family moved their home again. By now Charles had left long-haul shipping and was employed on a boat *The Sunlight*, which was involved in local coastal work based in Swansea, so the Evans family moved to the town. Swansea was important; it was part of the nation's 'workshop of the world' and also known as 'Copperopolis' because of the prominence of the copper trade. The family moved to Hoskin's Place, Swansea. They would have lived in one of the thousands of identical 'two up, two down' little terraced houses, with a communal back yard and 'privy'. It is not clear just how many of the family made the move to Swansea; only the four youngest are recorded as being in the house on the 1881 census, but it is unlikely that Edgar's 13-year-old sister Mary Anne or 11-year-old Annie would have left home by 1883, so it is probable that seven or eight Evans members (at least) shared the overcrowded facilities. Life was not easy. When coal could be afforded, the downstairs room was warmed by a coal fire, which was an integral part of an iron oven. Food was scarce: homemade bread and pies, meat once a week if possible, and potatoes. Water was heated by the stove and a tin bath (decorously concealed behind a clotheshorse decked with washing for privacy), was used for the weekly or fortnightly baths. Three or four members of the family used the same water.

With its population of over 50,000, busy streets, horse traffic, pollution from the copper works and noise, the town must have come as a shock to the country children; a huge contrast to sparsely populated Rhossili.

Young Edgar was enrolled at St Helen's School, Vincent Street, Swansea and remained there until he was 13. The school had just been enlarged when 7-year-old Edgar enrolled as a pupil and, with its 250 pupils, it too must have seemed huge. The life of the school and the education it offered is described by N.L. Thomas in a centenary booklet, *A Hundred Years in School, St Helen's 1874–1974*,[9] which shows how very fortunate Edgar and his fellow pupils were to fall under the influence of an enlightened, humane headmaster, Mr Lewis Schleswick. This was an opportunity certainly not enjoyed by all Victorian children. Mr Schleswick's service was stretched; he had a small staff, certified assistants, uncertified assistants and pupil teachers[10] and, to keep the teaching standards as high as possible, he taught the pupil teachers each morning before school began. The school remains. It is proud of its famous old boy and has Edgar's picture prominently displayed.

As the school year progressed, Edgar, no doubt with the other pupils, was tempted by those infrequent but exciting diversions which lightened the drab routine of the Victorian school room, and often (as the daily school roll recorded) cut school attendance dramatically. Many of the children had to work for their parents before and after school. By a young age they were accustomed to a life of repetitive monotony and any glamorous excitement must have been a glorious break. Such delights were visits by circuses to the St Helen's area, the occasional fair, regattas at Mumbles and Swansea, Saint Patrick's Day[11] celebrations (when school attendance was noticeably small) and, on occasion, processions. Once, after a Sunday school outing, over one hundred boys were absent. The reason given by the miscreants, according to Mr Schleswick, was that they were too tired to get to school.[12] Occasionally, however, absences were official. When General William Booth, the founder of the Salvation Army, visited Swansea in 1883, the school was given a half-day holiday and when there was a large public procession in relation to the Blue Ribbon Movement,[13] the boys were allowed time off to watch it. The headmaster wrote that not only the pupils but also the pupil teachers were given an official day's holiday as a reward for their 'unremitting zeal and energy'.[14]

Attendance could fall for more serious reasons. Mr Schleswick recorded that the summer of 1885 was exceptionally hot and it was difficult to keep the boys at their work as they were in a 'state of exhaustion'. The area around St Helen's was overcrowded, poor and susceptible to disease. Typhoid fever, that curse of unsanitary water supplies, attacked the school

in 1896 'in spite of the drains being regularly disinfected by the Urban
Sanitary Authority'. When Mr Schleswick inspected the drinking-water
cistern, he found that it was filled with a deposit, to the depth of an inch
and had a dirty filter.[15] Other infectious diseases extracted a heavy toll: an
outbreak of measles would close the school for three weeks,[16] scarlet fever,
that harbinger of rheumatic fever, sinus and ear infections, also visited
regularly. Boys from houses where infection lurked were sent home to
reduce the risk of cross contamination in this pre-antibiotic era, but death
was a common caller. In 1887, there was a drought which had an impact
both by causing dehydration and because the boys drank infected water.
On this occasion wily local entrepreneurs profited by collecting barrels
of water from springs in the countryside and transporting and selling the
water to whichever urbanite could afford to buy it.

The end of the school day was the signal for those boys, who did not
have to work for their parents, to escape to freedom. They made their own
entertainment; since there were no cars or buses, but only slowly moving
horse drawn vehicles, they could play on the street: trundling hoops,
whipping tops or just standing in the middle of the street and gossip-
ing. St Helen's was close to Swansea Bay, famous for oysters, but probably
of more interest to the boys as a glorious beach playground for football
and swimming. Sundays were rest days. Edgar went with his family to
Sunday school during the day and church in the evening. They all wore
their 'Sunday best' clothes for the church visit.

Soon after his tenth birthday Edgar became a 'half timer'. This exploita-
tive use of cheap child labour meant that school time was cut, so that Edgar
spent half the day at school, half at work. For his work he earned about
a shilling (approximately £5 in current value) a week. He was relatively
lucky. Fourteen years previously he could have been working as a 'half
timer' from the age of 8.[17] So Edgar's total education was five years full-
time (from 5 to 10), thereafter three years of half-time education. Nothing
highlights the difference between the privileged and working classes of
Victorian England better than their educational opportunities. By the
time he was 10, Edgar, an intelligent child, would have been competent
in the basic subjects: able to read, write to dictation and do arithmetic.
Later he would have been introduced to a smattering of more interesting
topics: geometry and geography.[18] He would have been used to the idea of
homework or 'home lessons'. He would have sung – the Welsh are natural
singers – and St Helen's had a tradition for music and singing and the

pupils were examined on their prowess.[19] But his formal education was virtually at its end. By contrast, Dr Edward Wilson, who served with Edgar on both Scott's expeditions as an officer and who came from a privileged background, was (although an average student) immersed in Latin, Greek, English, arithmetic and spelling by the age of 10.[20] And Wilson's education would continue for many more years. Education for the upper classes provided shibboleths to enter into a society that was virtually closed for people of Edgar's education. His was the class that sailed the ships, worked the mines, smelted the ore and so underpinned for Britain those social and economic foundations that maintained her pre-eminence in the world. But the country was (in the main) proud of the Empire and proud to serve Queen and Country, and Edgar would have imbibed this pride.

From 1886, Edgar worked as a telegraph messenger boy in Swansea's head post office. He carried his bag around Swansea delivering telegrams. His hours were long and tiring, and a fellow pupil from the 1880s recalls working till 10.30 at night.[21] After Edgar's death, his photograph, taken after his first Antarctic sortie, was displayed in the Swansea Head Post Office for many years. The photograph shows a good-looking young man. He was described as having blue eyes and a 'fresh' complexion.[22] He was clean-shaven with brown hair, a straight nose, a strong jaw and a generous mouth.

The Head Post Master of 1886 decreed that messenger boys began their day with musket-duty and Edgar, between the ages of 10 to 13, was drilled and marched in procession, carrying his musket on his shoulders. A big event of 1887 was the visit of W.E. Gladstone[23] (Victoria's former Prime Minister) to Swansea to open a local Public Free Library. By now the boys were sufficiently drilled to march in procession to the library. How much they appreciated Gladstone's speech on Irish Home Rule is not recorded.

Behind the post office was the North Dock. Here ships from exotic destinations would tie up and the boys were sometimes allowed on board. They would badger the sailors with questions, their imagination soaring along with stories of lands and adventures far, far beyond the confines of Swansea. Edgar had never been out of Gower. These visiting seamen and his father's stories nurtured his determination to see the world, to become a sailor. In his early teenage years he decided that he would join the Navy as soon as they would have him.

However, he had to curb his impatience for a few years. In the meantime his mother took him to visit her family in Middleton. The journey was a step back in time for the newly sophisticated urbanite. To get there they had to travel by road to Pitton Cross and then brave the rigours of a high-banked, muddy, narrow lane, just wide enough for a horse and cart. But the Gower Coast had attractions other than family visits for a young boy. It was littered with wrecks: schooners, paddle ships, barques, oyster boats and ketches.[24] Over fifty vessels – from a French vessel in 1557, to the Norwegian Barque *Helvetia* in 1887 – were known to have foundered in its treacherous waters. Edgar was 11 when the *Helvetia* ran aground in the southern part of the bay. He was enthralled at the story of her battle against the elements. On this occasion there were no fatalities, but her cargo of timber floated onto the beach and every available man, boy, horse and cart spent days loading the wood. *Helvetia*'s bare wooden ribs can be clearly seen today, sticking out of the sand in Rhossili Bay.

When he was 13, half-time work finished and Edgar left school for full-time employment in the Castle Hotel. Many of the captains of those copper ore barques berthed at North Dock actually frequented the hotel[25] and their stories must have strengthened Edgar's resolve to join the Navy. He read the *Boys' Own Paper* (a relentless recruiting agent for the Navy), too.[26] By now he was so keen to see the world that he actually tried to join up when he was 14. He was refused but returned to the Castle Hotel announcing, 'I am coming back to you for another year and then I am going to join the Navy.'[27]

His parents were dismayed. Sarah Evans had known the hardship of bringing up (and probably already burying) her children with a husband away for months at a time. Charles Evans also tried to dissuade his son; he had had to have a leg amputated after it was damaged in an accident on his ship. But Edgar was determined. As soon as he could, at the age of 15, he applied to join the Navy.

The die was cast.

Notes

1 Investigated in 1823 by the Reverend William Buckland (1784–1856), Professor of Geology at Oxford, an eminent palaeontologist, who, because he was a Creationist and thought that no human remains could be older than the Biblical Great Flood, hugely underestimated the age of his find.

2 Lundy, D., *The Way Of A Ship*, Jonathan Cape, London, 2002, p. 15.

3 Wild, J.R.F., Letter to Mrs Bostock. SPRI MS 1078/3/1;D.

4 Lee, S., *The Population of Rhossili* Gower, IV. Swansea, 1951, p. 27.

5 *South Wales Daily Post*, Tuesday 18 February: 'Consumption' is tuberculosis, then endemic and causing death in over half its victims.

6 Forster's Education Act. Drafted by William Forster, a Liberal Member of Parliament and introduced on 17 February 1870. The act provided elementary education for children aged 5–12. Parents were still expected to pay fees, though if they were poor, the board of each school would pay.

7 *Edgar Evans' Journal*, 27/1/11–12/3/11, SPRI: Ms 1487: BJ 9/3/11.

8 Thomas, N.L., *A Hundred Years in School, St Helen's, 1874–1974*, Souvenir Centenary Booklet, held at Swansea Library, 1974, p. 22.

9 Thomas, N.L., *A Hundred Years in School, St Helen's 1874–1974*, Souvenir Centenary Booklet, held at Swansea Library, 1974.

10 Pupil Teachers. Students who also taught.

11 The Patron Saint of Ireland.

12 Thomas, N.L., *A Hundred Years in School, St Helens 1874–1974*, Souvenir Centenary Booklet, held at Swansea Library, 1974, p. 2.

13 A Temperance Union.

14 Thomas, N.L., *A Hundred Years in School, St Helen's 1874–1974*, Souvenir Centenary Booklet, held at Swansea Library, 1974, p. 15.

15 Ibid., p. 17.

16 Ibid., p. 15.

17 Factory Act of 1874.

18 Thomas, N.L., *A Hundred Years in School*, St Helen's 1874–1974, Souvenir Centenary Booklet, 1974, held at Swansea Library, p. 22.

19 Ibid., p. 19.

20 Williams, I., *With Scott in the Antarctic Edward Wilson, Explorer, Naturalist, Artist*, The History Press, Gloucestershire, 2009, p. 25.

21 Thomas, N.L., *A Hundred Years in School, St Helen's 1874–1974*, Souvenir Centenary Booklet, held at Swansea Library, 1974. p. 22.

22 The National Archives, Service Certificate (No.160225) Ref. ADM 188/235.

23 William Ewart Gladstone (1809–1898). Liberal politician and repeatedly Victoria's Prime Minister. At the time of his visit to Swansea he was out of office, but was later to serve his final, fourth term.

24 *Gower, The Treacherous Coast*. Map based on the original idea and research by Mike Downie. © Mike Downie, 1985.

25 A three-masted ship.

26 Winton, J., *Hurrah For The Life Of A Sailor, Life on the lower deck of the Victorian Navy*, Michael Joseph Limited, London, 1977, p. 288.

27 Gregor, G.C., *Swansea's Antarctic Explorer, Edgar Evans, 1876–1912*. Swansea City Council, Swansea, 1995, p. 9.

2

The Boy Sailor: Naval Training

He did not have to wait long. The 5 April 1891, soon after his 15th birthday, saw Edgar attending his medical examination. Rules for medical fitness to enter the navy were laxer than today. A boy had to be without a physical deformity and to be able to speak clearly; he had to have good eyesight, colour vision and good hearing in both ears. There should be no obvious signs of injury to the head and he should not be of 'weak intellect'.[1] Boys who could read and write clearly were favoured.[2]

The navy wanted boys with 'good heart and lungs' and without any hernias or 'tendency thereto'. There should be no disease or malformation of the genital organs.[3]

Of particular interest to Edgar were the regulations concerning teeth. These stipulated that boys below the age of 17 could have *seven* defective (decayed) teeth. Entrants over 17 could have *ten* problematic teeth, the only proviso being that all ages had to have four sound, opposing molars (two in each jaw) and the same number of incisors similarly placed.[4] Dental hygiene was little practised in the 1890s and tooth decay was commonplace. Young people in the United Kingdom frequently had all their teeth removed as a 21st birthday present (an option clearly not open to would-be sailors), to avoid the infection, pain and expense of dental work. Edgar had eight decayed teeth.[5] He presumably had to have these (or at least some of them) attended to before he was finally accepted after a special application.[6]

His career began on the training establishment for Royal Navy Boy Seamen, HMS *Impregnable*, on the 15 April 1891 for three days.[7] After this Edgar Evans, Boy 2nd Class, official number 160225, was transferred to the wooden training ship HMS *Ganges*.[8] Edgar's Certificate of Service continued until 17 February 1912, when, as Chief Petty Officer, he was discharged, 'lost in British Antarctic Expedition'.[9] Roland Huntford denigrates Edgar Evans in his book *Scott and Amundsen*, by writing that over the years he turned into a 'beery womaniser', exposed to the risk of venereal disease.[10] This might imply absences during his training, but Edgar's naval Certificate of Service records no evidence of this, rather a seamless progress through the ranks.[11] His 'Character and Efficiency' throughout this time is described as being 'Very Good', except for 1897 and 1899 when it was 'Good'.[12]

Edgar started his new life at a time when Britain's commercial and imperial power was at its zenith and the navy an important guardian of that power. But as there had been no major sea battle since the Battle of Trafalgar, Britain faced no obvious rivals and the service was perceived to be stagnating and becoming hidebound by tradition.[13] It was also becoming a subject for national debate. The Naval Defence Act (1889) authorised the expenditure of £21,000,000 on the navy and the building of seventy-two new warships. The navy was to be on a scale 'at least equal to the naval strength of any other two countries'.[14]

The navy was becoming fashionable, too. The Royal Naval Exhibition of 1891 was hugely popular; visited by over 2.5 million people, it aimed to draw attention to important aspects of naval life and history. Attractions in the exhibition included a life-size model of the lower deck of HMS *Victory* at Trafalgar (showing the death of Nelson), an area for field gun drill and manoeuvres, a lake with two miniature battleships fighting out naval engagements, a 167ft model of the Eddystone lighthouse,[15] relics from Arctic expeditions and a fleet of fifty model silver ships.[16] In 1893 the Navy Records Society was first published. This publication featured historical documents that illustrated the prestigious history of the Royal Navy and in 1894 the Navy League[17] was established. This aimed to underline Britain's status as a world peace power, to promote public awareness of the country's dependence on the sea and to emphasize the fact that a powerful navy was necessary to maintain that power. The League stated that the primary aim of national policy was the command of the sea.[18]

Bluejackets (enlisted men with Edgar amongst them) were becoming the sentimentalised nation's darlings and nautical dramas, such as *Black Eyed Susan, True Blue and HMS Pinafore*, became popular.[19] Even Edgar, a 15-year-old 'boy', could share in this nationalistic pride. Indeed, in the popular imagination the British 'tar' was the envy of the world. Led properly, 'he would go anywhere, do anything and do it with a will'.[20] When Queen Victoria's Golden Jubilee Naval Review took place in 1887, the *Daily Telegraph* wrote that the people loved their navy and believed in it.

The reality of training was very different from this imperialistic, jingoistic attitude. Many a fond hope for adventure and excitement must have been irredeemably crushed within hours of entering the service. *Ganges*, which Edgar joined in 1891 with his parents' consent, was an old hulk in Falmouth, Cornwall, which served as a training establishment for Boy Cadets. Later, at 18, he signed for a further twelve years (in his case from 9 March 1894 to 9 March 1906) and then at the age of 30 he signed on for a further ten years. This second signing was essential because twenty-two years actual service (gaps due to illness or for other reasons were not counted) was the minimum required for a sailor to be eligible for a pension.[21]

Reading the accounts of life on the *Ganges* as recorded in extracts from the *Falmouth Packet Newspaper 1866–1899*, and reading personal accounts of the life endured by the Boys, is like looking through the two ends of a telescope. Both are undoubtedly true, but the training, aimed at toughening the boys, was harsh and often cruel. It must have often seemed overwhelming to the 15-year-old boy, now classified as Boy 2nd Class, and to the thousands of other Boys who went through the system.

There was no soft introduction. From the moment he was on board Edgar was caught up in the everyday routine. First he was told how and where to sling his hammock, then issued with his kit (for which he had an allowance: £6 in 1891, lesser amounts in 1893 and 1906).[22] His civilian clothes were sold and he was introduced to the overcrowded, under-ventilated, unsanitary ship that was to be his base for the next year. The kit issued was quite extensive; over sixty items are listed in the *Navy List* for 1891, including jacket, jerseys, trousers, hats and caps, boots, bed and covers, a knife and two lanyards (ropes worn around the neck for securing whistles or knives). Intriguingly, two 'cholera belts' are listed; these are bands of flannel, sometimes with strips of copper in them, to be worn around the waist and thought to increase 'bodily resistance'.[23] It is not clear whether these were issued routinely against the possible perils of the training ships or held back for use in the east.

The Boys all had a 'Housewife' containing needles, buttons, thread and cotton, so that they could keep their kit in the condition demanded by the service.

In their day-to-day existence the Boys were entirely at the mercy of their Instructors. Lionel Yexley, a Boy on HMS *Impregnable* just a few years before Edgar joined HMS *Ganges*, recorded an existence that would have been similar to Edgar's experience. The day began at 5.30 a.m. when, wakened by the shrill notes of the Bosun's pipes and with his hammock safely slung and his kit in place, he was given a ship's biscuit, plus a basin of hot cocoa with a little sugar. These biscuits were staple naval diet; they were routinely and famously full of weevils – little beetles, which swarmed out and floated in the cocoa when the biscuit was dunked in it. Breakfast came only after the Boys had worked for several hours scrubbing the decks. For this activity they had to pull their trousers above their knees and were not allowed to wear shoes or socks, even on the coldest days.[24] Breakfast was a hulk of bread with a scraping of butter or dripping (on another ship, HMS *Vincent*, at about this time, no Boy was allowed his bread ration until he had collected two hundred cockroaches to exchange for the food). The meal was followed by sail drill and mast and yard drill, considered important in spite of the fact that there were few sail-driven war ships by the 1890s, although, as it happens, this training was to be of particular relevance to Edgar. He was instructed in all aspects of sail maintenance: shortening and setting, loosing and furling sails. Later he would learn about the rigging, climb the mast and gain knowledge of the hull.

After this came the prayers, read by the Captain or Chaplain, followed by gunnery training, with the Instructors concentrating on muzzle loading cannons similar to those used at Trafalgar.[25] The Boys still had Cutlass drill.[26]

At 11.30 a.m. the instruction finished and the Boys fell in to witness the daily punishments. Flogging was abolished in Britain in 1891, partially due to the long-term efforts of a man with indirect connections to Edgar, Sir Clements Markham, 'father' of Scott's first Antarctic expedition, but the cane, the birch and the rope's-end (the stonnicky), were feared symbols of discipline. 'Miscreants' were whipped with a cane bound at both ends with waxed twine to prevent splitting. They were punished for offences that seem minor today: no chinstrap sewn on the cap, a button off the trousers or being 'slack' at falling in. For this ordeal, hammocks were lashed into a cross shape, the Boy to be caned had his shirt drawn up around his waist, leaving only his duck (heavy cotton) trousers to protect his buttocks from the vicious cane. Usually the punishment was six to nine cuts and the weals took about ten days to heal. Serious offences (theft or desertion) were punished by the birch, up to twenty-four strokes being permitted.[27] This was an appalling punishment. In 1892 on the training ship HMS *Boscawen* in Portland, the birch was pickled in brine; this made it tougher, so that it caused more tearing and laceration of the skin (on this ship, the Corporals apparently took it in turns to administer alternate strokes, laughing as they did so).

After this terrifying experience, those with any appetite had their dinner. The Boys prepared this themselves and took it to the overworked galley cooks to be put in the oven. They ate meat and potatoes with occasional helpings of cabbage or doughboys.

The final meal of the day was at 3.30 p.m., thus giving a literal interpretation to the word 'breakfast' the following morning. Tea consisted of bread and treacle (the treacle often being taken by the strongest bully, it was considered that actually getting hold of the food was a wonderful way of encouraging initiative), washed down by tea.

Even this meagre provision of foodstuffs depended on the weather being good enough for the supply boat to get to *Ganges*. If the weather was bad, the diet reverted to salt beef, canned pork and the weevily ship's biscuit. Although officially vegetables were provided every day, the food given to the Boys seems like a subsistence allowance and it is difficult to see how some of them did not succumb to deficiency diseases such as scurvy. However there was probably was no evidence of full-blown nutritional disorders; those who survived the system and wrote their memoirs do not record deficiency illnesses. No questions were asked in Parliament about malnourished Boys.

The afternoon was spent in further instruction; tying knots and splicing, more sail and arms drill, boat handling. There was also a little instruction in reading, writing, arithmetic, geography, religious instruction and also naval history, though Edgar's formal education had been virtually completed by the time he entered the service. After 4 p.m. there was recreation: drill, dumb bells, Indian clubs, football on the shore in the summer (though the time available was limited in Edgar's time as British Summertime was not introduced until many years later). When he went back on board *Ganges* he had to mend his own clothes and then he could pass the evening with draughts, ludo (a board game with dice) and reading. Remarkably Edgar remained a keen reader – his schoolmaster at St Helen's had done well.

Life on *Ganges* was endured without heating and with candles and oil lamps to light the evening hours. The Boys had a bath each week. *Ganges* had six baths; everyone went through them in turn with no change in the cold water and the Boys had to wash their clothes in the same water too, which quickly became black from their dirt and from the dye in blue serge uniforms. After the bath the Boys were lined up for inspection by their instructor. They were only too keen to look clean; the instructor was aided in his inspection by his stonnicky, the fearsome symbol of authority.

It was considered that sailors should be able to swim. Though this is entirely reasonable, the methods employed seem horrendous to the modern reader. A sort of bathing tray was lowered by the side of the ship, a large crate with the boards at the bottom set apart so that water got in. Barnacles (small organisms with sharp shells) were put on the bottom, so that once a Boy was in the water he was committed to try and swim if he wanted to avoid his feet being cut by the barnacles. In this respect Edgar was lucky; he was used to the sea whereas many unlucky Boys came from the countryside and had never been in water. Indeed, the authorities felt very strongly about swimming; in one training ship those Boys who still could not swim after thirteen months were flogged. A Parliamentary Question revealed that, after this, only six unfortunates still failed the test.[28]

It was not all repetitive training. There were other activities. Efforts were obviously made to enliven the Boy's lives; for example singing was thought to be good for the boys and Edgar was a tuneful singer. It was written that 'the songs of home never sounded sweeter than when heard far away from home'[29] and the Chief Instructor for Singing (under the School Board for London) visited Boys' training ships to recommend a suitable selection of songs; *A Life on the Ocean Wave, Britannia, the Pride of the Oceans* or *We'll soon sight the Isle of Wight my Boys* were popular. In 1890 the Bandmaster of *Ganges* edited the *Royal Naval Song Book*, a collection of fifty national melodies and a naval song book has been in print ever since. In the *Falmouth Packet*, newspaper reports on *Ganges*' activities, singing and recitations are mentioned frequently. Also there were concerts. Remarkably, Offenbach's one-act operetta, *The Two blind Men (Les deux Aveugles)*, was performed (in English)[30] and theatricals and lantern slides were put on, in addition to cricket matches, boat races, football matches and sports days (the name of 'Evans' appears in the report on the prize-giving of 27 May 1893 as coming second in the sack race,[31] but he did not shine athletically when he was training on *Ganges*).The Boys could have breaks from the ship, if they had anywhere to go to: half days on Sundays and, if their parents could afford it, two weeks in the summer and four weeks at Christmas.

This was the life that Edgar entered to. It is no wonder that years later he said that although he practically ran away to join the navy, he was sorry he had done so for the first two years were so arduous, despite getting used to it after that.[32] He was on *Ganges* for twelve months. By 1892, newly promoted to Boy 1st Class on 21 April, he would have enough practical knowledge to be sent to sailing brigs which cruised along the south coast of England and down to Spain for six weeks. His thin uniform offered poor protection against the conditions at sea. He had not yet reached his full height of 5ft 10in, and at 5ft 6in[33] he probably would have just been able to stand upright between the decks.

In spite of the modernisation to be introduced by that naval innovator, Admiral Sir Jackie Fisher,[34] for the likes of Edgar the discipline and routine remained horribly traditional. One contemporary, a lad named Fred Parsons, who was 15 in 1893 when Edgar was 17, described how he and his mates were fed with pork from a cask stamped 1805 and how, when he cried out when a marine stepped on his bare toe, he was disciplined to six cuts of the cane, for 'talking rather than hoisting'. He wrote that the cane was not struck straight down, but rotated in a half circle so that the exposed flesh was struck as the cane travelled upwards, which was more painful. Fred wrote that he held out till the third stroke when he let out a scream that brought the upper deck to a standstill.[35]

In January 1893 Edgar was transferred to HMS *Trafalgar*, a battleship of 11,940 tons, carrying twenty-nine guns of various descriptions and six torpedo tubes. *Trafalgar* was the second flagship of the Mediterranean Fleet and based in Malta. At 17 Edgar was at last beginning to see the world. A brief spell on HMS *Cruiser*[36] was followed by a return to *Trafalgar* where, in March 1894, he was promoted to Ordinary Seaman. This is the lowest rank in the navy and marks the beginning of his official naval career. He was 18 (and now described in official records as having 'a device' on his right forearm and a stabbed heart on his left forearm).[37]

The next stage up the promotion ladder from Ordinary Seaman is Able Seaman and Edgar, having presented himself to *Trafalgar*'s Captain for an examination of his skills in seamanship, sail reefing, knotting and his familiarity and ability to work on any part of the ship, was duly promoted in July 1895. He remained on *Trafalgar* for a further ten months, until May 1896, when he was transferred back to shore barracks in Portsmouth, firstly at HMS *Vivid*. *Vivid* was a new establishment, thought by some in the naval hierarchy to be so expensively and lavishly built that it was a complete waste of money (it had gas lighting, electric bells, good washing facilities and an immense drill hall where Edgar exercised). Edgar then had a barrack transfer to HMS *Victory*, whose most famous engagement, he learnt, had been the Battle of Trafalgar in 1805.

In September 1896 he was transferred to HMS *Excellent*, another shore establishment and the Royal Naval Gunnery School at Whale Island, where he was taught the principles and practice of firing and maintaining naval guns. Whale Island still values its connection with Edgar. An accommodation block for Warrant Officers and Senior Ratings was named after him in the 1960s, the first ever to be named after a Petty Officer (rather than an Admiral). The buildings were replaced in the 1990s; Edgar's name was honoured by a plaque commemorating his service. He remained at the shore base *Excellent* and another 'stone frigate' HMS *Vernon* until May 1898. *Vernon* was the home of the Royal Navy's torpedo branch, based independently but near to HMS *Excellent*. In his three months at *Vernon*, Edgar learnt about torpedoes and the art and purpose of firing these missiles from battleships. So by the time of his next posting, Able Seaman Edgar Evans had received training in gunnery and torpedoes.

Upward progression was continued when Edgar became a Leading Seaman. The Queen's Regulations and Admiralty instructions state that 'Men who are thorough seamen, good helms-men, able to assist in repairing sails and practical riggers capable of doing duty in any part of the Ship, may be examined for the rating of Leading Seamen. If found qualified, the Captain may rate them as such, as vacancies occur for that description of men in the complement'.[38] Edgar passed this milestone in June 1898 when he was on the shore establishment HMS *Pembroke*. The only blemish in his exemplary record occurred during a three-month stint on HMS *The Duke of Wellington*, a gun ship, from 1 April to 26 June 1899. He was demoted back to Able Seaman by his Captain for twenty days (6–26 June) and for a further three days when he was transferred to the battleship HMS *Majestic*.[39] After this he is re-registered as Leading Seaman again. As the time is of short duration, the misdemeanour must have been a minor one.

Majestic was awe-inspiring. She was the largest battleship in existence. She had forty-four guns of different sizes, five torpedo tubes and a crew of 700 and led the Channel and Atlantic Fleet. The Commander of the Fleet was Vice Admiral, Prince Louis of Battenberg, GCB, GCVO, KCMG, PC,[40] probably called something less respectful by the lower deck. The torpedo officer on this tremendous warship was the man who was to shape Edgar's destiny, Lieutenant Robert Falcon Scott. Edgar's basic training in gunnery and torpedo work immediately put him into contact with Scott as he served on *Majestic* in the Channel Fleet for the next two years.

When Scott was given command of the British Antarctic Expedition and of *Discovery*, the Admiralty gave permission for naval men to apply to join the expedition, which aimed to penetrate the unknown mysteries of the Antarctic and amass as much scientific and geographic information as possible, about that part of Antarctica that had been seen in the 1840s by James Clark Ross. Scott always felt that he wanted a Royal Naval crew; men in the Merchant Navy were less drilled in the rigid hierarchy of command than the Royal Navy. He knew that there would be volunteers and when Edgar, as well as Petty Officer David Silver Allan and Stoker Arthur Lester Quartley from *Majestic*, volunteered, all three were appointed. Edgar's long association with Scott and the Antarctic had begun.

Scott knew that the bluejackets would bring the sense of naval discipline with which he was familiar. In fact, as *Discovery* was not in government employment, her crew was not legally subject to the Naval Discipline Act, but they signed on voluntarily under Scott's command. Everyone on board must have been aware of the real position and the men, as well as the officers, deserve credit for observing this 'fiction'.

Edgar had one more step up the promotion ladder before he sailed in *Discovery*; he was promoted to Petty Officer 2nd Class on 18 November 1900. (Later, on Scott's recommendation on 2 April 1904, he was promoted to Petty Officer 1st Class and allowed to qualify as a gunner. To complete this advance he had to pass a further 'Education Certificate' in 1908).[41] Petty Officers were, and are, the Sergeants of the navy. They are in charge of the seamen and the daily working routine of the ship. They are selected from Leading Seamen, preference being given to those who had signed on for continuous service (as Edgar had done), and they may have special skills (for example a stoker or carpenter). Edgar was classified as a Seaman Petty Officer, Gunnery Class. For his promotion Edgar had to take the examination laid down by the Admiralty; he had to show knowledge of the King's

Regulations, he had to have an understanding of the principles of seamanship and be considered capable of enforcing regulations on board.

Edgar's service record shows a man of ability, intelligence and determination. Scott valued him from the start. He valued Edgar's intelligence, physical strength and practical ability, but also his kind spirit and good nature.[42] Edgar repaid him with a loyalty that lasted to their deaths on the ill-fated return from the South Pole in 1912.

Notes

1   The Queen's Regulations and Admiralty Instruction for the Government of Her Majesty's Naval Service. Her Majesty's Stationery Office, London, Regulation 1153: 1899, p. 514.

2   Ibid., 1861, Chapter IX, Para.2.

3   Ibid., Regulation 1154, section 6, p. 514.

4   Ibid., Regulation 1154, section h, p. 516.

5   Gregor, G.C. *Swansea's Antarctic Explorer, Edgar Evans, 1876–1912*, Swansea City Council, 1995, p.11.

6   *Cambria Daily Leader*, 13 February 1913.

7   HMS *Impregnable* was a training establishment started in Davenport in 1862. As ships were added to the establishment each was renamed *Impregnable*. The ship in Edgar's day had been previously named HMS *Howe*.

8   *Ganges* was commissioned in 1821. She had seen a good deal of action and was the last sailing ship to sail as a Flagship.

9   The National Archives, Service Record (No. 160225), Ref. ADM188/235.

10 Huntford, R., *Scott and Amundsen*, Hodder and Stoughton, London, Sydney, Auckland, Toronto, 1979, p. 328.

11 Edgar was kept on the ledger of HMS *President* when he was on Scott's second expedition of 1910–12. National Archives, Service Record (No. 160225), Ref. ADM 188/235.

12 Certificate of Service. D.N.A. 3A/S.R. Official number. 160225. Portsmouth Division.

13 Carew, A., *The Lower Deck of the Royal Navy 1900–1939,* Manchester University Press, 1981, p. xiv.

14 Winton, J., *Hurrah For The Life Of A Sailor, Life on the lower deck of the Victorian Navy*, Michael Joseph, London, 1977, p. 287.

15 Eddystone Lighthouse. Lighthouse built to protect mariners from the treacherous Eddystone rocks in Cornwall. This was the fourth lighthouse here. It was designed by James Douglas in 1880.

16 Winton, J., *Hurrah For The Life Of A Sailor, Life on the lower deck of the Victorian Navy*, Michael Joseph, London, 1977, p. 292.

17 The Navy League was established in 1894.

18 Winton, J., *Hurrah For The Life Of A Sailor, Life on the lower deck of the Victorian Navy*, Michael Joseph, London, 1977, p. 287.

19 Ibid., p. 288.

20 Ibid., p. 301.

21 Carew, A., *The Lower Deck of the Royal Navy 1900–1939,* Manchester University Press, Manchester,1981, p. xvii.

22 The National Archives, Service Record (No. 160225), Ref. ADM188/235.

23 *Navy List, corrected to March 1891,* Her Majesty's Stationery Office, London, 1891, p. 576.

24 Boys only wore shoes and socks with their best uniform or when they were ashore or visiting the sickbay. Summers, D.L., *One hundred years of training Boys for the Royal Navy.* HMS *Ganges,* Shotty Gate, Suffolk, 1966, p. 34.

25 Ibid., p. 35.

26 Phillipson, D., *Band of Brothers: Boy Seamen in the Royal Navy 1800–1956,* Sutton Publishing, Gloucestershire, 1966, p. 18.

27 Summers, D.L., *One hundred years of training Boys for the Royal Navy.* HMS *Ganges,* Shotty Gate, Suffolk, 1966, p. 35.

28 Ibid., p.40.

29 Winton, J., *Hurrah For The Life Of A Sailor, Life on the lower deck of the Victorian Navy*, Michael Joseph Limited, London, 1977, p. 297.

30 HMS *Ganges,* Mylor. Extracts from the Falmouth Packet Newspaper, 1866–1899. Compiled by Harwood, B. HMS Ganges Association, Cornwall Division. 05/03/1891.

31 Ibid., 27/05/1893.

32 Debenham, F., *Journal,* 19/01/1911–08/03/1911 MS 279/2: BJp, p. 15.

33 The National Archives, Service Record (No. 160225), Ref. ADM188/235.

34 Admiral Sir Jackie Fisher. When Edgar entered the navy Fisher was in charge of the Portsmouth Naval Dockyard.

35 Winton, J., *Hurrah For The Life Of A Sailor, Life on the lower deck of the Victorian Navy*, Michael Joseph, London, 1977, p. 297.

36 HMS *Cruiser* was an Osprey-class sloop that Edgar served on from May until August 1893.

37 The National Archives, Service Record (No. 160225), Ref. ADM188/235.

38 *Queen's Regulations and Admiralty Instructions 1861* Chapter VII. Regulation 13.

39 The National Archives, Service Record (No. 160225), Ref. ADM188/235.

40 Louis of Battenberg, GCB (Knight Grand Cross); GCVO (Grand Cross of the Victorian Order); KCMG (Knight Commander of St Michael and St George); PC (Privy Councellor); (1854–1921), Ist Marquess of Milford Haven and Grandfather of Prince Phillip, Duke of Edinburgh, the husband of Queen Elizabeth the Second.

41 The National Archives, Education Certificate number 1025/08.

42 Bernacchi, L., Saga, London, p. 96.

3

The *Discovery* Expedition

Much has been written about the Scott's journeys in the early 1900s yet relatively little about the contribution of the seamen to their achievements. Yet the expeditions' successes self-evidently depended on the men's huge contributions, amongst which Edgar Evans' input can be ranked with the highest.

Edgar was following Scott, his commander, rather than a geographical target when he joined the British National Antarctic Expedition, the *Discovery* expedition. Other destinations would have been as acceptable. Almost certainly he knew where the Antarctic was – that large white mass on the bottom of the globe – but if he knew little more than this, he was on par with the majority of British citizens. Antarctica had been described by Captain James Cook, on his second voyage of 1772–75, as lands doomed by nature to everlasting frigidness, never to feel the warmth of the sun's rays and the land mass had been identified by subsequent explorers. It had been visited briefly by a number of expeditions: the Norwegian Borchgrevink claimed to have planted the first footstep on its icy surface when he leapt out of his rowing boat in 1895. Later, in 1899, he led an expedition, funded by the British newspaper magnate George

Newnes, which landed and overwintered on Cape Adare. But sorties to the interior had been limited to a short trip on the Barrier; no expedition had penetrated into the heart of Antarctica. Its geography was obscure; was it the mythical seventh continent, or a series of islands? Was the South Pole on land or water? Edgar would probably have read about previous expeditions and would have known about these uncertainties; he would also have heard that more was known about the moon than about Antarctica.

But 1901 was planned as the year for exploration and discovery in Antarctica. There was to be scientific cooperation between nations: Great Britain, Germany, Scotland and Sweden planned explorations and aimed to pool their scientific findings. Of these expeditions *Discovery* was the most successful in making inroads into Antarctica, but the continent would take decades more to reveal her secrets.

Today we know that Antarctica is a continent; the coldest, windiest and most remote place on earth, it occupies a tenth of the world's landmass and is covered by an icecap that (as Scott's team discovered), flows slowly towards the surrounding oceans. It has very little rain (less than the Sahara Desert) and has few indigenous inhabitants, though visited regularly by varieties of penguins, seals, birds and whales. These facts would, of course, have become of interest to Edgar and his fellow crew-members, but in a peripheral way. Their focus was more immediate and practical: to obey orders, to maintain discipline, to be cheerful, and to rise to any crisis that might befall the ship or the expedition.

In Britain, plans for the expedition aroused national interest. Apart from grants from the government and The Royal Geographical Society (including a huge private donation from one of its Fellows), large and small donations were received from all over the country. Thousands applied to become part of the voyage; there were 3,000 applications from the navy alone[1] and Edgar was elated to be part of the patriotic voyage. When, on Tuesday 6 August at 11.30 a.m. precisely, *Discovery* slipped her moorings and sailed for Madeira, the young Edgar was an obscure, 25-year-old Petty Officer (2nd Class). By the time *Discovery* returned to England three years later, he had become a national hero, a local lad made good, written about glowingly in the South Wales newspapers,[2] a modest young man who had sailed to South Africa, New Zealand and Antarctica and remained on the Antarctic continent for over two years, enduring the worst conditions that it could throw at him. By 1904, he had contributed to seven sledge journeys totalling 174 days (a record only beaten by Scott) and experienced the horrors of man-hauling at sub-zero temperatures. He had become a man of new knowledge and experience.

However, in August 1901, none of the crew could be certain that *Discovery* would even reach Antarctica (in 1897 the Belgian vessel *Belgica* had been trapped in Antarctic ice for thirteen months). They did know, however, that in *Discovery* they had a ship that had been especially built for the Antarctic conditions. The ship was the brainchild of one man, Sir Clements Markham (1830–1916), who for years had pursued his vision of Antarctic exploration with determination, tenacity and astuteness. By 1900 Sir Clements had managed to get enough support from the government and other sources to commission his purpose-designed, 1,600-ton *Discovery* – a coal-fired ship, rigged as a barque.[3] Her name was deliberately chosen to 'continue the spirit of maritime enterprise' which Sir Clements felt had always been a distinguishing feature of the British nation.[4] She was painted black, her profile lightened by yellow masts and funnel and white boats painted with a 'D' in black and gold. She was constructed of wood (which would flex when ice pressed against it); her bow was essentially 11ft of oak with sheathing of ironbark, which allowed her to function as an icebreaker, and along her sides were two outer layers of wood, about 26in thick, to protect from glancing ice blows. Water could be drained from the engine to prevent freezing, and both rudder and the screw could be detached and brought into the ship if need be in icy conditions, as was done later in the voyage.

One reason that the expedition finally received government subsidies related to the need to advance work on terrestrial magnetism. The Magnetic Pole is not in a static position – it moves each year – yet an accurate assessment of its position was needed to calculate longitude. In the early 1900s movement of the Magnetic Pole caused significant problems (and therefore concerns for commercial shipping) in the Southern Ocean. Ships sometimes went miles out of their optimal routes and one of *Discovery*'s briefs was to investigate the location of the Magnetic Pole. Edgar was well aware of this difficulty; his father's Cape Horn voyages via the Southern Ocean to South America had all too much experience of the problem. So *Discovery* was equipped with a magnetic observatory, and to ensure accurate recordings no iron or steel was allowed within 30ft (fore, aft, either side, above and below) of the magnetic instruments. Inside the 30ft radius, copper was used and, instead of wire in the rigging, ropes were made of hemp and in the cabins the beds were made of rolled brass with wooden battens. Officers within the circle were threatened with having to shave with brass razors. The zoological and biological laboratories on either side of the meteorological observatory were not allowed any iron tools or even steel-wire bottlebrushes.

In 1900 Robert Falcon Scott, then a relatively unknown Lieutenant, was appointed to lead the British National Antarctic Expedition. There was never any question that Scott's expedition was to have scientific as well as exploratory ambitions; the support of the Royal Geographic Society and the Royal Society (who were interested in the behaviour of tides, currents, glaciers and southern weather), had been an important factor in Sir Clements Markham obtaining government finance. The expedition was instructed to investigate whether or not an Antarctic Continent actually existed, thereafter to investigate the position of the South Magnetic Pole, record those problematic southern winds and currents and study the geography, meteorology and physics of the region. A determination to claim as much land as possible for Great Britain would have been heartily endorsed by Edgar and his comrades.

Scott knew that bluejackets[5] would bring naval discipline to the venture. In total, thirty-two personnel were appointed to *Discovery* from the Royal Navy and two from the Royal Naval Reserve: Officers, an Officer/ Engineer, a Bosun, Petty Officers, Able Seamen, Royal Marines, Stokers, a Steward and a Carpenter.[6] Edgar, as well as David Silver Allan (Petty Officer), Arthur Lester Quartley (a Leading Stoker) and James Dellbridge, the 2nd engineer, had served with Scott on *Majestic* and were quickly appointed when they volunteered. Although *Discovery* was run as if she sailed under the Naval Discipline Act, she was not in fact in Government employment. This was not a problem for Edgar; his appointment was a simple continuation of his naval appointment (as was the case for the other naval men, a substantial form of government support). During the *Discovery* expedition his records show he was on the pay roll of HMS *President*, seconded to the National Antarctic Expedition. All the crew signed voluntarily under Scott's command. Scott wrote that the success of the expedition was not due to a single individual, but to the loyal cooperation of all the members. He paid tribute to the petty officers and men who had worked so cheerfully and loyally for the general good.

Discovery was launched in Dundee on 3 June 1901. The imagination of the nation was caught as she progressed around the coast towards the East India Dock in London, her progress cheered by thousands on land. Edgar joined his ship on 27 July 1901. He was immediately precipitated into the bustle and hustle of preparing the ship and storing the huge amount of provisions and equipment needed for at least a year in Antarctica. The work of the crew was interrupted and constantly delayed by dignitaries and members of the public eager to inspect the ship. Finally, the Bishop of London came on board to address and bless the officers and men. The Bishop spoke of the difficulties and dangers of the voyage but also impressed with his comments concerning the need to remember that God was with them always. Quoting from the psalms, he stated the necessity of good comradeship and sympathy for each other – 'Behold how good and how pleasant it is for brethren to dwell together in unity.'

Discovery sailed from London to Cowes in the Isle of Wight, an event of sufficient importance to be reported in *The Times*.[7] Cowes was to be her final port of call in Britain before she sailed away for three years.

Notes

1 Wild, R.F.J., Notes related to the British National Antarctic Expedition 1901–04, SPRI, MS 944/3: D.
2 *South Wales Daily Post*, 20 September 1904.
3 Three masts: two square-rigged masts, the third, (the aft 'mizzen' mast), rigged fore and aft.
4 Skelton, J.V., & Wilson, D.M. *Discovery Illustrated*, Reardon Publishing, Cheltenham, 2001, p. 10.
5 Seamen in the British Navy.
6 Markham, C., *Antarctic Obsession: The British National Antarctic Expedition 1901–1904*, Bluntisham Books and the Erskine Press, Norfolk, England, 1986, p. 18.
7 *Times*, Thursday, 1 August 1901, p. 6. Issue 36522.

4

From England
to South Africa

In Cowes, the newly crowned King Edward VII and his beautiful queen, Alexandra, came on board to inspect the ship and her complement. Edward's sister, Empress Frederick, had just died,[1] but he managed to speak well and impressed the lower deck with his comments. The King said that he was glad of the opportunity of saying goodbye to an expedition that was (for once), bound on peaceful aims for the increase of scientific knowledge. Seaman Thomas Williamson wrote that the King said 'we were a fine lot of fellows and before going he wished us God speed, a pleasant voyage and a safe return. We manned the rigging when he left, the Captain calling for three cheers for His Majesty which was heartily responded to'.[2] The men were, for the most part, patriotically enthusiastic about the venture. Marine Gilbert Scott said that the expedition was 'to remove any lack of the unknown from the map of the world and to press forward the frontiers of human knowledge a little further'.[3]

Although Edgar's local newspapers[4] do not report on *Discovery*'s departure, it was a national event. Government and official donations were complemented by small gifts and contributions from schools and individuals throughout the country. There were fundraising events and dinners.

Williamson included a ditty in his diary, written for a dinner in a London club and sung to the strains of *Auld Lang Syne*, which went:

> To night, my brother Savages we bid a warm adieu
> To Captain Scott and all the lot of his good ship's gallant crew
> They sail, as sailors sailed of yore, like Britain's brave and bold
> For a British crew is as stout and true as in the days of old
> So here's to Scott and all his lot
> With all his might and main
> And we'll meet them in the Savage Club
> When they come home again

It continues in typical populist fashion:

> They sail to find the Southern Pole and bring it safely home.[5]

The 6 August 1901 was a brilliant sunny day when Edgar left England. Thousands cheered and waved from the shore. Hundreds, on little boats, shouted and tooted. Bands blared. The noise and the sight of yacht racing at Cowes faded gradually into the distance as *Discovery* slowly sailed away.

Scott's planned route was from England to Madeira, then Cape Town and afterwards to Melbourne, Lyttelton and Antarctica. In the event several problems were to slow *Discovery*'s progress; it was obvious from early in the voyage that her speed was slower than expected, the sail area was small – 'it would take nearly a gale of wind to produce a respectable speed'[6] – and she was a glutton for consuming coal. In spite of continual attempts at repair en route, she also leaked throughout the voyage (probably due to unequal contraction of poorly seasoned oak in the main frames which shrunk and bent the rivet-like bolts[7] and, conversely, widening of the planking in the ship's sides close to the scorching engine room). In addition, she was 'a poor sailer', she had difficulty tacking into the wind and 'sagged leeward' (away from the wind).[8] These problems meant that Scott could not keep to his schedule.

From the start *Discovery* was run on the naval 'tier system' with a line of command from Officers (including scientists), Warrant Officers, Petty Officers (POs) and Ratings. Sir Clements Markham lists three Warrant Officers and six Petty Officers, including Edgar, in the ship's complement.[9] Each rank had its own quarters. POs were berthed in a separate, starboard-side area and had their own Mess. The Ratings lived and ate in their own quarters (which, being relatively near the stove, had an advantage in that it was warm in winter).[10] They slept on hammocks that were stowed away during the day; they used their lockers as seats and slung their tables between the beams when they did not need them. Plans of *Discovery* show six mess tables and total accommodation for forty-five crew (more than eventually sailed, which was thirty-five).[11] The average age of the Petty Officers was 27 (Edgar was 25); the crew members' 23.[12]

At sea, a routine was quickly established on naval lines with watches of four hours. In between duties Edgar read, mended his kit, got to know his new shipmates and slept. As a Petty Officer of the watch he gave orders to the seamen for the smooth running of the ship. When he was on watch he instructed the bluejackets to climb the rigging and climb out on the yards to unfurl and furl the sails. The diaries are full of details of working on the topsail yards, shortening cables, cleaning, painting, pumping out the main hold and clearing up in general.

Throughout the week duties followed the same routine, but on Saturdays the ship was given a thorough cleaning. This was for medical reasons as well as naval standards. In 1901, the cause of scurvy, the dreaded disease that had caused so many deaths in previous years, was still unknown. The value of citrus fruit juice, which had provided protection to earlier travellers, had become questioned as an effective defence,[13] and one of the many theories as to scurvy's cause was that it was exacerbated by dark, damp conditions; Scott was determined to attend to every precaution that might keep this horror from his ship. On Sunday, Scott did a full inspection of the men and the ship. A religious service followed, Scott reading the prayers; the men, with *Discovery*'s First Lieutenant Charles Royds (1876–1931) accompanying them on the piano, sang heartily. Scott used the time after the service to address the crew on specific problems or general matters, and, after this, the crew were (officially) at leisure.

On the first part of the voyage *Discovery* proved to be a 'remarkably comfortable ship'.[14] Scott described the voyage as 'most delightful'[15] and the officers were very satisfied with the morale and general bonhomie – a satisfaction that persisted throughout the voyage. As in many organisations, however, the views of the 'managers' were not automatically reflected by those in the lower echelons. Some of the crew were unhappy with their conditions and grumbles surfaced early. After only two days at sea, Thomas Williamson complained that he had 'six hours sleep in twenty-four hours of hard work'[16] and that the routine consisted of 'all day at work and keeping watch at night'. Later, he complained that the officers must have thought that the sailors were 'automobiles or traction engines, which only needed to be oiled to keep on the go, rather than human beings'.[17] But although Williamson commented freely in his logbook, his observations are by no means all negative. He liked the ship and thought she sailed well; he appreciated the novelty, the interest and (sometimes) the beauty of the places he was visiting. His day's log entry frequently ends with 'All's well'.

Another Able Seaman, Frank Wild (later to become a well-known Antarctic hero when he was on Shackleton's famous expeditions), also recorded his reservations. Wild wrote that the voyage from England was neither eventful nor happy because the crew were worked very hard, day and night, and often unnecessarily so. He wrote, puzzlingly, since he himself was a naval seaman, that this way of working was the naval way and 'as the Captain and most of the officers were naval men they could not get out of these ways'. Only when *Discovery* reached Antarctica did things 'work round to a reasonable state', and they had 'occasional glimpses of sunshine through the clouds of discontent'.[18]

Differences between ranks permeated many aspects of life on board. Although the same food was provided for officers and men, the men served themselves, whilst the officers were served at a table in the mess refined by oak furniture, linen on the table, silver cutlery and monogrammed china. Marine Gilbert Scott, one of the stewards, has left an account of his duties in the wardroom; he found the hours long and weary. There were differences in some supplies for officers and crew; for example, jam, marmalade, tea, coffee, tobacco and alcohol.[19] In relation to tobacco, *Discovery* carried 1,800 pounds, 1 and a half pounds per officer per month, 1 pound per man (the men smoked Navy Leaf, stronger tobacco than that smoked by the officers, and they rolled the leaf tobacco into 'pricks' with spun yarn, the traditional naval way).[20] In relation to alcohol, the provision was different too; the 30 gallons of brandy, 60 of port and 36 of sherry were presumably for officer consumption, as were the 28 cases of champagne (listed under 'medical comforts'). Cases of these had been brought on board *Discovery* from the king's yacht when Edward inspected the ship and had, most conveniently, been forgotten. The 800 gallons of rum were provided for the crew. Ratings were issued with grog each day – grog being a 'tot' of rum (an eighth of a pint), diluted with water, and the rum was a potent mixture of Demerara, Trinidad and other rums.[21] The addition of water made it virtually undrinkable after an hour, but Dr Wilson wrote that somehow the tots were occasionally saved and drunk in bulk, causing a comfortable fuddledness. Non-drinking seamen, such as William Lashly, a Leading Stoker, could opt for lime juice but probably rarely did. Lashly claimed his ration, which he either distributed to friends[22] or, more likely, traded for benefits such as a change of duties.

But the most important divides between men and their officers, present not only in the navy but in virtually every section of Victorian society, were education and pay. This combination of relative disadvantages created an almost impassable chasm for a man such as Edgar to cross. For most of the crew, their formal education had finished in their early teens. In relation to pay, there was little hope of Edgar ever achieving the remuneration received by the officers. In this instance, in comparison to Scott's annual pay of £865 (expedition pay £500, plus £365 naval pay),[23] Edgar received a total annual pay of £82 4s (£41 and 1s from the expedition and £41 3s from the navy).[24] Seamen received just over £55[25] (for comparison, General Labourers received £62, Porters £89, Surgeons and Medical Officers £475).[26] One man who did cross the divide was Able Seaman Frank Wild, who years after Scott's expedition and after heroic expeditions with Ernest Shackleton in the Antarctic, rejoined the naval forces in 1916, and in 1917 was given a commission as Temporary Lieutenant Royal Naval Voluntary Reserve (RNVR) and sent to the North Russian Front.[27] Another seaman, Garrett, became a Lieutenant in the RNVR.[28]

However, some links did exist. In the Victorian era, literature and poetry were important interests. There were hundreds of books on *Discovery*; publishers had given volumes, a 'well wisher' had given fifty novels and some authors had given copies of their works. There were also quantities of magazines,[29] and Edgar and his companions had ample opportunities to read the authors and poets. Edgar was well read and Scott found him superior to the other seamen in this respect. Edgar had firm opinions on the works he read; he did not like Kipling's poems and Dickens did not appeal, but he greatly liked Dumas (whose name he anglicised to Dummass), because the works had 'more plot'.[30] Also, when they were on later expeditions, there was no differentiation between men and officers as they struggled equally in their quest to explore new ground. In one of the longest sorties of the *Discovery* expedition, Scott spent sixty-six days in close proximity and complete equality with Evans and William Lashly, as they battled against Antarctica's awesome conditions. Scott felt he got to know his co-explorers well and had nothing but praise for them. Edgar, for his part, developed a deep loyalty to Scott that lasted until their deaths in 1912.

Although on HMS *Majestic* Edgar had served with Scott, he had to get to know the officers and scientists who would be making the long journey with him. He felt that the officers would be of importance to him, the scientists less so. Alongside Commander Scott, there were seven officers (plus the two doctors), who all took on specialist work in addition to their naval duties. The hierarchy was as follows: Second in Command was Albert Armitage, a veteran of polar work who had already been in the Arctic for three years. Armitage was Scott's navigator and ice master. The First Lieutenant was Charles Royds, who was in charge of the day-to-day running of the ship, allocating officers and men to the duties of the watch. His specialist area was meteorological observations and he had had training in magnetism. Royds had good contact with the men and was credited with achieving much of the relative harmony that existed on *Discovery*. He was a talented piano player and organised concerts for the men's entertainment. The Second Lieutenant was Michael Barne, a shipmate of Scott's on *Majestic*. He helped with magnetic observations and was in charge of the deep-sea sounding apparatus. The Third Lieutenant was a man later to become famous in the annals of Antarctic history – Ernest Shackleton. For the *Discovery* expedition he was trained up in seawater density and salinity studies. Reginald Skelton, an ex-shipmate of Scott's from his *Majestic* days, was the Engineer. Doctor Reginald Koettlitz, 6ft tall with a droopy moustache, who had already survived winters in the Arctic, took on the role of botanist. Dr Koettlitz had his problems with Edgar; although Edgar was always respectful in the presence of officers, his language, when he was working, was colourful. When Koettlitz heard some of Edgar's more florid expressions he reported him to Scott for bad language. Dr Koettlitz's junior was the recently qualified Edward Wilson, who was the zoologist and artist. The geologist was Hartley Travers Ferrar, aged 22 and also recently qualified.

Among the lower deck, Edgar's new colleagues were four Warrant Officers. The Boatswain (Bosun) was Thomas Alfred Feather, aged 31, who was in charge of seamen's duties. Scott was full of praise for his Bosun, writing that no rope or sail was lost on the three-year voyage under Feather's expert supervision.[31] The other Warrant Officers were James Dellbridge (29), the 2nd engineer who came from *Majestic*;

Fred Dailey (28), the carpenter who possessed an 'eye' for defects,[32] and Charles Reginald Ford (23), the ships steward, whose duties were to keep an exact account of the stores. Feather's deputy was David Silver Allan from *Majestic*, a Scotsman aged 31, who, with Thomas Kennar (25) and William MacFarlane (27), carried out the duties of Quartermaster – which means they had some responsibility for navigation and signals. Other POs for *Discovery*'s journey to Antarctica were William Smythe (24), Jacob Cross (26) and William Lashly (33), the Acting Chief Stoker (re-rated by Scott as Chief Stoker). An American, Stoker Arthur Lester Quartley was described by Dr Wilson as 'quite the finest figure of a man I have ever set eyes on, standing just over six feet and a perfect giant in strength and sinew'.[33]

Edgar himself was tall and big for a Welshman. He was nearly 6ft and weighed 12 stone 10lbs. He was strong, competitive and in 'hard condition'. Along with Cross, Kennar, MacFarlane and Smythe he was appointed as a supernumerary rating for the thirty-one-strong shore party.[34] The shore explorations were to include a balloon ascent. Lashly and Engineer Skelton had been sent to the Army Balloon Factory at Aldershot to be given instruction on balloon ascents, one of Scott's more unusual briefs for the Antarctic.

Eight days out of England the ship approached Madeira, and Seaman Williamson wrote that the scientists were hard at work doing their depth soundings (difficulties were encountered with the apparatus which frequently broke). In Funchal, Madeira's capital, *Discovery*'s crew took on 54 tons of coal. Coal was already being consumed more quickly than expected and this was to remain a concern throughout the voyage.

All the men took their turn with coaling – a filthy, backbreaking task. All the ventilators and any cracks had to be papered over before work began, otherwise the coal dust got everywhere, being most particularly unwelcome in the living quarters. In Madeira, a new worry relating to the ship's construction at Dundee surfaced, one that concerned Edgar. Various metal attachments for the sails had broken, and although these could obviously be repaired, the defect clearly made the crew anxious about the ship's performance in a severe gale.[35] Gilbert Scott, the Marine, wrote that some of the men got drunk and started rowing and fighting, 'which was caused by the same thing that causes most of the trouble'.[36]

Official plans for cooperation between *Discovery* and other European explorations are underlined by the fact that at the same time that *Discovery* was in Madeira, the German ship *Gauss* was departing from Germany for Cape Town and the Antarctic. In the case of *Gauss*, plans for collaboration were not as comprehensive as was hoped; she became trapped in the Antarctic ice.[37]

Discovery left Madeira bound for Cape Town with a stop planned in South Trinidad, a small island in the Atlantic. A few days out and Skelton's grumbling tooth abscess gave him so much pain that extraction became essential. As a sensible precaution Scott had arranged dental treatment for all the crew before *Discovery* sailed, an attention that Skelton had presumably missed. This was much in the way that prophylactic appendectomies may be performed nowadays on men and women who will be cut off from medical attention for months. In the check-up over ninety teeth were removed, and nearly 200 fillings put in (at a cost of just over £62).

Edgar's teeth remained far from perfect; he had two extractions and three fillings[38] (one unfortunate had ten fillings and five extractions).[39] In fact, very little dental trouble was recorded on the expedition and the doctors must have reflected with relief on Scott's forethought.

However, a problem was discovered when it was found that a serious new leak had developed.[40] Black, stinking, slimy water had seeped into the hold and covered and rotted the bottom layer of provisions. All hands were called on to help. They were not pleased, and were particularly furious with the men who had stowed the hold in London. One hand wrote, 'and by all the saints above, the man or rather the men who were responsible for the leakage ought to be strung up, for the greater part of the provisions are in a dilapidated state and those at the bottom are utterly destroyed'.[41] It was very hot (140°F in the engine room), but the gruelling work went on round the clock under a relentless tropical sun. Tins of cheddar cheese had gone putrid, eggs in unsoldered tins had gone rotten, and sugar had fermented. The holds had to be cleared and disinfected and the provisions stored above until a new platform was built in the hold.

Edgar was involved in this unenviable task, made particularly obnoxious by a stench that was so awful that they could only go on with the work when a ventilation hole had been made. In spite of repeated attempts to solve the problem of leaks the problem continued to plague *Discovery* as she sailed south, but this occasion gave the most trouble.

Discovery headed west to take advantage of the winds and currents sailing almost as far as South America before heading south-east towards Cape Town. On 31 August she 'crossed the line', the equator, a milestone associated with a rather violent initiation for those crew members crossing the equator for the first time[42] – although Williamson described it as 'good sport'[43] and likewise Lashly as a 'very good afternoon's sport'.[44] It may have been good sport to the onlookers, but hardly for the initiates. The oldest seaman (in this case PO David Allan, Bosun Feather's deputy), was 'Neptune' who 'visited' the ship. Initiates were introduced into his court 'in the most thorough manner'. The ritual could be humiliating and probably settled a few scores.

PO David Allan was resplendent in his crown and his oilskins were chalked all over with fish. His 'wife', merchant seaman John Mardon, was wearing a flowered silk outfit; he had pink cheeks, a mass of thin rope twist down his back and a hat with paper roses. The two were accompanied by attendants (tritons): Leading Seaman Arthur Pilbeam, Able Seaman Frank Wild and seven other crew members arrived to sit the initiates on a platform 12ft above a canvas bath, shave their heads roughly, wash their mouths out with soap, and finally to pull the chair from under them so that the victims dropped backwards into the water bath. The officers went first, uninitiated lower-deck men followed. Edgar had not 'crossed the line' and had to endure the ritual. Unfortunately he did not record his feelings or, more probably, his fury. The 'court's' activities were lubricated by two bottles of whisky, which were passed quickly around. The carnival atmosphere soon turned sour. Neptune's queen, Mardon, fell into the sail bath, the entire court became covered in soot, flour and soap, and when the men returned to the mess, aggressive complaining followed against the Officers and Quartermasters with Mardon becoming particularly obnoxious. The next morning one of the stokers collapsed in the boiler room and when Dr Wilson was called to the scene he found that the man's thumb had been bitten right through to the bone in a drunken brawl by his fellow Dundee citizen, James Duncan, seaman.[45]

Naval Regulations gave clear guidelines to cover excessive drinking and Scott had to respond with formal discipline. He discharged Mardon to be handed over to the authorities at the next port. He also, optimistically, ordered the lower deck to clean up their language. At least some of the lower deck agreed with him; Gilbert Scott thought that some of the men's behaviour was disgraceful.[46]

Drink was both a regular feature of sailors' routine as well as a curse. Events such as the 'crossing of the line' and shore leave were characterised regularly by drunken bouts, though drunkenness was unusual at sea. Although most sailors drank whenever the opportunity presented itself, and in the later expedition Edgar drew particular attention to himself with his drinking, there is no mention in the *Discovery* diaries, or in Edgar's naval record of this expedition, that he was prone to noteworthy overindulgence.

Life at sea was not all work. Scott understood the importance of trying to keep the crew entertained. In the early part of the voyage the heat was tropical and as they sailed away from Madeira, the men had time for deck games: boxing, tug-of-war, deck cricket. They sang, accompanied by the mandolin. They played with the animals on board: Scott's Aberdeen Terrier, Scamp; Armitage's dog, Vinca, a Samoyed (whose mother was an Arctic Veteran); and also with the cats and the rabbits. Lectures, such as 'Vegetable and Animal Marine Life' and 'The Causes of Phosphorescence', were organised. The opportunity to look at specimens under the microscope (magnified 500 times) was appreciated. Remarkably, a form of hockey was played on the upper deck; officers against scientists, keenly watched by the crew.

On 13 September, *Discovery* stopped at the small, uninhabited island of South Trinidad in the South Atlantic, approximately 500 miles east of Brazil and described by Wild as 'a very pleasant visit'.[47] Edgar saw a land covered with yellow-grey craggy rock that rose steeply from the shore to peaks of 1,000ft, covered with fern and scrub. Frigate birds wheeled overhead as some of the crew landed. A bluejacket was assigned to each of the scientists to aid in the collection of specimens. They found a shore alive with crabs, some large and red and green, with eyes that stared bulbously at their visitors; others were pale and globular, like black-eyed apples on legs. The stop was short but important for getting samples of the wildlife to send back to London, and sixteen types of bird were found. Not all the crew landed; Williamson, for example, was detailed to look after the transport boats. He passed the time by fishing, adding sixteen fish and one young shark to the haul of new treasures.

Many different birds followed the ship and Edgar became adroit at identifying them. Catching different types of albatrosses and the Cape pigeons became a popular pastime.

The run to Cape Town was made by sail as much as possible to reserve the coal supply. With a good wind, reasonable progress was made, though not at the speed that was hoped for (174 nautical miles on 26 September, 180 and 165 on 27th and 28th). *Discovery* weathered her first gale on 26 September; the topgallant sheet was carried away and the sails had to be furled 'after a hard struggle'.[48] The wind continued to blow very heavily till 2 a.m. in the middle watch, when it began to drop, and by 5.30 a.m. it had gone, leaving behind it a big heavy swell which made *Discovery* roll unmercifully. But Edgar and the whole crew were satisfied with the way their ship had stood up to her first gale, she had proved herself a good sea ship.

Apart from battling the difficult conditions, the crew were occupied with preparing for their arrival in South Africa. They painted the ship – that unending naval duty – and prepared the coal chutes. Scott told them what he expected in terms of dress and behaviour, and later he met them to help them make their wills. Edgar, dutiful son that he was, left everything to his mother.[49]

On the afternoon of the 3 October, *Discovery* entered Table Bay eight days behind schedule, in spite of the effort of the crew. The remarkable sight of Table Mountain impressed Edgar. The mountain was covered in a cloth of cloud, which moved continuously, so that the mountain tops showed variably in shade and in sunlight. Because of the difficulty in keeping to schedule, Scott decided that he would have to bypass Melbourne, a decision that meant that dogs and supplies waiting in Melbourne had to be transported to New Zealand. These were problems beyond Edgar's sphere as he had more pressing things to think about. Hundreds of visitors came to the ship in spite of the fact that the Boer War between the British and the Dutch settlers was continuing. Although Afrikaner guerrillas were close by and martial law was in place, *Discovery* and her crew were welcomed with open arms by the British community.

Edgar attended a garden party hosted by the Admiral in Cape Town and a picnic hosted by the Governor.[50] He visited a Boer prisoners' camp but, sadly, did not record his thoughts or impressions about the war, which was, by now, in its third year. His Warrant Officer, Ford, and others were hosted at a dinner given by the Chief Warrant and Dockyard Officers of the port. On this occasion Ford gave a speech saying that although doubtless many dangers would be met in the Antarctic, he dreaded more the last half hour knowing that he was about to speak. Ford said that *Discovery* was manned with volunteers motivated with that love of adventure and carelessness of danger, which was the birthright of every English man,[51] a view endorsed by Edgar.

Meanwhile Scott's disciplinary duties continued: Mardon, the merchant seaman who had caused so much trouble 'crossing the line' and the only one of the crew whom Scott thought was completely unsatisfactory, was finally dismissed. But in spite of this warning, drink-related concerns surfaced again. The relaxed discipline in Cape Town meant that alcohol was freely available to the crew and their new friends plied them with drink. This time two other crewmen, Donkeyman[52] William Hubert and Stoker William Page, were drunk and incapable. Worse, Page was grossly insubordinate to a superior. The two offenders were paraded before Scott. Such insubordination should have resulted in discharge and naval detention on shore, but at this stage Scott needed his crew. He merely stopped the men's pay, shore leave and rum allowance.

Work continued alongside the social activities. In spite of the numerous visitors on board, which naturally held things up, Edgar was busily involved in supervising the resetting of the rigging and the recaulking of *Discovery's* deck and sides above the waterline. A crew member wrote that it 'proved a very painful job but of course it must be done'.[53]

Other important duties continued: *Discovery's* magnetic observatory had to be recalibrated with the Cape Town observatory. This could not be done in the town because of the Cape Town trams, which distorted readings, so the observations were made on a plateau behind the town on the Cape of Good Hope peninsula. Guerrilla activity meant that the work could only be done in the day and the work extended to ten days, rather than the seven that had been planned.[54]

After taking on coal, *Discovery* sailed to the naval base of Simon's Town on the other side of the Cape on 5 October. As she made the short journey the ship again demonstrated her remarkable ability to roll, sometimes through nearly forty degrees, so that everything not carefully fastened down just flew about. When they arrived in Simon's Town, the crew received the customary friendly welcome; Edgar was allowed ashore in the evening even though he had plenty to do during the day. *Discovery* was refitted and supplied at no cost to the expedition.

On Monday 14 October 1901, *Discovery* left Simon's Town and steamed round the fleet. It was the grandest send-off. Some of the sentiments expressed by the crew as they left South Africa seem dated today. 'The ships in harbour gave us a splendid send off with all good wishes for a successful voyage and a safe return to dear old England'.[55] Williamson was positive, too. *Discovery* received 'three glorious cheers from each of the ships as we steamed past them, I think that this was the best send off ever I saw a ship get'.[56]

Notes

1 *South Wales Daily Post*, Tuesday 6 August 1901, p. 3.
2 Williamson, T.S., *Log 1901–1904*, SPRI, MS 774/1/1; BJ, p. 2.
3 Scott, G., *Journal during the British National Antarctic Expedition* SPRI, MS 1485:D.
4 *Cabbrian, Herald of Wales* and *South Wales Daily Post.*
5 Williamson, T.S., *Log 1901–1904*, SPRI, MS 774/1/1; BJ, p. 4.
6 Markham, C., *Antarctic Obsession: The British National Antarctic Expedition 1901–1904*, Bluntisham Books and the Erskine Press, Norfolk, England, 1986, p. 107.
7 Yelverton, D., *Antarctica Unveiled, Scott's First Expedition and the Quest for the Unknown Continent*, University Press of Colorado, USA, 2000, p. 94.
8 Markham, C. *Antarctic Obsession: The British National Antarctic Expedition 1901–1904*, Bluntisham Books and the Erskine Press, Norfolk, England, 1986, p. 113.
9 Ibid., p. 66.
10 *Times*, 20/03/1901.
11 Yelverton, D., *Antarctica Unveiled, Scott's First Expedition and the Quest for the Unknown Continent*, University Press of Colorado, USA, 2000, p. 378.
12 Markham, C., *Antarctic Obsession: The British National Antarctic Expedition 1901–1904*, Bluntisham Books and the Erskine Press, Norfolk, England, 1986, p. 67.
13 Williams, I., *With Scott in the Antarctic, Edward Wilson, Explorer, Naturalist, Artist*, The History Press, Gloucestershire, 2008, p. 86
14 Markham, C. *Antarctic Obsession: The British National Antarctic Expedition 1901–1904*, Bluntisham Books and the Erskine Press, Norfolk, England, 1986, p. 109.
15 Ibid., p. 106.
16 Williamson, T.S., *Log 1901–1904*, SPRI, MS 774/1/1; BJ. p. 3.
17 Ibid., p. 4.
18 Wild, J.R.F., *Letter to Mrs A.C. Bostock* (his cousin), SPRI, MS 1078/3/1; D.
19 Baughman, T.H., *Pilgrims on the Ice, Robert Falcon Scott's First Antarctic Expedition*, University of Nebraska Press, USA, 1999, p. 77–78.
20 Ellis, A.R., *Under Scott's Command, Lashly's Antarctic Diaries*, Victor Gollancz, London, 1969, p. 37.
21 Pack, J. *Nelson's Blood: The Story of Naval Rum*, Mason, Havant, Hampshire, 1982, p. 85.
22 Ellis, A.R., *Under Scott's Command: Lashly's Antarctic Diaries*, Baylis, London, 1969, p. 37.
23 Markham, C., *Antarctic Obsession: The British National Antarctic Expedition 1901–1904*, Bluntisham Books and the Erskine Press, Norfolk, England, 1986, p. 70.
24 Ibid., p. 90.

25 Ibid., p. 93.

26 Williamson, J.G., *The Structure of Pay in Britain 1710–1911, Research in Economic History*, 7, 1982, p. 1–54,

27 Afterwards Wild sailed with Shackleton on *Quest* in 1921 as second-in-command. When Shackleton died in January 1922, Wild took over command.

28 Abbott, G.P., *Letters to Cherry-Garrard*, SPRI MS 559/22/1-3; D, 13/04/1916.

29 Armitage, A.B., *Two Years in the Antarctic*, Paradigm Press, Bungay, Suffolk, 1984, p. 116.

30 Gregor, G.C., *Swansea's Antarctic Explorer, Edgar Evans, 1876–1912*. City of Swansea Publication, 1995 (Appendix 3, *The Martyred Hero*. Richards, H.S.) p.96.

31 Scott, R.F., *Voyage of Discovery*, Vol. 1, London, p. 54.

32 Ibid., p. 54.

33 Ed. Savours, A., *Edward Wilson, Diary of the Discovery Expedition to the Antarctic Regions 1901–1904*, Blandford Press, London, 1966, p. 286.

34 Yelverton, D., *Antarctica Unveiled, Scott's First Expedition and the Quest for the Unknown Continent*, University Press of Colorado, USA, 2000, Appendix 2.

35 Markham, C., *Antarctic Obsession: The British National Antarctic Expedition 1901–1904*, Bluntisham Books and the Erskine Press, Norfolk, England, 1986, p. 106.

36 Scott, G., *Journal during BNA Expedition* SPRI, MS 1485; D.

37 *Gauss* was trapped in sea ice for twelve months, many miles from the region the Germans had intended to explore.

38 Markham, C., *Antarctic Obsession: The British National Antarctic Expedition 1901–1904*, Bluntisham Books and the Erskine Press, Norfolk, England, 1986, p. 89.

39 Ibid., p. 97.

40 Yelverton, D., *Antarctica Unveiled, Scott's First Expedition and the Quest for the Unknown Continent*. University Press of Colorado, Colorado, USA, 2000, p. 76.

41 Williamson, T.S., *Log 1901–1904*, SPRI, MS 774/1/1: BJ, p. 8.

42 A traditional 'hazing' ceremony, in which initiates are subjected to a strenuous, humiliating and sometimes, dangerous ritual.

43 Williamson, T.S. *Log 1901–1904*, SPRI, MS 774/1/1: BJ, p. 11.

44 Ellis, A.R., *Under Scott's Command, Lashly's Antarctic Diaries*, Victor Gollancz, London, 1969, p. 17.

45 Ed. Savours, A., *Diary of the Discovery Expedition to the Antarctic 1901–1904*, Blandford Press. London. 1966. p. 73.

46 Scott, G., *Journal during BNA Expedition*, SPRI, MS 1485; D.

47 Wild, J.R.F., *Letter to Mrs A.C. Bostock* (his cousin), SPRI, MS 1078/3/1; D.

48 Ibid., p. 22.

49 Markham, C., *Antarctic Obsession: The British National Antarctic Expedition 1901–1904*, Bluntisham Books and the Erskine Press, Norfolk, England, 1986, p. 90.

50 Baughman, T.H., *Pilgrims on the Ice, Robert Falcon Scott's First Antarctic Expedition*, University of Nebraska Press. USA, 1999, p. 75.

51 Ibid., p. 74.

52 A sailor working in the engine room.

53 Williamson, T.S., *Log 1901–1904*, SPRI, MS 774/1/1; BJ. p. 26.

54 Yelverton, D., *Antarctica Unveiled, Scott's First Expedition and the Quest for the Unknown Continent*, University Press of Colorado, USA, 2000, p. 83.

55 Ellis, A.R., *Under Scott's Command: Lashly's Antarctic Diaries*, Victor Gollancz, London, 1969, p. 19.

56 Williamson, T.S., *Log 1901–1904*, SPRI, MS 774/1/1; BJ. p. 28.

5

The Southern Ocean
to Antarctica

When *Discovery* departed from Simon's Town on 14 October 1901, she was twelve days behind schedule, with Scott's route taking him away from the main shipping routes. He needed to investigate the magnetic fields in the area south of 40° latitude (his scientists were to record the intensity and dip of the magnetic forces), to comply with an important part of his instructions from the Admiralty. After making the scientific observations, *Discovery* would make for Lyttelton, New Zealand.

Discovery soon caught a westerly breeze and made way by sail alone. The atmosphere amongst the sailors was cheerful; they caught a good haul of fish in the trawling net but subsequently managed to tangle the net and lose their haul in the process. Edgar enjoyed the evening singsongs.

But the weather soon deteriorated and the run became cold, rough and wet. From late October to early November *Discovery* went through a series of storms of wind, snow and hail. These made for unpleasant conditions but impressive daily distances, 'nipping along' through the thousands of miles still to be covered: 207 miles on 22 October and 200 on the 28th, for example. The storms were a real test of the ship's sea worthiness; Gilbert Scott wrote that 'even the most experienced crewmen had never seen the like',[1] and the crew agreed that *Discovery* did well despite waves of 30 to 40ft rising as high as the Upper Topsail.[2] The ship lifted over them, though Williamson wrote that she was reeling 'like a drunken man'. He was concerned that she would 'roll her masts out of her'.[3] On the 28th a vast wave flooded on board, deluging the forecastle[4], mess deck and laboratories. The men had just brought their winter clothes up from the hold. They were soaked through, and the crew had a lively time bailing water out of the wardroom. To make matters worse, the men were wearing sea boots, and Williamson wrote 'it's a wonder to me that some of us did not break our necks, once during the day I thought my checks were in. I was flung from one side of the ship to the other, with such force that I thought I had stove my ribs in … All's well'.[5] But this second baptism confirmed to Edgar that he could have confidence in his ship.

Discovery continued south until, on 12 November, she was at a focus of magnetic interest at 52°S 131°E. Scott aimed to get even further south, as far as 65°, so that changes in the magnetic force and dip closer to the Magnetic Pole could be recorded. *Discovery* was now about 1,000 miles from land and well away from the shipping tracks, so the cry of 'ship afire' on the night of the 14th caused considerable alarm. A sailor's oilskin had been left too close to a lamp; the ship was rolling and a fire started close to some paraffin oil tanks. Tales from his father's 'Cape Horn' years of fires on wooden ships must have come flooding back to Edgar as the alarm was raised. However, the crew were well rehearsed and the fire was put out quickly, but it was a cautionary experience nevertheless.

On 16 November, Edgar saw his first piece of ice bobbing around on the sea – only the size of a soup plate, but indisputably ice. Soon the ship was surrounded by bigger pieces succeeded by strange weathered blocks. The crew hooked up some ice to taste. It was fresh.[6] Edgar was on deck when *Discovery* first 'charged' an ice block as she entered the pack (the band of ice that surrounds Antarctica). By the evening she was enclosed by ice. The pack's shrouded grey-white mystery could not fail to impress; shafts of light reflected as a ghostly shimmer, the occasional bird flitted silently through the gloom. But Edgar did not have much time for introspection. As Petty Officer he was busy as he supervised the removal of the topgallant sails at night (to reduce strains on the masts should there be collisions with ice) and their replacement in the morning.

Discovery punched through as far south as 62° 50'S 139°E on steam. Then, after the magnetic observations had been made, she had to turn northwards; neither time nor coal reserves permitted further southern ventures. A glass of rum was issued all round; the boundaries of science had been pushed a little further.

On 22 November the crew sighted Macquarie Island. Here, in only a few hours, more seals, birds and penguins were added to the haul on board. The skins were to be of interest to the Natural History Museum in London, while the flesh was to be eaten. This visit was made lively by an encounter with a very large seal which, reluctant to give up its life for the advancement of scientific knowledge, charged at Skelton's camera and stand while Skelton himself attacked it with the boat's foot spur. The crew had seen penguins on the sail to the island, but here there were thousands of birds: handsome King penguins and smaller, orange-crested Royal penguins.

As the ship approached New Zealand Scott wrote that no sail, rope yarn or supplies on the deck had been lost (though on the final part of the run, in a 56° roll, big waves damaged several cabins and a huge amount of china). Finally, on 28 November, *Discovery* was off Lyttelton, the port of Christchurch. She had covered over 1,500 miles under a whole variety of conditions: heat, cold and wind. The crew had performed well.

The New Zealanders were fascinated by their visitors and made a fuss of them. They viewed them as young heroes sailing away to unravel the unsolved mysteries of Antarctica. Thus hundreds of locals turned out to greet them, and the crew were impressed and appreciative, writing that there were always willing hands ready to do the least little thing to make things easier and that the New Zealanders would not be forgotten. One wrote, 'when we are in Antarctica there will be as many thinking of us in New Zealand as at home, perhaps more'.[7] Edgar attended a 'smoking concert' in a local Working Mans Club. There were other smoking concerts, on the ships and in Lyttelton. The mayor and people of Christchurch hosted a banquet for the crew,[8] and the Sydenham Working Men's Club invited the sailors to dinner. Railway journeys to Christchurch were provided free of charge. Indeed, the time in New Zealand passed quickly.

For Scott, though, the time was too long. He would have liked to bypass some of the hospitality and sail straight on to the Antarctic, but he had no choice – he had to remain (for nearly four weeks) because of some possible damage to the hull, which meant that *Discovery* had to go into dry dock for inspection. Visitors swarmed over the ship. Meanwhile, everything in the hull had to be unloaded, every item in every box recorded, and, after restowing, every box's exact location in the hull accounted. Stores shipped from England, including the unassembled magnetic huts, had to be squeezed in somehow. The Third Officer, Ernest Shackleton, was assigned this unenviable task and needed all the help he could get, but the crew, exhausted by their journey, keen to sample generous local hospitality and allowed to spend their evenings on shore,[9] soon reached the stage where many were incapable of doing anything practical. But although Lieutenant Royds wrote that there wasn't a sober man on board by early evening and Engineer Skelton recorded that, 'there has been a great deal of fighting and drunkenness and I hope two of the seamen will be discharged',[10] Edgar Evans does not rate a mention in relation to poor behaviour.

But poor behaviour was rife amongst other members of the crew. An Able Seaman (Baker) struck the Quartermaster Kenner (an arrestable offence), for some unknown reason, and deserted with Seaman Robert Sinclair and one of Edgar's fellow Petty Officers, William Smythe. Royds was sure that all three had deserted permanently but Smythe and Sinclair eventually reappeared; Smythe was reported to the Admiralty to be disrated from Petty Officer to Able Seaman.

Apart from these problems, New Zealand was a success for the lower deck. The city of Christchurch was greatly admired; it was beautifully laid out with wide streets and a river running through it, which enabled much boating and fishing. Maori ladies in local costume visited the ship and were given lunch. New Zealand sheep farmers offered as many sheep as the ship could carry (fifty); the farmers drew lots to see which farmer would have the honour of presenting them.[11] When questions were asked about the reason for the expedition, the reply was that the question missed an important point – 'how could they expect to know anything of the mighty universe of which the world is but an atom, if they didn't explore to the uttermost recesses of their own little globe?'[12]

Finally, on 21 December, Julius, Bishop of Christchurch, came on board to bless the explorers. The men in their working clothes sang their final land-based hymn, *O God our help in ages past*, lustily. The send off was a rousing event; cheer after cheer followed the ship as she sailed, bands played *Say Au Revoir But Not Good-bye* as *Discovery*, with her forty-four crew members, made her way to Port Chalmers – her last port of call before Antarctica. But the happy, noisy, band-blaring atmosphere was instantly destroyed when one of the young seamen, Charles Bonner, who had climbed to the top of the main mast, fell 100ft to his death from the mast truck.[13] He seems to have stood up, holding on to just a wind vane, and lost his balance at the first sea swell. There was a 'wild cry' as he hurtled headfirst onto the corner of an iron deckhouse,[14] spilling his brains over the deck. Skelton thought he was the worse for liquor when he went up and he hoped the death would be an object lesson to the men who had been drinking too much,[15] but records from the crew do not mention alcohol. They were dumbfounded; the accident cast a gloom over the ship's company – death had visited them in seconds, depriving them of a popular crew member who, they knew, had left a fiancée in England. Able Seaman Duncan wrote, 'Every one went about his work silently and quietly; they were afraid that the least sound would disturb the dead … Myself and another of his messmates washed poor Charlie and put a Union Jack over him and put him quietly to rest on the poop ready for internment at Port Chalmers.'[16] Bonner was buried with full military honours; his body was carried on a gun carriage.[17] Bluejackets from *Ringarooma*, another British ship in port, formed a funeral escort and firing party.

When *Discovery* sailed into the unknown, weighed down by personnel and scientific equipment, provisions, coal, terrified sheep, snarling dogs and livestock, *Ringarooma* (whose officers and crew had given a benefit concert for *Discovery*) gave the crew three cheers and crewman Williamson wrote that 'as Englishmen and brothers in arms, we could not hold it any longer, so we bucked up in spirit and gave them something of a return. The best possible under the circumstances. Good-bye civilisation.'[18]

Christmas Day passed without celebration; the crew had no heart for it. Just a religious service as they sailed over the Southern Ocean. New Year's Day also started with melancholy memories of those loved ones 14,000 miles away. A feeling of isolation permeated all ranks. Scott wrote of this, so did Seaman Duncan. But as the day progressed and the crew sailed under clear skies, they were diverted to a degree by a new phenomenon – icebergs. These came as a revelation to the men, most of whom could never even have imagined such extraordinary icy sculptures. Soon six or more icebergs were in view, each one a miracle of blue and green and white. Some bergs were tabular, flat topped and with perpendicular sides.

On 3 January 1902, *Discovery* crossed the Antarctic Circle at 66° 33'S and was now within the Antarctic Circle, the second major British exploration to be there since Captain James Clark Ross in the 1840s.[19] (Bernacchi recorded the custom, which allows seamen to drink a toast with both feet on a table.)[20] On that day the ship re-entered the pack ice. This belt of ice, which consists of the sea-ice from previous seasons and which is sprinkled liberally with icebergs, surrounds Antarctica. It is separated from the mainland by a rim of water in the Antarctic summer; in winter the whole sea freezes northwards for hundreds of miles. Edgar had aimed at adventure and excitement when he joined the navy, he must have felt fulfilled as he looked across the remarkable sight; hummocks of ice piled up in endless confusion, the surface white intensified by the greens and blues in the hollows and showing starkly against pools of dark water. The later calm of the sea was a big relief after the blustery Southern Ocean.

Time spent going through the pack was not wasted. As *Discovery* pushed her way through her crew took every opportunity to catch seals, and soon the upper deck looked more like a butcher's shop than His Majesty's Ship, as gory carcases of sheep and seal meat were hung on the rigging to freeze. Scott was determined that all the crew should eat fresh meat. He hoped this might be an added protection against scurvy, and the liver was often served at breakfast, the meat at dinner. Some thought the meat 'very good, better than beef, especially Bombay beef'[21], but Edgar could never get used to it and didn't enjoy it. The biggest seal caught on the pack was a huge crabeater seal that crew members Cross, Heald and Joyce and two officers bagged. It was nearly 8ft and over 1,200lbs. It certainly gave the crew enough food for a few days. Edgar saw Emperor penguins for the first time; the birds looked large, more like small seals, but they were indisputably penguins. One was standing on his hind legs, his characteristic beak and yellow throat clearly visible.

Discovery sailed close to the 170°E meridian in the direction of the hut where the explorer Borchgrevink had overwintered in 1899. As she battled through the pack the crew 'watered the ship'. They swarmed over the side armed with picks and shovels to cut blocks of snow from the top of the floe.[22] The ice was melted in long tanks fitted with steam coils. In this way tons of water could be collected in a few hours.[23] In 1901 Scott had no way of knowing how long *Discovery* would be in the pack (he knew that one expedition had been held in the pack for fifteen months and some of her crew had died before she was released without reaching her objective). In the event, she got through the pack in five days in spite of a few collisions with heavy pieces of ice. The crew picked a path through open patches of water whenever they could find them.

The 5 January 1902 was celebrated as the Christmas holiday. It was a Sunday and Edgar joined the morning service celebrating with Christmas and New Year hymns. On that day three memorable things happened:

firstly, the sun 'forgot to set' (and did not remember how to do so again till shortly before midnight on 15 February, to be followed by long days which gradually grew shorter until 'Old Sol' disappeared on the 24 April for four months).[24] Secondly, the skis that were to be used in Antarctica were tried for the first time. In 1901 skis were much longer than those used today and only one 150cm bamboo pole was used as a ski stick. The pole had an iron ferrule and a point at the end. This unwieldy combination must have been difficult to master but Edgar took to it well. He was competitive, athletic and strong, and by the end of the afternoon, in spite of collisions and falls, he felt confident enough to take part in races. Thirdly, the crew saw their first Adélie penguins. These birds, named after the French explorer Dumont d'Urville's wife, are quarrelsome and noisy, but the crew were instantly captivated by the way the Adélies ran eagerly and fearlessly up to them. Later, Dr Edward Wilson was embarrassed to record how a male Adélie made overtures to him by offering him a stone for a nest. In his collection of First World War writings, *Goodbye to All That and Other Great War Writings*, Robert Graves included the story of how a male Adélie passed Wilson, looked at him admiringly and returned to deposit his gift at Wilson's feet.[25]

After these new experiences, everyone congregated on the mess deck for a sing-along and a barrel of beer, presented before *Discovery* left England.[26] Cards were given to the men by Dr Wilson (a gift from his wife), and he gave the Petty Officers a box of crackers. They also received gifts from Royd's mother. The Mess desk was dressed and Scott wrote that it 'looked very nice'.[27] Celebrations ended with the men singing and cheering, and an extra tot of rum was served.

Soon open sea was visible beyond the pack, backed in the distance by the Antarctic mountains – mountains hitherto unexplored. For the first time Edgar could appreciate the awesome, austere beauty of Antarctica. Early on 8 January, basked in beautiful sunshine and surrounded by calm blue water, *Discovery* steamed into the open sea. A day later Edgar, with his companions, landed at Cape Adare. Crew member Williamson wrote, 'Soon all was excitement, we lowered the boats and were soon scrambling up the beach where the great man Borchgrevink spent that lonely and tiresome winter.'[28] Some local inhabitants were also excited; another colony of Adélie penguins gave the men their close attention. The birds jumped in and out of the water, squawking to their friends and managing to look both earnest and comical. Borchgrevink's hut impressed; Seaman

Duncan wrote that it was constructed on a log cabin principle and could be assembled quickly. Duncan thought it was better than the one they had brought.[29] Some useful provisions and coal remained from 1899.

The sun shone all night and the distant mountains gleamed as the crew left a tin cylinder on the Cape's stony shore. This contained records and private letters and was the first in the series of the hopeful paper chase of messages left so that the relief vessel could follow *Discovery*'s progress. Lashly left a letter for his wife; 'she may get it some day if the postman should happen to come this way'.[30]

Discovery sailed down the west coast of the Ross Sea looking for likely landing places and winter quarters. All too soon Edgar and his colleagues understood the power of the elements ranged against them. The crew kept a watchful eye on proceedings as the ship escaped from a chain of icebergs, then had to shelter from a raging snowstorm. Williamson later said it was, 'more like two gales lashed together'.[31] On the 15 January, once the wind had subsided, men were able to land to leave another of those hopeful messages, marked by a red pole, for the relief ship. These small containers were literally their sole method of communication with the outside world. As she sailed along the coastline *Discovery* passed close by icebergs and the crew captured a variety of seal that completed their collection of the 'set' of pack-ice seals: Weddell, Crabeater, Ross, Leopard.[32]

When ice blocked further exploration south on 22 January, *Discovery* turned eastwards, charting the coastline. Amongst the confusion of mountains that they passed, some named, others not, the crew saw the two volcanoes recorded by Ross, Mount Erebus and Mount Terror, at over 100 miles away. Mount Erebus was, and remains, an active volcano (the world's most southern). Mount Terror was thought to be dormant, but the crew decided immediately that during the expedition they would climb it and settle any doubts. *Discovery* passed Cape Crozier. This cape, home to thousands of Emperor penguins was a place that was to linger permanently in Edgar's mind after he was involved in an abortive expedition to reach it. But now it was merely the recipient of a third record of instructions and letters for the relief ship. This time two red cylinders were placed conspicuously in the centre of the penguin rookery.

From Cape Crozier, Edgar had his first view of Ross' famous Barrier, then one of the unsolved mysteries of Antarctica. The Barrier stretched as far as the eye could see in an irregular coastline. The crew were a bit let down – Gilbert Scott was 'greatly disappointed' at its appearance,[33] as they had heard so much about it from Ross' descriptions. Perhaps its contrast with the huge mountains they had just passed made it look smaller than they had thought, a bit like a flat sea broken up by wind furrows.[34] *Discovery* sailed east along the Barrier for seven days. New findings were made; the Barrier is 400 miles long and between 200–400ft high. Soundings were taken along the whole length, and on good days, with the sun shining, it was like a pleasure trip.

By 28 January the height of the Barrier was getting lower. Sea soundings recorded a depth of around 90 fathoms (at the other end of the Barrier the sea soundings were 640 fathoms) and on the 30th, two high peaks of land were seen. Ross had believed that there was land to the east of the Barrier but had been unable to prove it, so this was a big discovery. Lashly was unmoved, commenting laconically, 'so we have passed the ice barrier at last'.[35] But Gilbert Scott wrote that it was the first finding of land in the twentieth century 'which human eye had never seen before'.[36] It was named after King Edward VII, *Discovery's* patron.

Finding winter quarters was becoming increasingly urgent. It was time to turn back. However, the return was difficult and there was a close shave with icebergs.[37] On 1 February it was feared that *Discovery* would be trapped in rapidly forming ice, as she steamed round and round trying to find an opening. Still, discipline was maintained. Williamson grumbled; 'this monstrous idea of scrubbing decks every morning … in below freezing temperature … it seems as though they cannot forget that navy idea or commandment of thou shalt not miss scrubbing decks no matter under what circumstances, if it did any good I would not mind but as soon as you turn the water on it is frozen and then you have to come along with shovels to pick the ice up'.[38]

After this danger the emphasis to get back to secure winter quarters increased, but on the sail along the Barrier a stop was made to make a balloon ascent. *Discovery* was secured in a little bay called Balloon Bight (later the Bay of Whales), and this was the furthest south any ship had been; it was also the site from which Roald Amundsen was to make his successful sortie to the Pole in 1911. In 1902 all hands were occupied in filling the balloon with hydrogen. It was hoped that seeing the Antarctic from on high would yield information about her interior. Scott made the first ascent, he forgot the camera so, when Shackleton went up next, he became the first aerial photographer of the Antarctic. None of the hands were invited to ascend, not even those who had undergone special training in Aldershot. In the event the only finding was a view of miles and miles of snow, and the realisation that ballooning in Antarctica, in inexperienced hands, is a very chancy business.

By 8 February *Discovery* had reached the top of McMurdo Sound.[39] Scott decided to make his winter base in the shallow bay close to a tongue of land jutting out from the slopes of Mount Erebus (which steamed intermittently throughout the expedition). It was relatively close to the Barrier and gave access to the interior. The crew blasted the ice away with gun-cotton to get as far inland as possible and the ship was snug in snow and ice from 12–30ft deep. Here they landed. The shore party, with Edgar as Petty Officer, landed to erect a hut on a rocky promontory looking across to Mount Erebus – the base was known as 'Hut Point'. Edgar must have been relieved. Along with many of the crew he must have wondered if he would ever get this far.

Notes

1 Scott, G., *Journal during the BNA Expedition*, SPRI. MS 1485: D.
2 Duncan, J., *Journal kept during the British National Antarctic Expedition 1901–1904, 4/10/01–8/11/02*. SPRI MS.1415; D, p. 3.
3 Williamson, T.S., *Logs 1901–1904*, MS, 774/1/1: BJ, p. 47. p. 31.
4 Forecastle. The space at the front of the ship below the main deck where the crew's quarters were.
5 Williamson, T.S., *Logs 1901–1904*, MS, 774/1/1: BJ, p. 31.
6 Sea ice loses its salinity after about three years.
7 Williamson, T.S., *Logs 1901–1904*, MS, 774/1/1: BJ, p. 47.
8 Scott, G., *Journal during BNA Expedition* SPRI MS 1485: D.
9 Ibid.
10 Skelton, R., *The Antarctic Journals of Reginald Skelton*, Reardon Publishing, Cheltenham, England, 2004, p. 31.
11 James Duncan. *Journal kept during the British National Antarctic Expedition 1901–1904, 4/10/01–8/11/02*. SPRI MS.1415; D, p. 3.
12 Baughman, T.H., *Pilgrims on the Ice*, University of Nebraska Press, Lincoln and London, 1999, p. 85.
13 A truck – a guide for ship's ropes in the form of a disk with holes, fitted to the top of the mast.
14 Scott, R.F., *Scott's Voyage of the Discovery*, John Murray, London, 1929, p.84.
15 Skelton, R., *The Antarctic Journals of Reginald Skelton*, Reardon Publishing, Cheltenham, England, 2004, p. 33.

16 James Duncan. *Journal kept during the British National Antarctic Expedition,* 19011904. 4/10/01–8/11/02. SPRI MS.1415; D .

17 Ibid.

18 Williamson, T.S., *Logs 1901–1904*, MS, 774/1/1: BJ, p. 51.

19 Borchgrevink's British Antarctic Expedition of 1898–1890, which sailed in *Southern Cross* was British, but in name only. Only three of the thirty-one men on board were not Norwegian.

20 Bernacchi, L.C., *Saga of the Discovery*, Blackie, London, 1938, p. 23.

21 Ellis, A.R., *Under Scott's Command: Lashly's Antarctic Diaries*, Victor Gollancz, London, 1969, p. 21.

22 Scott, R.F. *The Voyage of the Discovery*, John Murray, London, 1929, p. 94.

23 Ibid., p. 95.

24 Wild, J.R.F., *Letters to Mrs Bostock*, SPRI MS 1078/3/1: D, p. 3.

25 Robert Graves, *Goodbye to All That and Other Great War writings*, Carcanet, London, Postscript, p. 280.

26 Williamson, T.S., *Logs 1901–1904*, MS, 774/1/1: BJ, p. 55.

27 Scott, G. *Journal during BNA Expedition* SPRI MS 1485: D.

28 Williamson, T.S., *Logs 1901–1904*, MS, 774/1/1: BJ, p. 59.

29 James Duncan, *Journal kept during the British National Antarctic Expedition 1901–1904*, 4/10/01–8/11/02. SPRI MS.1415; D.

30 Ellis, A.R., *Under Scott's Command: Lashly's Antarctic Diaries*, Victor Gollancz, London, 1969, p. 21.

31 Williamson, T.S., *Logs 1901–1904*, MS, 774/1/1: BJ, p. 63.

32 Skelton, R., *The Antarctic Journals of Reginald Skelton*, Reardon Publishing, Cheltenham, England, 2004, p. 43.

33 Scott, G., *Journal during BNA Expedition* SPRI MS 1485:D

34 Ed. Savours, A., *Edward Wilson, Diary of the Discovery Expedition to the Antarctic 1901–1904*, Blandford Press, London, 1966, p. 105.

35 Ellis, A.R., *Under Scott's Command, Lashly's Antarctic Diaries*, Victor Gollancz, London, 1969. p. 24.

36 Scott, G., *Journal during BNA Expedition* SPRI MS 1485: D.

37 Ibid.

38 Williamson, T.S., *Logs 1901–1904*, MS, 774/1/1: BJ. p. 79.

39 Ed. Savours, A., *Edward Wilson, Diary of the Discovery Expedition to the Antarctic 1901–1904*. Blandford Press, London, 1966, p. 112.

6

Early Months in Antarctica: February to September 1902

Work started on Hut Point immediately. Speed was essential in the construction; the magnetic huts, store huts, kennels, provisions, coal and water all needed to be on land quickly. Scott couldn't be certain that *Discovery* would not be torn away from her moorings, so any shore party had to be self-sufficient.

It was a hard job: the supports had to be dug deep into the frozen ground and it was difficult to locate all the pieces for making up the sides.[1] When the hut was finished its roof was felted and covered in heavy double wood and, surprisingly, it had a veranda around its walls (the men thought it was better suited to a colonial shooting lodge than a polar base). In fact, the original idea, that it should be the permanent base for the expedition, became unnecessary when *Discovery* stayed in Antarctica over the winter rather than returning to New Zealand. Thus the men lived on the ship, mainly using the hut for storage, drying clothes and putting on entertainments. Problems with the hut's construction became apparent; when the stove was lit, snow on the roof melted and leaked through, icing up clothes stored there for weeks. Some of the men were not too overwhelmed by Antarctica; Seaman Duncan wrote 'this seems like a dreary place to be spending twelve months in'.[2] Ross Island and the hut were to be their base for the next two years. Behind the land rose gradually towards hills of about 500ft. The crew named these 'Arrival Heights' and 'Harbour Heights', and they called the mass of rock north of these hills, which rose over 1000ft above sea level, 'Castle Rock'.

Scott was aware that the problem of keeping over thirty men occupied might become acute throughout the freezing, dark Antarctic winter, when poor visibility precluded any sorties and when small irritations could easily become magnified. Recreational activities were not neglected. With the continuing light in the Antarctic autumn (February–March), football and hockey were regularly played. Teams were imaginatively varied to cross ranks: married or engaged against singles, older men against the youngsters. Sometimes, Officers against Men (Officers 3, Men 2 on 13 February was a particular highlight). The rules were lax; there was no such thing as 'off-side'. Hockey matches lasted an hour and were played in temperatures of -30°C, or even lower. Improvising, the crew used light sticks and a homemade hardball. This was just as well with men such as Edgar on the attack. Big (just under 12 stone) and athletic, he dashed about, a misty vapour steaming round his head helmet, his stick high in the air, eager to attack the opposition with deadly intent; a fearsome opponent indeed. Skiing was encouraged also whilst the light held: in spite of the cumbersome equipment there was only one serious injury – a broken leg.

Edgar made himself useful immediately. Scott said he was a man of 'Herculean strength' and 'well muscled'. Equally important in a party isolated from the rest of the world, he had a cheerful nature and was reliable and practical, outgoing and gregarious but not boastful or pushy. On this expedition during the next twenty-three months, he was to take part in some of *Discovery*'s most important sorties. These would make him a hardened veteran of Polar exploration and one of Scott's most trusted colleagues.

Most of the outings would take him towards, or on to, the Western Mountains, that enormous range of mountains to the west of McMurdo Sound. On three expeditions he was with Scott on journeys (totalling ninety-four days), the last being a stupendous 950 statute mile journey into the mountains. This expedition was a sledging feat that conclusively proved the immensity of the continent. It was a feat equal to the huge journeys of the Arctic explorers half a century earlier.

The crew understood that Scott retained absolute authority and realised that he was prepared to use this authority. Two days after *Discovery* berthed he ordered that the cook, Charles Brett, should be put in irons for insubordination. One of the crew, Duncan, simply recorded 'Mr Brett getting troublesome'.[3] (Brett refused to report for duty; he was fed up with working in the galley all day.) The lively scene, as Brett fought his captors, before he was finally clapped in irons, was recorded in the diaries. But this was the only time that physical discipline was used on the expedition.

Naval routine continued on land. Whilst the light lasted, the crew worked from 7 a.m. until 8 a.m. when they had breakfast: porridge, followed by curry with rice/salmon/mince/sardines/rissoles/cold tongue, washed down with cocoa or coffee.[4] Work continued until midday when there was a break for an hour and a half for dinner (soup followed by ham/beef pie/seal/tinned meat with vegetables then a pudding).[5] Virtually all the food came from tins. Soon after they arrived the men continued work until 5 p.m., but as the light faded they finished for the day by early afternoon.[6] The provision of artificial light was a necessity as there were twenty-four hours of darkness during the Antarctic winter. Scott was very conscious of the necessity for light, both for psychological reasons and for health (darkness was thought to contribute to Polar Madness). An attempt to manufacture a windmill dynamo to produce electricity failed repeatedly (the windmill blades snapped in the wind) so an oxyacetylene lamp was used to give light for about eight hours, otherwise candles (provided or homemade) were used and gave enough light for the men to write up their logs, play cards, draughts or chess. Royds showed magic lantern slides.[7]

Edgar's first sledging expedition was a catastrophe. It highlighted total British inexperience in coping with Antarctic conditions and was notable for its lack of proper preparation and for its incompetence. It was a hard lesson in survival. On this expedition Edgar was one of the inadvertent but blameless causes of a domino-type series of disasters that left one crewman dead and that could have easily resulted in the deaths of seven other crewmen and the officer in charge of them, Lieutenant Michael Barne. None of the equipment had been tested before the expedition set out. It was to be, as Scott wrote, 'one of our blackest days in the Antarctic'.[8]

The sortie was to Cape Crozier, and its practical purpose was to update the messages for the relief ship on the position of *Discovery*'s winter quarters. When the expedition set out no one understood how weather in Antarctica could change in a very short time from reasonable conditions to howling blizzards. The expedition lasted a memorable fifteen days, from 4–19 March (autumn in Antarctica).

The party was under the command of Lieutenant Charles Royds. There were three other officers, including Lieutenant Barne, and also nine crew members. Scott wrote later that the packed sledges 'presented an appearance of which we should afterwards have been wholly ashamed'.[9] The party took two sledges and four tents, with Edgar sharing a tent with Stoker Frank Plumley and Seaman William Heald. They slept in a three-man sleeping bag for extra warmth (but extra discomfort) and quickly understood the horrors of Antarctic journeys in the autumn.

They took pyramidal tents, big enough for three people to lie down in but for only one person to stand in comfortably. To erect the tent they firstly had to spread and stabilize bamboo poles on the ice and then cover them with the tent cloth: when a high wind was blowing, this would involve a long struggle with flapping canvas and collapsing poles. With the tent erected, snow was piled around its base to stabilize it. Edgar and his companions kept their woollen underwear on throughout the sorties but changed into their reindeer fur suits for sleeping (a prolonged business as the furs got as stiff as boards) and slept on a canvas cloth. Anything they took off had to be put in the shape it needed to be in the following morning, since garments froze (in a few minutes) into whatever shape they were left in. Unlacing the leggings was another ordeal. The men had to use their bare fingers which meant putting their hands back into their mitts every few minutes. One of the most important aspects of the night routine was foot care: frostbite could progress to gangrene so the utmost care had to be taken. The night socks were carried next to their skin during the daytime march; at night the innermost pair of day socks was changed with this pair and in turn put next to the skin. Grass was also used to absorb sweat and was often put next to the skin at night. Long fur boots reaching to the knee were worn with the fur nightwear. When they eventually got into their sleeping bags, they shivered and shook for hours, rime inside the tent from the evening cooking dripping onto their faces. Morning was always a welcome relief.

On the Cape Crozier Expedition, following three exhausting days and 21 miles progress, the work of finding the trail and keeping to the course was passed from the officers to Able Seaman William Heald and Edgar. But, after a short time, as conditions remained so difficult, the officers changed the plan again, unwisely deciding that those party members with skis – Royds, Skelton and Koettlitz (who had previous experience of Polar conditions in the Arctic) – should go on, leaving the inexperienced Barne to lead the nine men home (the Royds trio did not reach Cape Crozier).

On 9 March, Lieutenant Barne set off to return to the ship. The party made good progress initially, but on the 11th they ran into such atrocious flying drift that they stopped and pitched their tent for protection. Miserably they ate biscuits and solid, cold pemmican (the stove was broken). Two of the seamen, Vince and Hare, had such problems with frozen feet in the leather ski boots that they changed them for fur finnesko.

They were only about 4 miles from the ship, but the wrong decision was made when the group decided to abandon the tent, let the dogs loose and go on by foot in the direction which they thought led to *Discovery*. This was unwise because blizzards only last for two to three days in Antarctica and they would probably have been safe if they had stuck in their tent. But they had no way of knowing this; they were exhausted, freezing, frightened, hungry and thirsty with no means of heating ice for drinking water. As the wind thundered against the tent, they thought they could be blown away with every gust and they decided that it would be safe to make a dash for the ship, just a few miles away. In fact Lieutenant Barne, in the negligible visibility, miscalculated their position; they were actually close to cliffs on the north side of the Hut Point peninsula. The group of nine progressed cautiously along a steep icy slope with snow swirling around them. Vince and Hare in finnesko (no grip) slipped and slithered on the icy surface. When Hare decided to return for his boots he disappeared almost immediately. Lieutenant Barne and the remaining eight spread out to try to find him, and as they did so Edgar lost his footing and disappeared down a steep slope. Showing more courage than reason, Barne threw himself down the slope after him. He found himself accelerating down an ever-increasing gradient until he was, miraculously, stopped by the same snow bank that had halted Edgar's descent.

When the American seaman Arthur Quartley made the same decision to go down the slope to find Barne and Edgar, he left behind him, on that exposed hillside, six Polar novices in a blizzard that reduced vision to a few feet and with no idea of where they were. As they attempted a diagonal descent down the slope, they too began to slip, Wild said, 'at a fearful rate with no idea where they were going and no hope of stopping'.[10] Vince was first, Seaman Wild second, the other three close behind. Suddenly Wild stopped with a jerk on a snow ledge. The men behind all slid down helplessly and landed on his ledge except for George Vince, who was unable to stop, probably because he was in finnesko, who shot on and disappeared. The men could see a ledge 20ft from where they had landed. As they crawled cautiously towards it, the drift lifted and they saw, to their horror, the drop of 90ft into the sea that Vince had spiralled down. Shouting had no effect in that howling hurricane. They had to leave Vince to his dreadful fate.[11] The young seaman was to be Scott's only Antarctic fatality on the *Discovery* expedition.

Edgar, Lieutenant Barne and Arthur Quartley had no hope of getting up the slope to rejoin their companions. They cautiously made their way in what they hoped was the direction of the ship. At one point Barne was just saved from joining Vince in the sea by the quick thinking of Quartley who pulled him back from the edge of the cliff. Barne's compass was not working and the three men walked and crawled along until they finally saw a landmark they knew. Then they progressed more confidently, aided by the blaring of the ship's siren.

When they stumbled across a search party, the three were virtually unrecognisable. They could not speak intelligibly (Dr Wilson writes that one of them was talking rubbish),[12] and they were all dazed. Barne was so affected by the cold that he could hardly speak at all, intelligibly or otherwise, and the trio had to be identified by Quartley. Edgar's ear was badly frostbitten. It looked like an apple, but he said it felt like a cabbage.[13] He had frostbite of his fingers and feet, and his nose was swollen to a prodigious size. He was to continue to have problems with his nose on later expeditions; he would refer to it as his 'Old Blossom'. All three were put in the sick bay and looked after by Dr Wilson. The experience had no long-term physical effect on Edgar, though by now he undoubtedly understood the necessity for thorough preparation.

But what of Hare, the man who had first left the party to get his ski boots? He had an extraordinary adventure, reappearing uninjured, even without frostbite, after being caught in below-freezing temperatures for two days with no protection. Hare was put in the Magnetic Laboratory at 17°F and the temperature was gradually raised to freezing point. Remarkably he suffered no long term effects and could only have survived because he stopped near to the shelter of a pile of rocks, pulled his arms into his woollen blouse (under the gabardine wind jacket) and covered the opening to his helmet. He must have been covered in snow, which left enough space for him to breathe, a sort of primitive snow hole.[14] When he got back to the ship Scott was so relieved he looked 'as if he thought the dead were walking in'.[15]

By 19 March *Discovery* was firmly frozen into her winter quarters. Good Friday, 28 March, was celebrated with hot cross buns 'or bricks, could hardly tell which'.[16] By 3 April the ship was in darkness. Throughout the winter the doctors examined the men carefully with blood tests, chest measurements, waist, biceps, forearm and calf measurements, weight and a record of blowing power.

There was one further expedition in the autumn of 1902. Edgar was not on it. It was also unsuccessful because the conditions were simply too bad for expedition work. Called the Southern Depot Attempt, the expedition from 31 March to 4 April 1902 was to lay a series of depots to the south in preparation for exploration the following year. The expedition took eighteen dogs and four sledges, but the horrors of sledging in late autumn were again all too apparent. The temperature was between -26° and -40°F. If the men touched any metal it stung like a hot iron and left a white mark; the dogs would hardly pull; the snow surface was awful and the wind made progress terrible. The trip lasted three days with the men enduring miserable nights. Scott decided to depot the provisions early and turn back. On the way home the dogs pulled for all they were worth.

The 23 April was the official beginning of the long winter. Although the moon's movements (disappearing and returning every month), the rotation of the stars and the shortening of each day told them that time was actually passing, the sun, a vital force, had disappeared from their lives. On the 25th, the first edition of the *South Polar Times* was produced – 'The paper is a very good one quite interesting and amusing'.[17] Editions were to continue throughout the expedition. A single copy of an alternative paper, *The Blizzard*, was produced for those submissions not quite up to the standard of the *South Polar Times*. Unfortunately entries were anonymous, and if Edgar made an attempt it is not recorded. Scrap albums were popular, as was making metal models, but it was cold in the workshop and the men had to wear mittens to avoid a skin burn when the cold metal was touched.[18] The winter blizzards raged with gusts of over 100 miles an hour.[19] However, Edgar never tired of looking at the auroras, those brilliant undulating lights which lit up the pitch-black sky.[20]

By mid May, there was only half an hour of twilight in the whole day. A good moon meant that they could get about a bit, and the crew played football by moonlight when they could (though the doctor said it was injurious to health at such low temperatures). They played until 14 June, only a few days before Midwinter's Day.

As the winter months progressed some resentment creeps into the diaries; things were allegedly 'slack' with the officers who had intended to work wonders to keep the men entertained during the winter, but had not even started when the winter was nearly half gone (only one concert having been performed). The crew wanted the promised classes and information about the scientific work. The Lower Deck felt hard done by.

But the bleak months passed without any serious problems and the men were soon to hear Scott's plans for the expedition. He may have been aware of the rumbles. On Sunday 22 June, Midwinter's Day, he spoke to the men. He said firstly that he was pleased with the general health of the ship's company and he emphasised how each man must continue to look after his own health so as to be fit for sledging. He went on to say that he wanted all the men to have their chance to take part in expeditions and explained how different parties would go south, west and towards the Magnetic Pole.

Midwinter's Day was indeed a welcome diversion. The mess was beautifully decorated with coloured paper and draped in flags, garlands, wreathes and the men's photographs.[21] The stokers had carved an ice block into the shape of a frost king with his crown. More photos were taken. The crew had bloaters (soaked, smoked herrings) for breakfast (they needed a lot of water afterwards), and little toys and puzzles had been sent by Mrs Royds, which helped to pass the time, as did cards from Mrs Wilson. Dinner was real turtle soup; ham, kidney beans, potatoes and plum pudding with brandy sauce washed down with bottles of Bass ale, this showing that the crew were served a good and varied diet. After this largesse and a post prandial nap, there were ices made of condensed milk and chocolate vanilla, cakes and sweets, before the day was rounded off with grog and, finally, a concert in the Royal Terror Theatre. Some of the crew went to the Captain asking for more lubrication. Unsurprisingly, Scott had no difficulty in refusing.[22]

On 6 August, the anniversary of *Discovery* sailing from England, a minstrel show was held in the Royal Terror Theatre (The Hut); the singing was 'very fair indeed',[23] and in the later part of the winter months there were lectures on geology, wireless telegraphy (very interesting), 'Sledging To-day', the 'Wonders of the Deep' and magic lantern shows.[24] These probably received a varied reception, but in general the bleak months passed without any serious problems. Lashly wrote that he had plenty of work to do, and that everyone was preparing for the sledging journeys and weeks passed very well.[25] Alterations and improvements were made to the furs, their sleeping bags and the sledging equipment in general.

On Friday 22 August 1902, the sun returned at last. Most of the men climbed the hills to get a glimpse of it. Its first appearance for four long months, a brilliant red and the sky all around it, looked, as Williamson said, 'something beautiful.'[26] As daylight increased so everyone's mood improved. The sledges and automatic sledgemeters were tested. Edgar became, unsurprisingly, an excellent sledge hauler; he was soon considered one of the best.[27]

Notes

1 James Duncan, *Journal kept during the British National Antarctic Expedition 1901–1904. 4/10/01–8/11/02*, SPRI MS.1415; D, p. 45.

2 James Duncan, *Journal kept during the British National Antarctic Expedition 1901–1904. 4/10/01–8/11/02*, SPRI MS.1415; D, 10 February.

3 Ibid., 10 February.

4 Yelverton, D., *Antarctica Unveiled*, University Press of Colorado, 2000, p. 154.

5 Ibid., p.154.

6 Williamson, T.S., *Log 13/07/01–23/06/02* SPRI MS 744/1/1: BJ, 22–30 April 1902.

7 Ibid., 1 May 1902.

8 Scott, R.F., *The Voyage of the Discovery*, John Murray, London, 1929, p. 173.

9 Ibid., p. 170.

10 Wild, J.R.F., Letter to Mrs A.C. Bostock (his cousin), SPRI, MS 1078/3/1; D

11 Ibid.

12 Ed. Savours, A. , *Edward Wilson, Diary of the Discovery Expedition to the Antarctic 1901–1904*, Blandford Press, London, 1966, p. 123.

13 Ibid., p. 124.

14 Williams, I., *With Scott in the Antarctic: Edward Wilson, Explorer Naturalist, Artist*, The History Press, Stroud, Gloucestershire, England, 2009.

15 Ed. Savours, A., *Edward Wilson, Diary of the Discovery Expedition to the Antarctic 1901–1904*, Blandford Press, London, 1966, p. 125.

16 Ellis, A.R., *Under Scott's Command, Lashly's Antarctic Diaries*, Victor Gollancz, London, 1969, p. 35.

17 Ibid., p. 40.

18 James Duncan, *Journal kept during the British National Antarctic Expedition 1901–1904. 4/10/01–8/11/02.* SPRI MS.1415; D, p. 45.

19 Priestley, R., Lecture, *The Psychology of Polar Exploration*, SPRI, MS 1097/16/1; D.

20 Auroras are phenomena related to the sun because of its emission of electric particles. Protons and electrons originating in the sun are caught by the terrestrial magnetic fields. When these electrical particles meet the ionised gases in the higher layers of the atmosphere a light is produced in the sky.

21 Ed. Savours, A., *Edward Wilson, Diary of the Discovery Expedition to the Antarctic 1901–1904*. Blandford Press, London, 1966, p.155.

22 James Duncan, *Journal kept during the British National Antarctic Expedition 1901–1904. 4/10/01–8/11/02*. SPRI MS.1415; D. 23 June.

23 Ed. Savours, A., *Edward Wilson, Diary of the Discovery Expedition to the Antarctic 1901–1904*. Blandford Press, London, 1966, p. 168.

24 James Duncan, *Journal kept during the British National Antarctic Expedition 1901–1904. 4/10/01–8/11/02*. SPRI MS.1415; D. 23rd, p. 41.

25 Ibid., p. 42.

26 Williamson, T.S., *Log 13/07/01–23/06/02* SPRI MS 744/1/1: BJ 22 August 1902.

27 Ed. Skelton, J., *The Antarctic Journals of Reginald Skelton*, Reardon Publishing, Cheltenham, England, 2004, p. 109.

7

The Antarctic Spring:
September to October 1902

Edgar's first spring expedition was south-west, towards the mountains bordering the west coast of McMurdo Sound, which were such an important feature of *Discovery*'s exploratory and scientific itinerary. In fact the Western Mountains were to be the main destination for Edgar's expeditions throughout the *Discovery* expedition. The aim of this first sortie was to find a southerly route into the interior of Victoria Land; in addition the team were to study ice formation and geological features. But the expedition soon ran into trouble. Six men set out – two officers, Lieutenant Royds and Dr Koettlitz, with four from the lower deck, Edgar, William Lashly, Frank Wild and Arthur Quartley. Quartley and Lashly were Stokers and Wild was an Able Seaman. The four were recognized as an impressive combination. As the party set out with two sledges, one behind the other, Skelton wrote that the four were the 'best possible you could pick out of the ship. I wish I was going with them',[1] a comment echoed by the mess deck who already called them the Guarantee Party.

Even with the Guarantee Party, the team soon encountered problems as they aimed towards Black and Brown Islands, two islands engulfed by the great ice Barrier to the east of Mount Discovery and just over 20 miles from Hut Point. Snow ridges split the sledge runners, the light was awful, the temperature dropped to -56°F and they were engulfed in a violent blizzard. Although the party did manage some survey work in the area around the two islands, they found the going terrible. Wild, in particular, was unimpressed: the party, he wrote, 'did little except getting frost bitten and bad tempered and had a miserable time for ten days, for two of which we were confined to the tents whilst a glorious blizzard played Old Harry with things in general'.[2]

As the blizzard whirled around them and they started to shut the camp down, Lashly left his sleeping bag beside his tent and went back to collect more gear. He saw his bag being swept away into the swirling whiteness. On this sortie Lashly was sleeping in the officers' tent and had a single sleeping bag. In 1902, opinions varied about the relative benefits of one-man and three-man sleeping bags. Some thought the three-man bag warmer (though more uncomfortable than the single bag). Also, one-man sleeping bags for all would be excessively heavy, so whilst officers and scientists had single bags, the men usually shared a three-man bag. Lashly, since he shared a tent with the officers, had been issued with a single bag, but when it disappeared he had to crowd in with Edgar, Wild, and Quartley. When one of them said 'turn', they all had to turn. Lashly, in a phlegmatic understatement, said that it 'was rather crowded'.[3] As the blizzard raged the men had to sit in the tent with their backs against the canvas to stop it tearing to pieces. The following day the bag was still missing and the party decided to retreat – the men were fed up and frostbitten. They decided that they were every type of fool to have ever come to Antarctica and swore that nothing would bring them back … and yet, the glamour of the vastness of the place, the scenery, the anticipation of finding something new, the satisfaction of winning against nature 'remain with one and call men again and again to, *"that stark and sullen solitudes, that sentinel, The Pole"*.'[4]

Before Edgar's next sledging party a problem surfaced that was to surprise and worry the entire crew. Second-in-Command Armitage had led an expedition to the interior of the south-western mountains. His party was also searching for a route that would lead into the interior of Antarctica. Six days into his trip and on a glacier high in the mountains, the team were held up by storms and deteriorating health (one man, Ferrar, had aches in his legs, another a troublesome ankle and another sore gums). Armitage suspected scurvy. He left two men behind in the camp and continued to explore the glacier valley before leading the team back to Hut Point. Confirmation of the disease caused considerable anxiety. The belief that scurvy was due to putrefaction in tinned food had been proved wrong and despite all the efforts that had been taken to avoid the problem (cleaning the ship, taking as much exercise as possible,[5] providing as much light as could be managed and carefully examining every tin of food before it was eaten for possible contamination)[6] scurvy was 'an unwelcome surprise'.[7] The advice Scott had been given was wrong.

As we now know scurvy is a deficiency disease due to a lack of vitamin C. It appears when the vitamin has been absent from the diet for about three months. Vitamin C is mostly present in fruits, green vegetables and potatoes. Although 'vitamins' were an unknown concept in the early 1900s, *Discovery* in fact carried many tinned vegetables on board: artichokes, Brussels sprouts, carrots, cauliflower, haricots verts, petit pois, tomatoes and many dried and preserved fruits (for example, apples, apricots, peaches, pears, rhubarb).[8] According to Hawk and Bergeim's *Practical Physiological Chemistry* of 1924, some canned vegetables remained rich in vitamin C[9] (the canning methods used were apparently less destructive to the vitamin than boiling).[10] But even if this is true and the men ingested some vitamin C with the tinned vegetables and fruit, Armitage had only been away from the ship for a short time so the diet clearly provided less than the 125mg now thought to be required in a male smoker (less in the non-smoker).[11] When, as a result of this outbreak, fresh, rather than tinned meat was provided, this too was to prove ineffective. Vitamin C is present in offal (liver and kidney), but meat itself has little of the essential vitamin.[12] But in 1902 this information was tantalizingly unknown, though the symptoms, of lassitude, fatigue, spongy gums, swollen joints, aching muscles and swollen, red spots (which could later break down and rot), were all familiar. Armitage's party's symptoms were characteristic.

This diagnosis could clearly have dreadful consequences and radical action was called for. The ship was thoroughly cleaned, the bilges disinfected, overcrowding was reduced by some men sleeping in the hut and exercise was insisted on. Tinned meat was given up except for Tuesdays when the cook, Brett, had a day off ('Scurvy Tuesdays'), otherwise some form of fresh meat or, importantly, liver and kidney, was served daily, plus porridge each morning, 'liberal' jam and extra portions of bottled fruit.[13] Since it was thought that the problem was made worse by Brett's cooking, Armitage informed him that his (Brett's) bonus depended on an improvement. Suddenly, palatable, even tasty food appeared; and thereafter the men mostly enjoyed the meals and some thought the seal liver was delicious. An exception was Edgar, who never took to seal meat. But he must have eaten some offal and may have made up his vitamin intake with the tinned foodstuffs. Certainly he never developed scurvy on *Discovery*, in spite of all his sledging miles.

On 4 October, Edgar was off again, this time a return to Cape Crozier, the Cape where messages for the relief ship were left. In addition the party aimed to survey the land in general and, if possible, to climb Mount Terror to confirm whether it really was, or was not, an extinct volcano. This was a smaller party than the expedition in March, which had started out with thirteen members. It had two officers and the Guarantee Party, Edgar, Lashly, Quartley and Wild, who all went on skis pulling two sledges. It took a week's hard pulling for them to reach Cape Crozier, but on 11 October, Edgar and Engineer Skelton climbed down to the mail post on Cape Crozier and fixed their tin below the one already there, writing on the binding: 'planted 2.45 PM, 11th October 1902'. Then they both added their signatures.

The 11 October was productive. The two men were to make an important natural history discovery. They saw Emperor penguins on the shore and noted a track they thought was worth investigating. Emperors were a fascinating mystery in 1902; their life cycle obscure. It was assumed that no animal could possibly have evolved to breed in the caterwauling gloom of Antarctica and that the birds probably migrated north in the winter. When Skelton returned the following day he and his companions saw 300 Emperors squawking together on the sea ice. Skelton was convinced that he had made a significant discovery, but it would take another six days (18 October) before he could prove this, when with Edgar and Quartley he reached the rookery and captured two young birds. Dead chicks of various ages were strewn over the colony. This proved conclusively that Emperors did, indeed, breed in Antarctica.

Those five days delay between the visits to the shore was due to another blizzard. Wild wrote that the wind was 100mph. He said that the weight of snow bent the tent poles alarmingly. It also reduced the space inside the tents so much that the men could not lie straight in their bags; instead they had to take turns to keep the 'doorway' open and they could only cook one hot meal a day and that was with difficulty. Wild wrote that his companions' tent got completely snowed up and had to be dug out, its occupants having existed on biscuits and a little sugar for three days (another version is that they all lived on biscuits and sugar for five days and had nothing to drink in that time).[14] But Wild writes that the 'other' tent was revived by brandy and a good hot meal!

When the six men reached home base on 24 October, proudly carrying their young birds, all the men were suffering so badly from snow blindness that they did not recognise Dr Wilson who went out to meet them. They recorded their lowest temperature on the sortie had been -58.6°F. Unsurprisingly they had not attempted to climb Mount Terror.

They had a wonderful meal: seal liver and bacon. On the same night the sun started its 'shameful routine of forgetting to go to bed and staying out all night'.[15]

Notes

1 Ed. Skelton. J & Wilson, D., *The Antarctic Journals of Reginald Skelton* Reardon Publishing, 2004, p. 109.
2 Wild, J.R.F., Letter to Mrs Bostock. SPRI MS 1078/3/1; D.
3 Ellis, A.R., *Under Scott's Command, Lashly's Antarctic Diaries,* Victor Gollancz, London, 1969, p. 53.
4 *The Lure of Little Voices*, by Robert W Service (1874–1958) published 1907, Songs of a sourdough, Quotation written by Wilde, J.R.F., in Letter to Mrs Bostock. SPRI MS 1078/3/1;
5 Carpenter, K.J., *The History of Scurvy and Vitamin C,* Cambridge University Press, Cambridge, 1986, p. 138.
6 Scott had been strongly advised that the main cause of scurvy was ptomaine poisoning, putrefaction in tins. Dr Wilson's duty every morning was to sniff and taste the contents of all the tins to be eaten that day and discard any that were 'tainted'.
7 Wilson, E.A., *The Medical Aspect of the Discovery's Voyage to the Antarctic*, British Medical Journal, 1905 2 p. 77–80.
8 Information supplied by the Discovery Centre, Dundee, (Julie Millerick).
9 Hawk, P.B.; Bergeim, O., *Practical Physiological Chemistry*, Blackiston's Son. Philadelphia, 1926, p. 817.
10 Ibid., p. 818.
11 Food and Nutritional Board. Institute of Medicine, Vitamin C, Dietary Reference Intakes, National Academy Press: 2000: 95–185.
12 Personal communication. Professor Jeffrey Wood. Professor of Food and Animal Science, Bristol University, 2006.
13 Armitage, A.B., *Two Years in the Antarctic*, Paradigm Press, Bungay, Suffolk, 1984, p. 138.
14 Ed. Savers, A., *Diary of the Discovery Expedition to the Antarctic 1901–1904*, Blandford Press, London, 1966, p. 205.
15 Ibid.

8

The Antarctic Summer: October 1902 to January 1903

Commanded by Lieutenant Armitage, and with Chief Engineer Skelton and nine lower-deck companions, Edgar was on the Main Western Party from 29 November 1902 to 18 January 1903. The aim of the journey was to get as close as possible to the Magnetic Pole and to make recordings.

In 1902 the exact location of the South Magnetic Pole had not yet been identified,[1] and when the Main Western Party set off Edgar was well aware of the importance of its location to navigation. This related to the fact that magnetic compass readings differed significantly from the true north and by different amounts in different parts of the world. Charts showing magnetic declination, the difference between magnetic north and true north, were first produced in the 1770s. These charts had to be updated regularly (as is still done today), because the magnetic field pattern and the Magnetic Pole position change continuously, whereas the Geographical Pole remains fixed.

Historically, in spite of the charts, navigation errors had led to calamitous losses. Failure to correct a ship's compass accurately for the magnetic declination could result in the ship navigating a course miles from its intended land destination. This frequently led to disaster. Recordings made at sea were not as accurate as land-based recordings so the *Discovery* expedition was a unique opportunity to make many land-based recordings close to the Magnetic Pole, so that accurate adjustments could be made to the charts. The work, which was to be coordinated with the German and Swedish records, fulfilled an important part of *Discovery*'s brief.

It was a well-manned party: the Main Western Party comprised two officers (Skelton and Armitage), ten men (three from the Guarantee Party, Edgar, Wild and Quartley) and seven others. There was a Supporting Party of nine (two officers, seven men), who were to return after an anticipated three weeks, leaving the Main Western Party to continue. The ten sledges and four teams started off under a cloudless sky, pulling a total of nearly 5,000lbs, which included just under 2.5lbs of food per man per day and 112lbs of seal, mostly liver, which unfortunately had been cooked in fat and then oven dried in order to reduce weight. This reduced its vitamin C content to a minimum, a problem that was completely unsuspected at the time.

On any expedition enough food has to be carried for safe survival but not an ounce more. The basic sledge ration included: Pemmican, a concentrated rich mixture of fat and protein, soup squares and 'Red Ration' (a mixture of bacon and pea-flour to thicken the food), sugar, Bovril (a beef and yeast extract), rations, small amounts of chocolate, plasmon (a concentrated powder milk preparation), cheese and cocoa. The food was all individually marked; 'R' (Red Ration), 'Choc', etc, and was carried in weekly bags. Edgar shared his bag with Quartley and Horace Buckridge, a laboratory assistant.[2] Tea and matches were carried in a tin.

As they set off, the ship gave three cheers. Photographs were taken. The twenty-one-man party started off in good fettle with sails flying. Armitage's aim was to get to the south side of the Ferrar Glacier, the glacier he had been forced to return from a few months earlier, and thence onto the Polar Plateau. This glacier is enormous, bigger than all the European glaciers,[3] and Armitage thought it would be impossible to get straight onto it from the sea ice. He aimed to make the early part of the ascent via another glacier (later named the Blue Glacier) and then cross onto the Ferrar Glacier via a pass running between the two.

This expedition was to try everyone's stamina, including Edgar's, but his good nature and quick-wittedness survived intact. The teams started well; a stiff wind allowed them to use sails initially, but all too soon the wind dropped. On the hard, irregular sea ice, the teams found that wooden runners pulled badly in comparison to the German Silver (an alloy of copper and nickel) runners and had to be removed. By the end of the first day, 8 miles had been covered. When they camped Edgar did the cooking in his three-man tent; he was always practical and resourceful.

Victoria Land had never been charted, and it was hoped initially that if it was narrow the expedition might even reach as far as its western coast. But the Main Western Party that Edgar was on only had provisions for eight weeks and progress was slow. Reaching the Magnetic Pole quickly became an impossible goal, so repeated magnetic observations became the priority.[4] A dipping compass will incline downwards to 90° when directly over the Magnetic Pole. On 1 December, Skelton recorded a set of 'dips' of 86°32 (almost 2° higher than the recording on the ship),[5] i.e. they were closer to the Magnetic Pole.

It had taken them three days to get off the sea ice and onto the Blue Glacier. Pulling the sledges up the slope was heavy work, but with steady dragging they were 600ft above sea level in a day. But the glacier itself was steep and variably snow-covered or icy. It became so difficult to pull the sledges that the men had to relay; this happens when the surface or the incline makes man-hauling impossible with a full load. The men had to take half a load from the sledge, travel a certain distance, unload it and return with the empty sledge to load the remainder, thereby covering three times the distance they would cover normally. This was a time consuming and exhausting business, made worse on this occasion by their boots continually slipping on the treacherous surface so they had to keep changing from crampons to skis, and back again. But Edgar remained stoic and practical. He had a good memory and an excellent grasp of detail; when the teams stopped to make a camp, Edgar and three others were detailed to make a survey of the terrain before the others climbed out of their pulling gear.[6]

After six hard days the team had climbed 2,480ft and at last the surface levelled out in a big open valley filled with ice and snow. Mountains gleamed in the distance. Armitage's plan was to push through the valley and find a pass through the mountains and towards the Ferrar Glacier. After one more day (6 December) they had reached 3060ft. The scenery was breathtaking.

When Armitage skied off to investigate the pass to the Ferrar Glacier, Edgar was reorganising the sledges for the Support Party's departure. Two of his party's 11ft sledges were changed over with two of the Support Party's 9ft sledges, and he unpacked and repacked them. For once he was despondent; the loads the Main Western Party were to pull were too large for the 9ft sledges; the straps wouldn't go around them. Skelton told him he just had to make the best of it.[7] They named the site Separation Camp and left a depot of provisions there. The ongoing party separated from the nine men of the support group on 10 December.

Armitage found his Descent Glacier. It looked perilously steep. Its lower reaches out of sight, its upper part a steep icy slope. He, along with Dr Koettlitz, decided that it would be madness to try and get their heavily loaded sledges down that way, so five precious days were wasted in trying to find a better route through the mountains and down to the Ferrar Glacier. In this abortive search the sledges had to be hauled one by one, and Edgar spent two days easing six sledges up a slope by block and tackle over a rise of about 800ft in half a mile.[8] When the attempt was abandoned, Edgar and his companion had to lower the sledges down that almost 40° slope.[9]

Rather than give up, the team decided finally to try the Descent Glacier. Although it looked impassable from its upper parts, it is known now that the glacier is made up of a series of 'steps', which slope down to the Ferrar Glacier over a distance of approximately 3 miles. The upper step, which is very steep, slopes down for 400 yards and ends in a small shelf. The lower slopes are less extreme. So the glacier is actually a series of decreasing but significant gradients, interspersed with shelves.

The trial descent, on 16 December, was hair-raising. Edgar, Wild, Armitage and Skelton set off with ice axes, a long rope, and an empty 9ft sledge. They found that the upper slope was initially relatively easy, with no crevasses or ridges, but then it became very steep and dangerous. Edgar, Wild and Skelton put on crampons and tied themselves together to act as an anchor for Armitage (a heavy man), who was attached to the rope and lowered, with the sledge, down the slope. When the rope had been let out to its limit, Armitage secured himself and the sledge with an ice axe and the three went down cautiously to join him. They continued this way for about 700ft. Some of the stretches were very steep and they eventually ended up in a fog of clouds, which blocked out any further vision. But they had shown the initial descent was possible. To climb up the slope to the top again pushed them to their limits.

But, amazingly, on the very same day, all twelve men got down that fearful descent. The sledges were tied together in pairs; one 11ft–7ft pair with Edgar, Quartley and two others, and a 12ft–9ft combination. The first four fell and slipped down the slope for yards before bringing the slithering mass to a halt, thus the second group, with Edgar in it, started cautiously. They also lost control and slipped down helplessly onto the ledge (Armitage wrote that the run was more exhilarating than the water-chute at Earl's Court in London).[10] The next slope took three hours by which time they were over a third of the way down. A series of less horrendous gradients followed.

They got down the Descent Glacier in a day and a half. They had conquered the first great obstacle by reaching the Ferrar Glacier.

The remainder of the exploration of the Ferrar Glacier reads like the trials of Job. The team were trapped by blizzards, sticky snow made pulling awful, freezing fog engulfed them, snow blocked visibility, but still they kept going with stoicism and determination. On Christmas Eve, the men asked Armitage if they could have a holiday over Christmas Day: 'definitely not' was the response. But they were determined to mark the occasion and hid the small gifts they had carried in their kit under the snow. When the wind scattered the snow, exposing the little offerings, Wild wrote they were rewarded by 'a thorough wigging' for carrying extra weight![11]

The Ferrar Glacier continued unendingly. Whenever they thought they had reached the summit they found they were still on another of the series of icefalls. By New Year's Day they only had enough provisions to last a few more days, but at last, on 2 January 1903, a final icefall saw them on the summit, the Polar Plateau. The party was the first to set eyes on that vast ice plain and comprehend the enormity of the Polar Plateau icecap. This was a significant advance in Antarctic exploration.

They went on for a few miles taking further magnetic readings. But food supplies and illness determined their return. One man had collapsed with breathlessness and chest pains. He may have been suffering from altitude sickness, secondary to the relatively low oxygen levels at high altitude, which can cause problems at a height of 10,000ft. Even today men regularly need to be evacuated down to sea level because of problems at this height. In 1903 others felt unwell too, but there is no record of Edgar suffering.

The descent meant going down the Ferrar Glacier, ascending the daunting Descent Glacier and returning via the Blue Glacier. As he went down the Blue Glacier, Edgar fell 20ft into a crevasse, the lower parts of which were so deep as to be out of sight. The rope attached to his harness was not thick. He did not panic. Another rope was lowered round him and he was hauled up, though with some difficulty.

The team got back to the ship on 19 January. They had broken through the Western Mountain chain to the immense Antarctic Plateau, reaching nearly 9,000ft, and in doing so had made important magnetic recordings.

They had achieved a remarkable exploration: they were to find that others also had achieved remarkable feats. On one of the most important expeditions of the *Discovery* years, Scott, Wilson and Shackleton had made a pioneering sledge journey, towards the Geographic South Pole. They were away from November 1902 until February 1903. The three hoped to get as close as possible to the Pole. Although they failed to reach it, in fact they did not get off the Barrier, they did reach a notable 82° 11' S, by far the furthest south achieved, they formed an impression of the nature of the Barrier (one of *Discovery*'s briefs) and they made a record of the mountains fringing the Barrier on Victoria Land. All three suffered with scurvy, with swollen spongy gums, knees that would not bend and swelling of their legs. Shackleton was the worst afflicted and became very breathless. Much against his will, he was sent home on the relief ship SS *Morning*.[12]

Indeed, these two expeditions yielded significant new knowledge about the mysteries of Antarctica.

Notes

1 The location of the South Magnetic Pole was to be found in 1909, by Douglas Mawson, Edgeworth David and Alistair Mackay on Shackleton's *Nimrod* expedition.

2 Ed. Skelton, J., *The Antarctic Journals of Reginald Skelton*, Reardon Publishing, Cheltenham, England, 2004, p. 136.

3 Cherry-Garrard, A., *Journal* SPRI, MS 559/18/1–4; BJ VOL 2, 24/08/1911.

4 Yelverton, D., *Antarctica Unveiled*, University Press of Colorado, 2000, p. 203

5 Ed. Skelton, J., *The Antarctic Journals of Reginald Skelton*, Reardon Publishing, Cheltenham, England, 2004, p. 138.

6 Ibid., p. 138.

7 Ibid., p. 140.

8 Yelverton, D., *Antarctica Unveiled*, University Press of Colorado, 2000, p. 204.

9 Ibid., p. 205.

10 Armitage, A.B., *Two Years in Antarctica*, Paradigm Press, Bungay, Suffolk, 1984 p. 171.

11 Wild, J.R.F., Notes related to the BNAE, 1901–1904, SPRI, MS 944/3:D

12 Wilson, E.A., *The Medical Aspect of Discovery's voyage to the Antarctic*. British Medical Journal, 1905, 2, p. 77–80.

The End of the *Discovery* Expedition, 1903–04

Edgar was on three expeditions to the mountains that led to the interior of Antarctica: the Western Depot Party, 9–20 September, the Western Attempt, 12–21 October, and the Western Summit, 26 October to 24 December 1903.

The ship's company were now experienced Antarcticans, and the Antarctic winter of March to September had lost its power to frighten or astonish. The men endured the months of freezing darkness and howling blizzards with grim determination. Even the *South Polar Times* had become a routine. Edgar played cards, wrote letters, looked forward to the return of the sun. The monotony was broken when the King's birthday was celebrated with a sports day, despite, the *South Polar Times* wrote, 'that ever constant friend the wind, squalling with its constant shrillness'. A large silk Union Jack was hoisted on Hut Point and a Royal Salute fired. Edgar led a tug of war team, generously allowing the opposition to take the best ground (his team lost two to one), but he won the 2 mile flat ski race easily. His team lost the sledge-dragging competition by 20 seconds; here, rival teams on skis, pulled sledges loaded with 900lbs of iron. The day was a big success. It was rounded off by a concert after a magic lantern show, where views of New Zealand and Maoris were shown and Engineer Skelton showed views of the ships in which he had served, followed by a concert.[1]

Scott spent the long winter planning a second sledging campaign. He aimed to have all the sledging parties back by Christmas (the Antarctic summer). He wanted to avoid a further year in Antarctica and needed to have the men free to concentrate on *Discovery*'s release from her icy manacles. Since Antarctica's low temperatures made major sledging expeditions impractical before October, this only left about ten weeks for exploration before the teams needed to return to base and release *Discovery* for her return to England.

Scott's object was to find a new road to the Ferrar Glacier and lay a depot on it; then he planned to push on from Armitage's furthest west, over the inland Plateau, and, hopefully, find the western shores of Victoria Land.

The Western Depot Party was important, both for laying a depot for subsequent exploration and for its success in finding a direct route to the Ferrar Glacier. The glacier descends gradually to an inlet called New Harbour; an inlet that Armitage had thought would be impassable for sledges and so had reached the glacier via the Blue Glacier and the awful connection between the two, the Descent Glacier. Scott hoped that a route could be found via New Harbour that would make exploration to the west easier and quicker.

The inlet of New Harbour was indeed an awesome sight when Edgar and the team first saw it on 14 September. Gigantic ice blocks and high masses of earth and rock debris blocked the entrance. Boulders looking like giant tabletops rested on ice columns. But when Scott, Edgar and Skelton reconnoitred cautiously into the maze they did find a route, which led gradually from the inlet to the lower part of the glacier. As they followed this course the team had to carry their sledges and loads (430lbs of provisions) across the jagged ground until they reached a trail on the north side of the glacier,[2] which twisted and turned until it finally arrived on the Ferrar Glacier itself. The glacier looked like 'a smooth polished road – a ribbon of blue, down the centre of which ran a dark streak caused by a double line of boulders'.[3] The team pushed on up its smooth icy surface until they came to an area below Cathedral Rocks[4] where, surrounded by glorious pinnacles reaching to over 3,000ft, they established their depot of three weeks provisions for six people, by a big boulder.[5] They turned for home on 17 September. Scott's hopes for greater speed had been fulfilled. The 140 miles had been completed in twelve days rather than the twenty-one days that had been allowed,[6] and it was possible that it could be done in even quicker time. Armitage's party had taken three weeks to get to the depot spot the previous year.[7]

The Western Depot Party was followed about a month later by the Western Attempt, an abortive effort to actually get through the Western Mountains and onto the Plateau. Twelve men in three sledge groups left base on 12 October. Edgar's group was led by Scott and included Engineer Skelton, Boatswain Feather, Stoker Lashly and Able Seaman Handsley. There was a second group, which planned to make a geological survey of the region. A third group of three men was a support group. Scott's party was to be away for nine weeks, the other groups were to return earlier. The four 11ft sledges, carrying 200lbs per man, were cheered off from *Discovery*. The party left with high hopes, but they were to be back at base in nine days.

Scott set a cracking pace which Edgar kept up with well. In spite of their heavy loads the party covered the 45 miles to the cape of New Harbour in two days. They called the cape Butter Point because Scott thought this would be the highest point that the group would get fresh meat on their return – and so left butter there to cook the meat.[8]

It was probably on this sortie that Edgar caused Scott an irritation that he told his skiing companions about years later. As the temperature was -47°F, Scott told the party to put on three pairs of socks. Edgar put on two. His feet were soon frostbitten and the party had to stop. Scott asked him, 'How many socks have you got on?' Edgar replied respectfully, 'Locks, sir. How many pairs did you say, sir?' To which Scott replied wearily, 'Why three.' He told Edgar to take his boots off and get the circulation back. Edgar dropped out of sight, but Scott came up to hurry him up. Trying to avoid Scott's observant eye Edgar tried to take his two pairs of socks off as if they were three. He fumbled away but without success. Scott accused him of disobedience. 'Can you count?' 'Yes, sir, fairly well.' 'Did you think you had put three socks on?' 'Well sir, I was a bit sleepy when I put them on.' Finally Edgar had to own up and was told off sternly. When he came to put his boots on they were as stiff as iron and he had to bend them with a geological hammer. The ice at the bottom of the boot was impossible to get out.[9]

They continued at such a pace that they reached their depot on 16 October (four days) and camped on the glacier in the valley under Cathedral Rocks. If Edgar, in his imagination, had ever considered Antarctica's majestic, severe beauty, he must have been impressed by the view in front of him that evening. The sunlight pinnacles of Cathedral Rocks showed a rich dark brown; lower down the rock became greyish-black, splashed with lighter areas. There were patches of snow, and here and there a glacier gleamed, sparkling white and contrasting markedly with the bare rock.[10] The glacier itself could be seen curving down towards the sea. Beyond this was the sea itself, pearly grey in the distance. There was complete stillness.

Continuing the punishing pace they reached the enormous boulders below the Knobhead Moraine, reaching this landmark in six days rather than the twenty-seven days of the previous year.[11] But, at 6,000ft, disaster struck. The German silver covering the wooden sledge runners had split to shreds on two of the four sledges; one was less damaged, the fourth intact. The men knew that without metal protection, the wooden runners underneath would disintegrate on the hard sharp ice. There was nothing for it but to leave the sound sledge and stores and return to base for repairs. Their return was as near to flying as was possible. They covered nearly 90 miles in three days.

The definitive expedition, the Western Summit, left on 26 October. It was a smaller party than the Western Attempt as there were just nine members: Scott's Advance Party and Ferrar's Geological Party. Again, rapid progress was made. On this run they reached the Knobhead Moraine in three days (rather than six), in spite of the runners still giving problems and having to be repeatedly mended by Lashly, Skelton and Edgar. Unexpectedly they were careless about leaving things outside the tents to dry and on 27 October they only narrowly escaped a serious problem when a sudden blast of wind scattered sleeping bags, socks and finnesko left out on the ground to dry. But at the depot on 1 November, they found 'a loss, the gravity of which could scarcely be exaggerated'.[12] The lid of the instrument box had not been fastened securely and had blown open. The wind had whirled away Scott's copy of *Hints to Travellers*.[13] This was hugely important. Skelton wrote 'it contains all the data for the skipper to work out his sights for time and position'.[14] The explorers had no landmarks to rely on accurately and made observations of the sun to work out their latitude and longitude. Edgar, familiar with his father's stories of the problems of navigation around the Horn, appreciated the importance of the loss all too well.

The team had intended to work out their latitude by observing the sun's height above the horizon at noon and adding a calculation for the sun's declination.[15] This calculation involved the tables in *Hints for Travellers*. The calculation of longitude involved time. We all know that as we travel around the globe the local time changes (for example there are five hours time difference between London and New York). To calculate their longitude, the explorers made a comparison between the time at whatever position they were at – usually at midday, when the sun was at its highest and, at the exact same moment, the time on their chronometer was standardised to Greenwich Mean Time.[16] The difference between the two was used to calculate their longitude position. Since the earth takes twenty-four hours to revolve through 360°, one hour is one twenty-fourth of that spin, or 15°, so if, for example, the difference in the readings was three hours, then the explorers were 45° away from the north-south meridian, i.e. 45° east or west. Logarithmic tables were required here also; at the equator, where the girth of the earth is at its biggest, those fifteen degrees equal 1,000 miles, but as the lines of longitude converge, the distance each degree represents shrinks until it is nothing at the Geographic Pole. If the explorers' course deviated by even a few degrees of longitude, they needed to be able to convert those degrees into miles. This, too, needed the tables in *Hints for Travellers*.

So the loss was a most serious blow, but Scott could not consider returning again. He thought that he could measure the sun's altitude at noon and use this to work out latitude. He planned to keep the party on a due west course on the ascent. He asked his group if they agreed to go on, and Edgar and his companions agreed, though Skelton wrote 'now we shall never know exactly where we are'.[17] They were marching away into the unknown without having any idea of their precise position or how to get back.

They had food for over six weeks, pulling 230lbs per man.[18] They struggled to climb towards the summit, repeatedly needing to repair the metal on the sledges, avoid ice falls and move from hard ice to snow (which made pulling harder but was kinder on the runners). They were frostbitten and engulfed by driving snow and icy blasts of wind sweeping down from the summit. Edgar lost all sensation in one foot, a known precursor of frostbite, which could become gangrenous. Progress was halted whilst his companions rubbed and warmed the injured foot until he could feel it again. The weather deteriorated, and on Wednesday 4 November, at 7,000ft, they were imprisoned by a violent gale and thick suffocating snow for seven days. 'Desolation Camp' was their name for this base. Edgar endured the gale but found inactivity even worse than hauling. Apart from managing to cook two meals a day he spent most of the day in his sleeping bag looking up at the fluttering green canvas, unable to sleep because of the gale. He spent his time reading William le Queux and *The Red Magazine*. Communication between the tents was only possible when there was a lull in the storm. Edgar's usual cheerfulness deserted him and he merely endured.

On 11 November they escaped. Ferrar's Geological Party split off (Ferrar's group was to make startling and important finds of fossil plant remains that would prove that Antarctica was once a part of a temperate climate, the first confirmatory find of this nature from this part of Antarctica). The remaining nine plodded westwards and upwards. Comments such as 'dragging heavy' and 'surface bad' occur with depressing frequency in the records.

By 15 November, the twenty-first day out, Skelton wrote that the surface was 'practically on the level all day'.[19] On 16 he wrote they were 'on practically level surface at 900 feet'.[20] As the vast level snow plain stretched out before them at 8,900ft they could congratulate themselves. They had achieved a remarkable 'first' and they still had five weeks of rations, enough to cover a good many miles over the Plateau before returning. Scott wanted to discover with certainty if the high land was just the plateau of an island (the island of Victoria Land) or part of a vast continent. But plans to locate the Magnetic Pole had been abandoned, despite magnetic records being made regularly.

Scott decided to pull the sledges separately; Edgar pulled with Scott and Boatswain Feather (whose back was giving him trouble). Skelton led the other two men. But by the end of the morning's march on the 16th, Skelton's team was three quarters of an hour behind the other team and he wrote on the following day, 'the work was really too hard for us'.[21] On the 19th this observation was confirmed; one of the men, Handsley, felt ill, and subsequently collapsed, unable to breathe (and probably not helped by the brandy that was administered).[22] Three days later Scott decided to split the party, changing Feather with Stoker Lashly and progressing forward as a threesome, leaving the others to return. It was their twenty-ninth day out; the start of what Scott described as 'three weeks of the hardest physical work that I have ever experienced, and yet three weeks on which I can look with unmixed satisfaction, for I do not think it would have been possible to have accomplished more in the time'.[23]

Lashley, Edgar and Scott shared a single sleeping bag. They endured the hardships, the dangers and the hunger equally. Scott was the leader but always consulted his two companions, whom he grew to like and admire, over big decisions. He always said 'we' not 'I', when referring to the journey. He wrote, 'with these two men behind me, our sledge became a living thing and the days of slow progress were numbered.'[24] But in spite of this apparent equality it might be questioned whether Scott, having lost his instruction manual, was not foolhardy to proceed, risking his own and his companions' lives. It would be interesting to know what Edgar and Lashly, who knew the risks, really thought. But being lower deck they would have been unlikely to question their leader.

Everything the three men recorded was new information; the surface of the mostly smooth, though variably broken up by sastrugi, sharp ice edges like waves whipped up by the wind. On this surface their progress resembled a small boat at sea, climbing up a wave and then diving down into the hollow. They recorded that the wind blew from west to east across the Plateau during the winter.

That wind was terrible. It blew continuously and cut them to pieces. Things were worse in the mornings but got slightly better as they warmed up on the march. Edgar had a deep cut on the side of a fingernail and his finnesko wore out. His face was cracked; his cheeks and lips were sore and raw. Eating was difficult. Laughing, if he had wanted to, was impossible.

They turned back on 30 November. They had kept going simply because they wanted to last out to the end of the month. They were 300 miles from the ship and had nineteen days' provisions and sixteen days' oil to get them back to their depot where they had cached another ten days' food and oil. Going through the fields of sastrugi was exhausting; they fell often and as they fell the harnesses jerked them. But they found no sign of the west coast of Victoria Land in spite of the fact that, as they reflected, they could have crossed Greenland in many places on a trek of the length they had covered.[25] They had shown the immensity of the Plateau and recorded its conditions. Antarctica was clearly not a series of islands but truly continental in size. Man had now penetrated its silent snow-topped plain.

The month they took to return was grim. The sledge capsized repeatedly, they fell time and again and Scott was worried that they had overestimated their marching abilities. But the phlegmatic characters of his two companions shone throughout. When poor visibility marooned them in their tent at a time when an hour's delay was critical because of their limited food and fuel supplies, it was a blessing to have Edgar stick his head out of the tent and announce in his usual matter-of-fact tone that the sun was now shining;[26] the calm, solid reassurance of the British lower deck representatives was a relief to the overwrought mind. Scott thought they were undefeatable and wrote, 'however tiresome our day's march or however gloomy the outlook they always find something to jest about. In the evenings we have long arguments about naval matters and generally agree that we could rule the service a great deal better than any Board of Admiralty. Incidentally I learn a great deal about lower deck life – more than I could hope to have done under ordinary conditions.'[27]

By 6 December, concern about the oil supply got worse. They were getting more and more hungry. They were gaunt. Edgar looked wild with sunken cheeks, frostbitten face and a bulbous frostbitten nose. They were so eager not to miss the smallest scrap of food that they used Shackleton's 'noble game of shut eye' to allocate each man his share;[28] one man turned his head when the food was divided and he decided who would eat which portion. They dreamed of food; Edgar's idea of happiness was roast pork, Lashly's apples and vegetables, while Scott thought continuously about bowls of Devonshire cream.

The snow surface varied but was often abysmal, and on 9 December it was like sand; the sledge felt like a log and they could hardly cover a mile in an hour. Edgar had never done such hard pulling. It took all his energy; for once he could not talk. Skis were hopeless to move the sledge in these conditions. They were worried about food but more worried about oil which was now down to one can, also Scott and Edgar's tobacco supply was at an end (Edgar had been on half a pipe per day). Although they were certain that they were near the edge of the Plateau they were uncertain of their precise location on this never ending plain. Scott suggested that they increased the marches by half an hour each day and he halved the oil allowance, (which meant a cold lunch). Edgar and Lashly would not disagree with a suggestion from Scott and indeed, under the circumstances, there was no alternative. They were travelling by the rule of thumb, but Scott wrote that Edgar's face fell dismally – he only believed that food was beneficial when it was warm and had 'a chance of sticking to the ribs'.[29]

On 10 December they slogged away for five hours, had a cold lunch and started again. But in the afternoon, as he peered through the unending snow, Edgar's sharp eye spotted land. They knew the end of the Plateau was within reach, but where were they precisely? There were innumerable glaciers falling down from the mountains but which was the Ferrar? Time and food made the right choice vital.

On 13 December Edgar's nose was badly frostbitten. The threesome had to stop to massage it back to life. It had given trouble for weeks and by now looked like a large, swollen potato. He always talked about this member as if it was something that was not actually his, but something he had to look after, 'my poor old nose again; well there, it's chronic'.[30] As they held to an easterly direction the land began to slope downwards. They really had no idea where they were.

The 14 December was a date that Edgar would remember for the rest of his life. They were heading east and, although they were lost, they decided to keep going; a snowstorm was brewing and incarceration in a tent, in a blizzard, might well mean death from starvation. So they advanced into the unknown, steering their sledge through great ice hummocks and crevasses. As they progressed, Scott in front, Edgar and Lashly behind, the slope grew steeper and smoother. Lashly lost his footing, Edgar was pulled over and the three men and the sledge careered into the unknown like an unstoppable express train. The surface became rougher and, as they bounced onwards and downwards, they must have thought that death, or at the very least serious injury, was on its way. But as they eventually came to a halt on hard, rough, windswept snow, amazingly all three were able to struggle to their feet. They had careered down 300ft. The first question Edgar and Lashly asked Scott was if he was all right (sir).

Luck seemed to be with them. As they looked around they recognised their own glacier and other familiar landmarks. In the distance they could see their friend, the volcano Erebus, smoking away. Their food depot was within reach. After all their tribulations they thought they were safe. But malicious fate had not given up yet. Soon after setting off, Edgar and Scott fell into a crevasse. Lashly, left on the surface to mastermind the rescue, used one hand to hang on to the broken sledge, straddling the crevasse and his other to slide skis under the sledge to support it. As Scott and Edgar hung in their traces, surrounded by blue ice walls and with an unfathomable gulf below, Scott asked Edgar how he was doing. The reply, from a man facing death for the second time in a day, was characteristically calm. He was 'good enough'.[31]

Scott had to climb up a rope to escape first. This was hugely difficult. His fingers were frostbitten, his clothes were thick and cumbersome, and he hadn't climbed a rope for years. But he took his gloves off, and in the subzero temperatures he hoisted himself up slowly. A harness was swung down to Edgar and he was hauled up, frostbitten but unbowed, 'Well I'm blowed' was the (unlikely) official report of what he said.[32]

That night, black and blue with bruises, frostbitten, sore and exhausted, he mused over his extraordinary day; Scott wrote that Edgar ruminated continually on the day's experience, 'My word but that was a close call. My word, but that WAS a close call'.[33]

They picked up supplies from the depots, and on the 16th they were at their old quarters at Knobhead Moraine in the large glacier basin. Instead of rushing back to base Scott decided to investigate the direction of ice streams from the basin. He wanted to follow a glacier tributary that sloped north and then eastwards. The team were about to make one of the great geographical finds of the expedition.

They negotiated the steep ice slope roped together and continued until they found a shallow frozen lake resting on deep layers of mud; 'what a splendid place for growing spuds'.[34] The glacier, it seemed, did not end by pouring icebergs into the sea, as had been assumed. Instead it ended in a lake high in the mountains. The three could not find any moss or lichen, though it is now known that far beneath the icy surface these lakes remain unfrozen and support colonies of bacteria and phytoplankton.[35] Microbes, bacteria and pollen have been found in the ice. This was information well beyond the explorers' wildest imagination and would take about another century to be discovered.[36]

But there was more. Progressing further down, through the valley of startling beauty and ruggedness, they came across stretches of undulating sand, then areas covered by rocks of different colours and sizes, more sandy stretches and boulder heaps. Extraordinarily there was no snow or ice, though the surface seemed to be the result of ice and water action. As they advanced, Edgar, always mindful of his stomach, asked if there was any point in carrying the lunch any further. The three had their lunch, sitting at a place that gave them memorable views up and down the valley. Except for the mountain summits there was no ice or snow in view. They ran their fingers through the sand and drank from the streams. It was amazing to think that they were less than 100 miles from their terrible experiences on the summit. They saw nothing alive, just the skeleton of a Weddell seal. Scott named this dry area a 'valley of the dead'.[37] The trio had discovered one of the extraordinary Dry Valleys of Victoria Land[38] – they were in what was to be later named the Taylor

Valley. The find was one of the major geographical discoveries of the entire expedition.

The trio returned. The Western Summit expedition was now over. Having managed to fry up some meat at Butter Point they got back to *Discovery* on Christmas Eve 1903. They were very thin and exhausted. The steward made a celebratory meal of steak and tomatoes, after which the three seemed to put on weight with every meal. They could congratulate themselves that they had achieved a remarkable sledging feat of nearly 1,000 miles. They had travelled by far the furthest into Victoria Land.

These expeditions, which opened up the Western Mountains, made Edgar a true veteran of Antarctic exploration. He was away from the ship for nearly sixty days on sorties that would tax the most experienced modern-day explorer, confirming (if this was needed), his strength, his alert intelligence and his composure.

When *Discovery* returned to England a number of the men were singled out for special mention. One of these was Edgar, who was promoted to PO 1st Class. Another was Stoker Lashly. Scott described them as men of magnificent physique. He wrote that the journey to the interior of Victoria Land reached the limit of possible performance under such awful conditions and that it could not have been accomplished had either man failed in the slightest. Scott recorded that Edgar's and Lashly's determination, courage and patience were often taxed to the utmost yet the two men were always cheerful and respectful. The outings cemented the loyalty and mutual respect between Scott and Edgar.

Notes

1   *South Polar Times*, vol. 2, VI, April 1903, p. 28.
2   Scott, R.F., *Scott's Voyage of the Discovery*, James Murray, London, 1929, p. 563
3   Ibid., p. 563.
4   The four abrupt cliffs surmounted by sharp peaks thought to resemble a cathedral. Named by Armitage in 1902.
5   Ed. Skelton, J., *The Antarctic Journals of Reginald Skelton*, Reardon Publishing, Cheltenham, England, 2004, p.184.
6   Ibid., p. 184.
7   Scott, R.F., *Scott's Voyage of the Discovery*, James Murray, London, 1929, p. 564.
8   Ibid., p. 574.

9 Debenham, F., *Journal*, 19/01/1911–08/03/1911 MS 279/2:BJp, p.78.

10 Ibid., p. 575.

11 Ibid., p. 576.

12 Scott, R.F., *Scott's Voyage of the Discovery*, James Murray, London, 1929, p. 587.

13 *Hints for Travellers*, a publication issued by the Royal Geographical Society of London which supplied the data to locate altitude and longitude accurately.

14 Skelton, R., *Sledging Diary* SPRI MS 342/2/6;BJ, 01/11/1903

15 The angle between the magnetic north and true north at a particular point on the Earth's surface.

16 Greenwich is at 0° longitude. This cut Harrison's Clock.

17 Skelton, R., *Sledging Diary*, SPRI, MS 342/2/6;BJ,01/11/1903.

18 Ellis, A.R., *Under Scott's Command: Lashly's Antarctic Journals*, Victor Gollancz, London, 1969, p. 71.

19 Skelton, R., *Sledging Diary*, SPRI, MS, 342/2/4;BJ, 15/11/03.

20 Ibid., 16/11/1903.

21 Ibid., 17/11/1903.

22 Ibid., 20/11/1903.

23 Scott, R.F., *Scott's Voyage of the Discovery*, James Murray, London, 1929, p. 601.

24 Ibid., p 602.

25 Ibid., p. 605.

26 Ibid., p.609.

27 Ibid., p. 609.

28 Devised by Shackleton on the Southern Journey 1902/03 which was undertaken by Shackleton with Scott and Wilson.

29 Scott, R.F., *Scott's Voyage of the Discovery*, James Murray, London, 1929, p. 613.

30 Ibid., p. 615.

31 Ibid., p. 621.

32 Ibid., p. 621.

33 Ibid., p 622.

34 Ellis, A.R., *Under Scott's Command: Lashly's Antarctic Journals*, Victor Gollancz, London, 1969, p. 83.

35 Subglacial Lake, a lake under an ice cap or ice sheet. There are over 120 subglacial lakes in Antarctica; Lake Vostok is the largest known at the current time.

36 Small free floating aquatic plants have now been identified.

37 Scott, R.F., *Scott's Voyage of the Discovery*, James Murray, London, 1929, p. 627.

38 A row of valleys in Victoria Land with low humidity and without ice or snow.

1. Edgar as a young adult showing his proficiency badges. (Courtesy of Swansea Museum)

2. Edgar's father in 1893. By this time he was a Quartermaster, sailing up the west coast of England from Swansea to Glasgow. (Courtesy of Keith Roberts)

3. St Mary's church, Rhossili. (Courtesy of G.C. Gregor)

4. Rhossili Bay. (Courtesy of G.C. Gregor)

5. HMS *Ganges*, a Training Hulk in Cornwall. (Wikipedia)

6. SS *Discovery*. (By kind permission of Dundee Heritage Trust)

7. The pack ice. (Courtesy of D.J. Williams)

8. The ice Barrier. (Courtesy of D.J. Williams)

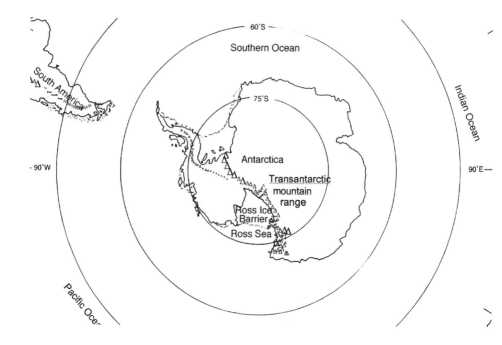

Map of Antarctica showing Transantarctic mountain range

- 60°S
Southern Ocean
- 75°S
Antarctica
Transantarctic
mountain
range
Ross Ice
Barrier
Ross Sea

South America

Pacific Ocean

- 90°W

Indian Ocean

90°E—

9. Map of Antarctica showing Transantarctic mountain range. (Courtesy of D.J. Williams)

10. A general view of the hut and *Discovery* at the bayside of Hut Point. (By kind permission of Dundee Heritage Trust)

11. Southern depot parties preparing to start, 1902. (By kind permission of Dundee Heritage Trust)

12. Sastrugi formed by the wind on Crater Hill. (By kind permission of Dundee Heritage Trust)

13. Scott's hut at Cape Evans (named after Lieutenant 'Teddy' Evans), with Mount Erebus in the background. (Courtesy of Scott Polar Research Institute – SPRI)

14. The Emperor penguin colony in Cape Crozier. (Image by Reginald Skelton. Courtesy of the Skelton Bequest to SPRI)

15. *Discovery* and the Aurora Australis. (Edward A. Wilson painting. Courtesy of Dundee Heritage Trust)

16. The foot of the Ferrar Glacier. (NASA image)

17. Modern picture of the field gun run which Edgar's team won for Portsmouth in 1907. (Courtesy of HMS *Excellent*, Portsmouth Museum)

18. The Western Depot Party, 1911. *From left to right*: Griffith Taylor, Charles Wright, Lieutenant 'Teddy' Evans, Lieutenant 'Birdie' Bowers, Captain Scott, Frank Debenham, Sub-Lieutenant Tryggve Gran, PO Edgar Evans, PO Thomas Crean. (Courtesy of SPRI)

19. Edgar on tour. (Courtesy of Adrian Raeside)

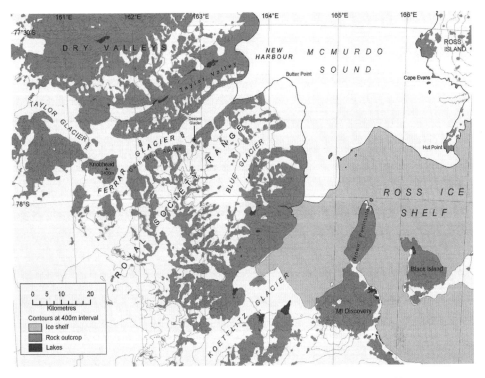

20. The Ferrar and Koettlitz Glaciers, Cape Evans, Hut Point and the Dry Valley Map. (Courtesy of Peter Fretwell)

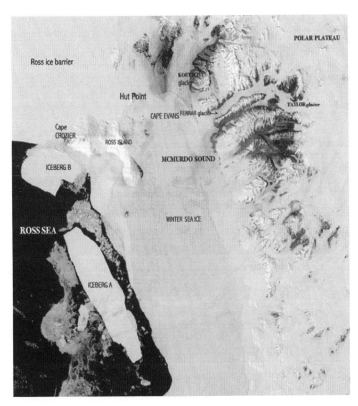

21. Satellite image of the winter ice around Ross Island. Note that two large icebergs, A and B, have calved off the Ross Ice Shelf. A is nearly as big as Ross Island. B is approximately 178 miles long. (NASA image annotated by D.J. Williams)

22. Edgar dressed for exploration. (Courtesy of SPRI)

23. A dry valley. (NASA image)

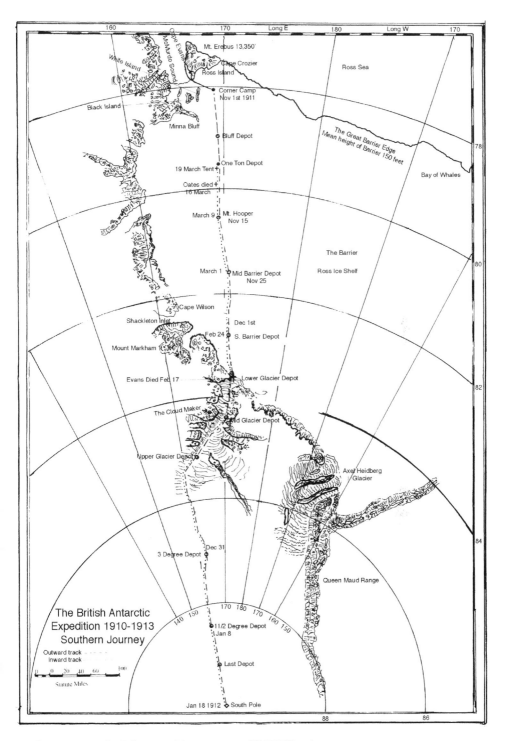

The British Antarctic
Expedition 1910-1913
Southern Journey

Outward track - - - - -
Inward track

0   20   40   60   100

Statute Miles

24. The journey to the Pole, 1911. (Map courtesy of D.J. Williams)

25. The motor party led by Lieutenant 'Teddy' Evans, October 1911. (Courtesy of SPRI)

26. Edgar Evans, 'Birdie' Bowers, Edward Wilson and Robert Scott in the tent. (Courtesy of SPRI)

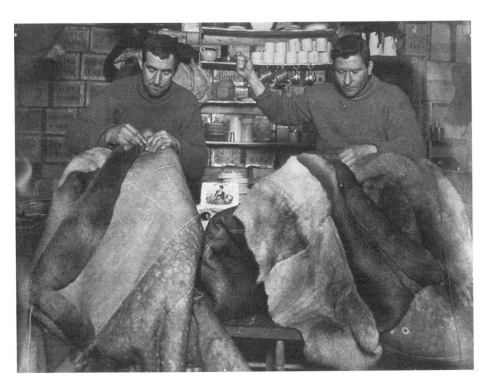

27. Tom Crean (left) repairing sleeping bags with Edgar Evans, during the winter months 1911. (Courtesy of SPRI)

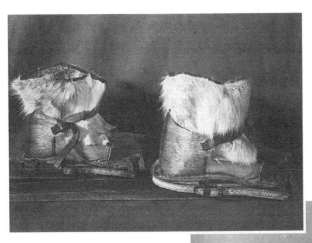

28. Edgar's modification to enable finneskoes to be securely fitted to skis, Antarctic winter 1911. (Courtesy of SPRI)

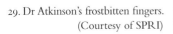

29. Dr Atkinson's frostbitten fingers. (Courtesy of SPRI)

30. Edgar Evans dressing Dr Atkinson's fingers. (Courtesy of SPRI)

31. Edgar's naval memorial plaque fixed to an accommodation block named after Edgar in 1964 at HMS *Excellent*, an important piece of Royal Naval social history. (Image courtesy of Jane Gregor)

THIS BUILDING IS NAMED
IN PROUD AND HONOURED
MEMORY OF PETTY OFFICER
EDGAR EVANS
WHO GAVE HIS LIFE RETURNING
FROM THE SOUTH POLE
17TH FEBRUARY 1912

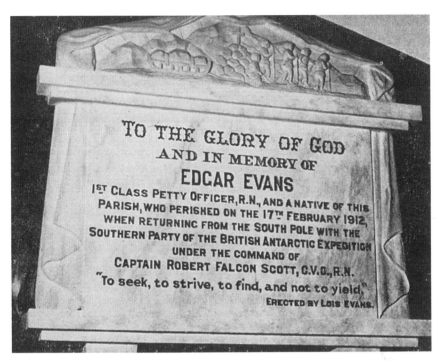

32. Lois' memorial for Edgar. In the memorial the men are shown using one ski stick rather than the two that were used in the *Terra Nova* expedition. The quotation from Tennyson's *Ulysses* should read: 'to strive, to seek, to find and not to yield.' (Courtesy of Jane Gregor)

33. Edgar's widow Lois with Norman, one of their sons, at the premier of *Scott of the Antarctic*, in 1948. (Courtesy of John Evans)

34. Edgar's Polar medals taken to the South Pole by Swann in 1987. (Courtesy of G.C. Gregor)

10

Return from Antarctica, then Home Again, 1904–10

Discovery was still incarcerated in miles of ice when the explorers returned and open water was yet 20 miles away. Second-in-Command Armitage had ordered highly organised teams to blast and saw through the ice to try and speed up its dissolution. It was hoped that *Discovery* could escape in January 1904, and 'Saw Camp' was well established by the time Edgar got back to the ship on Christmas Eve. The aim was to saw and blast a path through the ice (in the event a hopeless task, the ice was 7ft thick and any crack froze up almost immediately) and three shifts worked round the clock. When Edgar arrived at 'Saw Camp' with Scott he was happy not to have to joined the band of 'unwashed, unshaven, sleepless, swearing, grumbling, laughing, joking reprobates',[1] because Scott, seeing that the attempt was futile, stopped the work. Two days later all hands returned to the ship except for Scott, Dr Wilson, Edgar and Lashly, the cook Charles Clark and Seaman William Heald. They were to kill penguins. It seemed likely that *Discovery* would remain stuck for another year and her larder needed stocking.

On 5 January, bewilderment was rife. Not one but two ships came into sight. One was *Morning*, the relief ship, but Edgar joined in the wild guessing about the second: was it *Gauss* (the German vessel); a private yacht; a man o' war?[2]

Morning brought mail with much missed news of the family at home. Edgar had no personal bad news, but *Morning* carried orders that were dumbfounding to the hard-pressed crew of *Discovery*. Scott was ordered to abandon *Discovery* if she could not be freed from the ice (the government did not want the expense of yet another rescue attempt on a third year) and to facilitate the repatriation of *Discovery*'s crew and equipment, the government had sent a whaling ship, the *Terra Nova*, to accompany *Morning*.

Scott read orders to the crew that they could hardly believe. Although the royal societies and the Admiralty were apparently satisfied with the achievements of the expedition, the government had now taken over complete control. This was because the expedition had run out of money; there were no funds for a further year in Antarctica if *Discovery* could not be extricated from the ice. *Discovery* was now public property. Scott confirmed that if *Discovery* could not be freed, she was to be abandoned to the mercies of Antarctica. The men saw that Scott had tears in his eyes and Edgar, deeply loyal to Scott, was outraged. The crew all thought that there had never been orders framed to give an officer less option; they were full of 'you are on no account' and 'you are to distinctly understand'. Scott said that he had not fully taken in the idea of abandoning the ship but he thanked everyone for the way they had stood by him loyally. The men responded with three cheers. Williamson wrote, 'and there's no doubt that he deserves it if ever a man did',[3] and Ford agreed, 'I think it is very hard times that he should be given no option at all after proving himself such a capable Polar Commander and it is a pity this work should be spoilt by quarrelling at home'.[4]

Work to abandon *Discovery* began on 14 January; supplies and equipment were hauled over the ice to load into the relief ships, a miserable task. The crews met midway to transfer the loads and Edgar's strength was put to good use. But nature is capricious. In 1904, the ice, which had remained solid the previous year, started breaking up. On 3 February 7 miles separated *Discovery* from *Morning* and the *Terra Nova*. Hopes for a release started to rise. The men wondered if the ice's break up was helped by the weight of heavy snow that pushed it under water.[5] Edgar was involved in further blasting, the idea being to make a crack in the ice between Hut Point and the relief ships and then create a 'lake' that *Discovery* could escape to. By the 13th, the sea was only 2.5 miles away and on the 14th, the ice finally split as the swell broke up the ice and *Terra Nova* butted it again and again, her crew using the old whalers dodge of rolling the ship by running backwards and forwards across her deck to widen the crack. Finally *Terra Nova* sailed through triumphantly with *Morning* 'following meekly behind'.[6] The men hoisted the Union Jack on Hut Point and rushed onto the floe and onto the ships. Scott sent a case of whisky for the two ships.[7]

But still nothing was easy. When *Discovery* finally escaped into the water she was caught immediately by irresistibly strong winds, which pushed her back onto the shoreline at Hut Point where she lay stranded, pounded by wind, waves and tide for over eight hours. Edgar thought that there would be permanent damage to his ship; that having finally escaped the ice the sea would break her up. It must have been awful to see the way her decks buckled under the strain and to see planking from the ship's bottom floating to the surface. As heavy seas broke and washed over the ship, there was frozen ice all over the deck. But when at last the storm subsided and *Discovery* got off the sandbank, mercifully no permanent damage had been done.

Edgar gave a lingering look to those familiar landmarks that he thought he would never see again: Mount Erebus (still smoking), Castle Rock and Observation Hill. Then *Discovery* retraced her route up the coast of Victoria Land. The voyage to New Zealand was notable for gales and *Discovery's* penchant for heavy rolling, sometimes through 50°, as she tossed about like a cork. In storms she leaked 'everywhere', the bedding was soaked, the ship was shaken, and, wrote Williamson, the top gallants were left on her until it was too late to take them in and the 'jib blew out of bolt ropes with a loud report'. Several of the men were seasick. They all 'stood by to turn out'.[8] In a lull the topgallants were furled. This took two hours work and then the gale returned and continued all day, rolling the ship abominably. The men were utterly fed up, but they were, Williamson wrote, 'doing it for King and Empire and we are taking it joyfully!! … Pumping all day. How we are looking forward to Lyttelton and civilisation again.'[9]

They had some days of relative rest in Auckland Islands preparing for the grand arrival. All the ships were freshly painted as *Discovery*, with *Morning* and *Terra Nova*, entered Lyttelton harbour on 1 April, serenaded by the strains of *Home Sweet Home*. No one was sorry to be back in civilisation with hospitable friends. Gifts flowed on board, boxes filled with mutton, potatoes and greens. The ship overflowed with well-wishers. After two months in New Zealand *Discovery* (with a further twenty sheep on board and gifts from New Zealand farmers), sailed towards South America. She went through the Straits of Magellan[10] and called at Chile, Port Stanley in the Falklands and the Azores, where the Prince of Monaco, a distinguished scientist, came on board on 2 September. Passing ships signalled to the crew, congratulating them on their achievements and wishing them a safe return home. The scientific programme continued throughout.

On 10 September 1904, *Discovery* docked in Portsmouth. She had been away for thirty-seven months. *The Times* wrote that there need be no reserve in the welcome extended to the *Discovery* when she arrived in Portsmouth from an expedition 'full of hazard. The scanty knowledge which we possessed of an area of several million miles, Captain Scott and his companions have succeeded in dispelling our ignorance'.[11] The Mayor of Portsmouth welcomed the new knowledge of the character and interior of the continent, the geological collections, the penguins, the meteorology and terrestrial magnetism (the last two of practical importance). There was national unanimity (at least initially) about the value of Polar research to the nation.[12] Sir Clements Markham said that the *Discovery* expedition was 'the best-conducted and most successful expedition that had ever entered the Polar regions, Arctic or Antarctic'.[13] The sailors, interviewed by the *Daily News*, were enthusiastic: they had reached further south than any other expedition, they were glad to be back but 'didn't have a bad time of it' – they had got their mail every twelve months.[14]

The public were fascinated to meet those who had experienced the actuality of this place of mystery. People wanted to shake the heroes' hands; they wanted to hear them speak. There was support for the medals granted to the crew. Edgar, on Scott's recommendation, received the highly prized 'Silver Medal with Clasp' (a duplicate medal was issued to his widow in 1914)[15] and a small silver medal for success in an Antarctic sports competition (the ski race). Many years later a posthumous Royal Geographical Medal was added to this distinguished collection.[16]

He was given two months leave and was delighted to be home. Friendly and outgoing and with a great supply of new anecdotes, he was happy to return to Swansea, his family and friends. When *Gower Church Magazine* interviewed him, the reporter wrote that he was, 'robust and courageous to a degree and has during his voyage added much to his previous knowledge and attainments'.[17]

In the *South Wales Daily Post* he reflected on his Western Journey:

It's an uncanny feeling standing there, surrounded by everlasting snow, gigantic nunataks[18] all around you and dead silence, which is almost deafening. Not a sign of life, no birds to speak of, only a melancholy seal to look at, and his blessed hide not worth a cent in the European market. Six of us were chosen to do this trip, which was 300 miles from the ship, and lasted nine weeks and three days: but three went back. We saw absolutely nothing. We were 9,200 feet on the ice cap and away towards the Pole was a range of unclimbable mountains. Nobody knows what lies beyond it.[19]

He went to London to be 'Paid Off' from the expedition. The Certificate of Discharge states his date of discharge as 30 September 1904; importantly the certificate grades both his 'Character for Conduct' and 'Character for Ability' as 'Very Good'. He continued in full-time naval employment as a Petty Officer. His Certificate of Service records the date of his promotion to 1st Class Petty Officer as 2 April 1904 (when *Discovery* was in New Zealand) and this provided a modest financial boost; pay for a 1st Class Petty Officer was £39 10s 10d.[20] Although he had assured the reporter of the *South Wales Daily Post* that he had no marriage plans, he was in fact going back to Middleton regularly to pursue his friendship with his pretty cousin, Lois Beynon. He had been away from any domestic comfort for three years. Lois was a girl from a similar background (her father William, was Edgar's uncle, his mother's brother), who had been brought up in the public house in Middleton. She was someone who understood him. She was spirited, attractive, and musical. Edgar was a well-known young man, intelligent, good looking, affectionate and musical. A marriage was arranged in a very short time and was solemnised on 13 December 1904, just a little less than fourteen weeks from Edgar's arrival back in England.

Welsh interest in the marriage was not only directed towards the now famous Swansea boy but also to Lois. As well as being familiar to patrons of the Ship, Lois was known in Rhossili for her lovely singing voice. Evening entertainment then was often in the form of musical soirées and Lois frequently contributed to these; duets (often with the daughter of the Rector who had married Edgar's parents), *Blow Gentle Wind*, and solos, *O'er Life's Dark Sea*, were regularly performed and, more cheerfully, Arthur Sullivan's *Three Little Maids*. When she married her explorer on 13 December, 'Rhossili was agog with excitement'.[21] Lois was described as the youngest daughter of Mr and Mrs Beynon of the popular Ship Inn. Edgar, as a man who had 'sprung to prominence by reason of the fact that he was one of the crew of *Discovery* sent out for the purpose of Antarctic exploration'.[22]

He described himself modestly, according to the clearly impressed *Gower Church Magazine*, 'as a simple mariner'.[23] The Rector, The Reverend Lewis

Hughes, performed the ceremony and the celebrations were noisy. A 'feu de joie', a rifle salute with rifles fired in quick succession so that the sound is continuous, added to the boisterous festivities.[24] Lois looked delightful. She wore white silk, trimmed with cream chiffon with a matching picture hat. She carried the ivory-bound prayer book that Edgar had given her and was attended by two bridesmaids whom Edgar presented with dress rings. One of Lois' brothers, Enoch, was best man and the full choir gave vocal support. A wedding breakfast in the Ship Inn followed and the happy pair departed for London, their departure serenaded by coastguards and farmers who vied with each other by firing more gun salutes.[25]

The *Gower Church Magazine* reported inaccurately on Edgar's perilous Western Journey saying that he had been '270 miles further south than all the rest of the crew',[26] but enthusiastically describing his modesty; 'like every truly brave man he is far from being boastful and requires considerable persuasion to make himself relate anything about himself'. The article went on to say that Lois' contributions to local concerts were much appreciated 'as evidenced in the numerous and costly wedding presents given her by a large number of friends and relatives … the singing was worthy of the bright occasion, the voices in chanting the special psalm and the two well-known hymns were wonderfully sweet and one could feel that the hearts of all were full … May every blessing follow them in their new home'.[27]

A few days in London was exciting beyond Lois' wildest imaginings: the noise, the traffic, the people, the entertainment and Edgar; Edgar who was used to large cities, who knew about traffic, omnibuses, theatres, who could navigate confidently through the confusing whirl. Edgar was her hero.

After London came Portsmouth, the naval town on the south coast of England. The family were to be here until Edgar left again for the Antarctic. Married life began at 12 Walden Road, in the Tipner district of Portsmouth. Walden Road is a long terrace built over a number of years from the 1890s. Number 12 was an Edwardian house, first listed in the early 1900s. It had a bay window at the front and was 'modern', in that it probably had its own 'privy'.[28] There were shops: a fruiterer, a general store, a grocer (3lbs of sugar, just over 5 pence; 1.5lbs butter, 1 shilling 6 pence; a pint of beer, 2 pence; 2oz tobacco, 6 pence) and a confectioner conveniently close, also the local doctors,[29] but the change from rural Gower must have been a tremendous challenge for Lois. The only point of similarity was the sea; the dock was only about half a mile away, but for the first time she was away from her family and lifelong friends and thrown into a life of a very different pace. She had to manage long days on her own, to act independently, to cope with pregnancy and to look after babies. The couple had three children: Norman Edgar (18 August 1905) and their daughter Muriel (9 November 1906) were born when the family was at Walden Road. Edgar then moved his family to 52 Chapel Street, in the Portsmouth suburb of Buckland, where their second son, Ralph, was born on 4 December 1908. Both boys were to be baptised at home in Rhossili by the Reverend Lewis Hughes.

Edgar was fully occupied. After postings for a total of nine months on HMS *President* and HMS *Firequeen*, Petty Officer 1st Class Edgar Evans was posted to HMS *Excellent*, the Royal Naval Gunnery School in Portsmouth, on 15 January 1905 to train as a gunnery instructor. Apart from a three-month period in 1906, he remained on *Excellent* for two years and then stayed in other shore bases in the Portsmouth area until he left for the Antarctic again in 1910, having qualified also as a Torpedo Instructor. He was based at HMS *Barfleur* from April to July 1906 (*Barfleur* was the Flagship of the Rear Admiral of the Portsmouth Division of the Reserve Fleet), *Excellent*, again, from July 1906 to January 1907 and HMS *Victory* from February 1907 to April 1910.

In 1906 the Royal Naval and Military Tournament opened in Olympia in London. This tournament was a national entertainment with competitions, massed bands, musical rides and historic battles, but undoubtedly its centrepiece was the field gun run. This was a competition that had evolved after Royal Naval involvement in the relief of the South African town of Ladysmith[30] during the Boer War.[31] At that time naval personnel hauled guns from HMS *Powerful* up to Ladysmith to defend the vulnerable town against the Boer attack. Edgar knew of this notable achievement; he had been in South Africa before the Boer War ended. In 1906, in Olympia, as HMS *Excellent*'s Gunnery Trainer, he led his eighteen-man gun crew in a display of dismantling and reconstructing the heavy guns as they were hoisted over walls and bridges. This was no easy task. The guns used were 12-pounder 6cwt,[32] the weight of the gun barrel was 896lbs, the carriage 350lbs and the wheels 120lbs, so the total weight of the equipment to be taken over the course was approximately 1 ton (1,016kg, over 2,000lbs).

In the following year, Edgar led his crew to victory in the field gun competition (as apposed to display).[33] This took place during each afternoon performance throughout the tournament. It involved two crews vying with each other to initially haul the field gun and its carriage across the arena towards 'a wall', dismantling the gun to get it over the obstacle, reassembling the gun, and then getting it across a 28ft 'chasm'. For this the gun had to be dismantled again, some of the team swinging across the chasm carrying the 120lb wheels, the others sweating to get the carriage and gun barrel over the gap before they swung across themselves. The gun carriage was then put together again and raced towards a gap in the 'enemy wall' – too narrow for the gun to get through with its wheels on, so they had to be removed and put on again before a stiff contest to get to the enemy line, fire a round of ammunition and repeat the process in reverse to get back to the starting line. The team that crossed the original starting line first was awarded a point, and whichever team achieved the biggest number of points during the entire tournament was deemed victorious. The competition, accompanied by the virtually delirious shouts of support from loyal devotees, was hugely demanding and required relentless rehearsal, and a strong coordinated team. Here Edgar clearly excelled. The Royal Tournament, including the field gun exercise, continued until 1999 when it was axed, but currently there are plans to revive it.

Years later he told another story about the gun run. Whilst the training was in progress he was stationed in Corfu for a short while. With six friends he hired a ramshackle four-wheeled cart for trip into the country. Having somehow deposited the driver, some brilliant 'idjit' thought that it was a good time to carry out a gun run practice. They broke up the cart, reasonably scientifically, into about twenty pieces and then charged back with all the bits. An Officer appeared, 'What is this tomfoolery?', 'Gun Practice, sir, dismounting and retiring with gear.' And then, Edgar concluded to his spellbound audience, 'We couldn't make the bleeding fool see how important it was and he sent us back to the ship without letting us set the gun up again.'[34] The driver's reactions are not recorded.

Edgar's five-and-a-half years of married life were full of action and excitement. In relation to the navy, in February 1906, King Edward VII launched HMS *Dreadnought* in Portsmouth as part of the modernisation reforms instigated by Admiral Sir 'Jacky' Fisher. This was thought to be the most powerful warship in the world, a ship that would make all others obsolete. Later that year there was rioting in Portsmouth Barracks.[35] This extraordinary and much publicised event was precipitated when young recruits were kept on the parade ground for an inordinate length of time in appalling weather. They decamped, without permission, to the gymnasium where the Duty Officer (a gunner) dismissed the lesser offenders but kept junior stokers back for a reprimand. Unfortunately he started with a short, curt order of 'on the knee', apparently a common command in the gunnery division and given so that men at the back could hear what was being said. But the order and the way it was given caused indignation amongst the stokers who responded with a resounding 'No'. The stokers' arrest and subsequent disquiet continued for days, with stokers ransacking the canteen before finally mutinying. The gates of the barracks were barred. There was no movement in or out. The event finally culminated in over 200 stokers being arrested and the Duty Officer and Senior Officers being relieved of their commands. After this, 'on the knee' was used for drill only. The mutiny would not have affected Edgar directly (except for him being unable to get into barracks), but the tension, uncertainty and excitement must have been intense and spread throughout the ranks.

But Portsmouth offered attractions beyond naval and domestic duties. Apart from enjoying a drink in the pubs, for the first time Edgar sampled the novelty of cabaret shows, sometimes going to the 'artistes' door to see and talk to the performers as they left the theatre.[36] There were several theatres to choose from: The Hippodrome, The Royal, The People's Palace where performances were often twice nightly (so giving time to be home at a reasonable hour) and presenting 'all the latest novelties from America and the Continent … no expense is spared to present a bright and exhilarating entertainment'.[37] There were entertainments on the pier, too, such as marine bands and vocal concerts.[38] Lois wrote later that Edgar had been a good husband. But although he was an affectionate husband and father who worked hard, it was difficult to chain him to domesticity exclusively. It was still less than two years after his battles against Antarctica's worst excesses. Gregarious and outgoing, he needed new experiences. The field gun run was only one of these.

He may have been the father of two other children, twins, born a few months before his daughter Muriel. Beatrice Louise Pharoah was a teacher who, at the time of the twins' birth, lived in Sultan Road, about five roads along from Chapel Street, the Evans' home. Following Beatrice's history through several changes of name and address is a challenge. She was born in 1873, the daughter of a farmer, James Enos Pharoah. Her father died in 1877 and by the 1881 census Beatrice Pharoah is listed as the stepdaughter of Edward James Anderson and his wife Martha (although in fact the actual marriage of Edward and Martha does not appear to have taken place until 1883).[39] Beatrice seems to have taken her stepfather's name and the 1891 census lists her as Beatrice Anderson, living with her now widowed mother in 298 Commercial Road, Portsmouth. Ten years later, in the 1901 census, Beatrice, still known as Anderson, was living with her mother in Lake Road, Portsmouth.

Beatrice married Thomas Henry Glazier in 1902 (giving her name as Beatrice Louise Pharoah). Her husband died after just over two years of marriage. She was to marry again. In 1914, after Edgar's death, she married Charles James Amsden, recording Anderson as her father's name.[40] When Beatrice's daughter married in 1928, she recorded her maiden name as Amsden, but withheld details regarding her father's name and profession (although her new husband supplied details of his own father).[41]

Beatrice gave birth to twins, confusingly named Kathleen Lillian[42] and Lillian Kathleen,[43] on 31 July 1906 at Albert House, Albert Road, Cosham. Beatrice Louise Evans (formally Anderson) is recorded as the mother, the address as 39 Sultan Road. Edgar Evans, Petty Officer RN, is listed as father. This is possibly true. Beatrice was between marriages and Edgar was a virile, active young man. Lois, preoccupied with domestic commitments, her pregnancy and baby Norman, may well have been unable to satisfy him sexually. Whatever the truth Beatrice undoubtedly had a tough time with her twins. Lillian Kathleen (aged seventeen months) died at Sultan Road on the 23 January 1908. The father was registered as Edgar Evans, 1st Class Petty Officer Royal Navy, HMS *Victory*. The certified cause of death was 'Dentition' (presumably problems with teething) and bronchopneumonia.[44] Beatrice was with her daughter when she died, but there is no mention of Edgar being present.

In 1907, the erstwhile Third Officer of *Discovery*, Ernest Henry Shackleton, returned with his own expedition to Antarctica on *Nimrod*. Shackleton reached to within 97 geographic miles of the South Pole, having ascended onto the plateau via a momentous, 150-mile haul up a glacier, which he called the Beardmore after his principal financial backer. A group from his expedition reached the Magnetic South Pole and he was hailed as a hero. When Scott had first heard of Shackleton's intentions, he was back in the navy and marooned in the Atlantic. He wrote to Shackleton saying that he felt he had 'cut right across my plans' (for a return) and that he had the 'right to my own field of work in the way that Peary claimed Smith's Sound and many African travellers their particular locality'.[45] He wrote that foreigners had 'conseeded [sic] that the sphere of the Ross Sea was English', surely therefore 'the English must admit the same argument to apply amongst themselves'.[46]

When Shackleton failed to reach the Pole, Scott wrote that a sportsman is not jealous of his record or slow to praise those who surpass it, but there was surely *Schadenfreude* behind these comments. Shackleton's failure left the prize open for him. His new expedition, the British Antarctic Expedition, was announced on 13 September 1909, and aroused immense public interest; 8,000 people applied to join. Preference was given to those with Antarctic experience and to members of the Royal Navy. Scott wrote to Edgar in March 1910, saying that he (Scott) had applied for Edgar's services on the proposed expedition and that he expected that Edgar would be appointed in two weeks. He wanted Edgar to be at the ship to help in fitting her out. Edgar decided to accept the offer and started working for the expedition in its headquarters in Victoria Street, London. Funding for the expedition was a huge task. The British Government, weary of requests for polar exploration, initially refused financial support. Also, Lloyd George's 'Peoples Budget' had significantly increased taxation on the wealthy, making them less likely to donate money to philanthropic causes. *Discovery*, now owned by the Hudson's Bay Company, could not be got for a reasonable price so Scott bought the whaling ship *Terra Nova* for his expedition paying £12,500. Refitting and a thorough cleaning were needed (her hull was full of seal blubber and the stench was overpowering). Edgar was also fully occupied sorting the gear for the sledges. During the refit he shared lodgings in London near the dock.[47] By now he was a big, burly man at 5ft 10in, and nearly 14 stone.[48] He certainly made an impact on Griffith Taylor, the geologist of the expedition, when he visited expedition headquarters in 1910. Taylor said that Edgar, who was sorting the gear for the sledges, almost filled the room and that he (Taylor) looked at Edgar with considerable respect. Taylor's friend Charles Wright, a physicist, had just had his application to join the expedition turned down, so Taylor, fired up competitively by the sight of Edgar's sturdy proportions, decided to show that some of the scientists could at least 'walk' up to naval standards. The two walked 50 miles in twenty-four hours from Cambridge, to resubmit the application.[49]

Should Edgar have accepted Scott's offer and left Lois and their three children? When Admiralty released him from the navy to join *Terra Nova*, he and his colleagues were taken off the naval payroll, though they kept their place on the promotion list. Edgar's Certificate of Service records that his 'home' base, from 20 April 1910 until 17 February 1912, was HMS *President*, when it finishes with the words, 'Lost in British Antarctic

Expedition'. But the loss of naval pay meant that, unlike his *Discovery* days, Edgar was dependent on expeditionary funds.

There were obvious reasons against him going. He knew there was no guarantee that he would ever get back to England, having had all too vivid experiences of the dangers of Antarctica. He knew his wife would need him, having seen his mother bringing up her children single-handedly when his own father was at sea. But the lure of Antarctica remained strong; he was not the only married man or father to go with Scott (who had only recently got married himself). He knew that the *Discovery* expedition had brought him recognition well beyond the dreams of a lad from Gower, and he knew there would be a Pole attempt and thought he would be chosen for that party. Further recognition and fame beckoned. It was a chance worth taking. In the words of one of the *Terra Nova* explorers:

> I hear the white wastes calling
> Across the restless seas
> Civilization's palling
> The wanderer's disease
>
> I wish that I could once again
> Around the cooker sit
> And hearken to its soft refrain
> And feel so jolly fit[50]

The die was cast.

He certainly did not foresee that Lois was to face difficult financial circumstances. He had signed on for extra years to secure a naval pension. And his family supported him. After he had died his father-in-law (whose loyalty might be expected to be directly focused on his daughter and her struggles and conversely stretched towards his son-in-law) said, 'He was a fine boy. He was a good husband and a good son to his old mother.'[51] Indeed, Lois did not falter in her loyalty.

Edgar's father Charles had died in 1907 and before Edgar left, he and Lois returned to Gower. Scott had decided that Cardiff would be the place of departure for the *Terra Nova*. He visited his mother, now living in the village of Pitton with her sister, and then walked 16 miles to visit his older brother, Charles, at Cwm Farm, Sketty. This visit was made memorable to one of his nieces when Edgar swept her up in his arms and promised to visit her again on his return. When he left, Lois and the children stayed on with her sister in Cardiff.[52]

He told Lois he would be back with her and the children in a year. But the parting was sad and was to be final. She would never see him again.

Notes

1 Ed. Savours, A., *Edward Wilson, Diary of the Discovery Expedition 1901–1904*, Blandford Press, London, 1966, p. 331.
2 Ford, C.E., Journal 10/12/03–14/03/04, SPRI, MS 1174; D, 02/02/1904.
3 Williamson, T.S., Journal 1901–1904, SPRI, MS, 774/1/2; BJ. 10/01/1904.
4 Ford, C.E., Journal 10/12/03–14/03/04, SPRI, MS 1174; D, 10/01/1904.
5 Ibid., 02/02/1904.
6 Ibid., 14/02/1904.
7 Williamson, T.S., Journal 1901–1904, SPRI, MS, 774/1/2;BJ. 13/02/1904.
8 Ibid., 07/03/1904.
9 Ibid., 07/03/1904.
10 Ibid., 02/07/1904.
11 *Times*, Editorial, Saturday 10/09/904, Issue 37496, p. 9.
12 Unknown newspaper clipping. SPRI, 24/04/1906.
13 Unknown newspaper clipping. SPRI, 12/09/1904.
14 Unknown newspaper clipping. SPRI, 12/09/1904.
15 Yelverton, D., *Antarctica Unveiled, Scott's First Expedition and the Quest for the Unknown Continent*, University Press of Colorado, Colorado USA, 2000, Appendix 8.
16 Ibid., Appendix 8. The Royal Geographical Society Medal was awarded in 1913.
17 *Gower Church Magazine*, January 1905.
18 A mountain or peak sticking up through an ice sheet.
19 *South Wales Daily Post*, 20 September 1904.
20 Information from Royal Naval Library, Portsmouth.
21 *South Wales Daily Post*, 14 December 1904.
22 Ibid., 14 December 1904.
23 *Gower Church Magazine*, January 1905.
24 *South Wales Daily Post*, 14 December 1904.
25 Ibid., 14 December 1904.
26 *Gower Church Magazine*, January 1905.
27 Ibid., January 1905.
28 Multimap.com. Postal code PA2 8PJ.
29 Information from the Local History Section of the Portsmouth Library.

30 A town in Natal besieged by the Boers between 2 November 1899 and 28 February 1900. Relieved by Sir Henry Buller. Named after the Spanish wife of the Governor of Cape Town.

31 Boer War, 1899–1902.

32 Cwt is a hundredweight, 50.80kg.

33 Personal communication, 2010, Lieutenant Commander Brian Witts, Curator, HMS *Excellent* Museum, Portsmouth.

34 Debenham, F., *Journal*, 19/01/1911–08/03/1911 MS 279/2: BJp p. 56.

35 04/11/1906, the 'On the Knee Mutiny'. The most serious and widely publicised breakdown in naval discipline. It was confined to the Royal Naval Barracks, Portsmouth.

36 John Evans, grandson, personal communication, 2010.

37 *Portsmouth Guide*, The Hippodrome, Commercial Road, Portsmouth, 1907. (Prices 3*d*, 6*d*, 1/-, 1/6, 2/6, 10/6, 15/-).

38 Ibid., p. 93.

39 Information from the Museums and Records Service, Portsmouth City Council, 2010.

40 Certified Copy of an Entry of Marriage, Registration District Portsmouth, 23 September 1914, TE 159326.

41 Certified Copy of an Entry of Marriage, Registration District Portsmouth, 3 May 1928, TE 159292.

42 Certified Copy of an Entry of Birth, Registration District Fareham, 31 July 1906, No. 269, CJ 735173.

43 Certified Copy of an Entry of Birth, Registration District Fareham, 31 July 1906.

44 Certified Copy of an Entry of Death, Registration District Portsmouth, 23 January 1908. HC 326019.

45 Scott, R.F., *Letter to Ernest Henry Shackleton*, 18/02/1907, SPRI, MS 1456/23: D.

46 Ibid., Undated letter, but soon after 18/02/1907.

47 Cheetham, A.B., *Letter to Mr and Mrs Brewer*, 14/02/1913, SPRI, MS 1365/1/1-2: D.

48 Debenham, F., *Journal*, 19/01/1911–08/03/1911 MS 279/2: BJp p. 17.

49 Taylor, G., *Letter to H.S. Richards* 11/06/1962, Swansea Museum. Wright was successful.

50 Cherry-Garrard, A., *Diary, The Barrier Blight by One Who Has Not Had It*, SPRI. MS 559/4; BJ.

51 *South Wales Daily Post*, 11 February 1913.

52 Johnson, A.M., *Scott of the Antarctic and Cardiff*, The Captain Scott Society, Cardiff, 1995, p. 23.

11

Terra Nova

The *Terra Nova* expedition lasted from 1910–13. The ship was to return to Cardiff without Edgar Evans and his four companions, Robert Falcon Scott, Edward Wilson, 'Birdie' Bowers and 'Titus' Oates. The five men died in Antarctica in 1912.

The journey to Antarctica was full of incident for Edgar. He came near to dismissal in New Zealand and *Terra Nova* came near to disaster soon after leaving her last port of call. If Edgar had retired from Antarctic challenges after the *Discovery* expedition he would have disappeared gently into the quiet backwaters of historical oblivion. But he chose to follow Scott again and so became, after his death, nationally famous and, to an extent, nationally defamed.

He had an unfortunate start to the expedition. Scott had chosen Cardiff, the capital of Wales, as the point of departure simply because the Welsh had offered generous financial and practical support to the expedition. For their part, the dignitaries in Cardiff were quick to appreciate the publicity and commercial advantages offered to their city by the expedition, Cardiff had only been granted city status by Edward VII in 1905, and national exposure was a bonus. In Cardiff, Scott and his officers were invited by the Cardiff Chamber of Commerce for a farewell banquet at the Royal Hotel (fillets of beef *Terra Nova*, soufflé Captain Scott, South Pole ice pudding).[1] The crew were entertained at a nearby hotel (unfortunately no record of that menu remains), and after the meal the men were invited to join the officers. Scott requested that Edgar, the local South Wales hero, who had been lionised in Cardiff,[2] should sit between him and the Lord Mayor of Cardiff. No doubt Edgar's glass had been well filled throughout the evening when he rose to his feet to give an impromptu, but effective speech. The event was reported fully by *The Cambrian*:

Edgar Evans' Cardiff Speech

Abertawe Boy who is Southward Bound
Breezy Speech at Cardiff Banquet

Captain Scott C.V.O and the officers of the British Antarctic Expedition vessel, Terra Nova, were entertained to dinner on Monday evening by the commercial community, the President of the Cardiff Chamber of Commerce in the chair. The crew were also entertained to dinner and £1,000 for the funds of the expedition were collected at the former ceremony, at which an event of special interest to Swansea also occurred, when the Lord Mayor presented to the Expedition a banner emblazoned with the arms of Cardiff.

Chief Seaman Edgar Evans of Swansea, one of the biggest and burliest members of the crew, was received with three times three as he rose from his seat between the Lord Mayor and Captain Scott. With the typical modesty of a Jack Tar and an unmistakable West Wales accent, he said;

I think it's out of place for me to sit up here with Captain Scott, but like Lord Charles Beresford, whatever I have to say I'll say it in as few words as possible. (cheers)

Every man in the ship has confidence in Captain Scott. I know him well and he knows me very well—(laughter)—and I know Lieutenant Evans very well. (cheers)

Every man in the Expedition is heart and soul in the business, and it has got to be a success this time-- (cheers)—every man will do his best.

As a representative of Wales I am pleased to meet you all, but whether Wales or Ireland if Captain Scott had only said he was going again I would go too. (cheers) No one else would have induced me to go again, but if there is one man in the world who will bring this to a successful issue, Captain Scott is the man, (renewed cheers)

As regards the flag, if Captain Scott wants to know the English translation of the Welsh mottoes, here it is: 'Awake, it is day' and 'The Welsh dragon leads the van'.

The crew appreciate what you have done for them; I hope we shall meet again—and we shall. (Cheers) Of course that depends on Captain Scott bringing back the Pole, (loud laughter). We cannot put it in the museum, but if we do bring it back I hope you will let it go to Swansea. (loud cheers and laughter)

Everyone has great confidence in Captain Scott and Lieut. Evans, and if we do ever come back we hope to meet you again in Cardiff again. (loud cheers)[3]

It was a big occasion for Edgar; the dark, oak-panelled room glowed in the candlelight. The great and the good of Cardiff paid him attention, their badges of office shining. His officers, their medals gleaming on their chests, listened. He was bedazzled. He was excited. He was plied with drink. No wonder he got more than well lubricated.

It took six men to get Edgar back onto the *Terra Nova*.[4] He was not aggressive,[5] just incapable. His niece said later that he did tend to drink too much on occasions; she thought it was understandable considering his hazardous career.[6] He was also, almost certainly, not the only man worse for wear on this occasion. Sixteen months later, Lieutenant Henry Bowers wrote to Kathleen Scott when the British team were leaving for the Pole, saying that he was glad that by then the men would have had a certain amount of experience which would be of help in the approach to the job, with – in the case of some of them – 'a little less of that spirit that did not do us credit on our departure from Cardiff.'[7] Yet this story is repeated whenever Edgar Evans' story is told.

The dinner was actually a great success financially. The £1,000 collected towards expedition funds was of great importance, because it went some way to relieving Scott of the embarrassment of departing from the United Kingdom still unable to guarantee the wages of some of his officers and men.

The *Terra Nova* was the trusty whaling ship, the unexpected relief vessel that had accompanied *Morning* in Antarctica in 1904. Now she sailed under the white ensign rather than a merchant flag because Scott had been elected as a member of the Royal Yacht Squadron and she was registered as a yacht under Scott's name.[8] The expedition was expensive, about £50,000, mainly because of the personnel numbers, sixty-five men, eleven of whom were scientists or doctors. There were three motorised sledges that Scott hoped would be of use in pulling supplies across the Barrier, sixteen Siberian ponies, dogs, equipment and supplies for several years in Antarctica.

Although after his death the *Western Mail* printed a photograph of Edgar and Lois aboard *Terra Nova* in Cardiff,[9] Lois did not go to see Edgar off on 15 June. She had three children under five, the youngest only eighteen months, and she may have thought that the pressure of seeing him off from the dock would be too much. It was probably a wise decision; a truckload of coffins clearly visible to the crew hardly encouraged cheerfulness.[10] But his niece, Sarah Evans, travelled from Swansea for the departure which was viewed by thousands. Scott was clearly not fazed about Edgar's perform- ance the night before. Sarah recalled that he called Edgar into his cabin to receive the Mayor of Cardiff's final good wishes and that he (Scott) gave her a sledging biscuit as a memento.[11] Edgar was clearly back to his normal self; described as 'burley Chief Seaman', he hoisted Cardiff's flag to the foremast. As the breeze shook out the flag to show its Welsh dragon 'rampant and confident', the crowds 'burst into a mighty roar', particularly when a Welsh leek fastened onto the masthead joined the Cardiff flag.[12] Sarah was on a steamer following *Terra Nova* as, surrounded with tugs and pleasure steamers, the ship started down the Bristol Channel. When the last tugboat departed, Edgar is reported to have said in a 'thunderous' whisper; 'Goodbye we shall always remember you'.[13] Members of Edgar's family waved from the Gower cliffs at Rhossili as *Terra Nova* made her way towards the open sea. They would never see their man again.

Terra Nova followed the same route as *Discovery* had taken but she did berth in Melbourne rather than bypassing Australia: she sailed via Madeira, South Africa, Australia and New Zealand to Antarctica. She left England without her Captain; Scott remained behind to continue fundrais- ing engagements and the journey to South Africa was commanded by *Discovery*'s Second-in-Command, Lieutenant Edward 'Teddy' Evans. Edgar knew several of the people on board: Chief of Scientific Staff was the erst- while Junior Doctor and Zoologist on *Discovery*, Dr Edward Wilson. There were others who had been on that expedition: Petty Officers Thomas Crean, Thomas Williamson and William Heald, and Chief Stoker Lashly. Other crew members had journeyed south before: Lieutenant Evans had been second-in-command of *Morning*, a trip that irrevocably whetted his appetite for Antarctic exploration. Engineer Bernard Day had been on the *Nimrod* expedition with Shackleton in 1907. Bosun Alf Cheetham was the veteran of Antarctic travel; he had also been on *Morning's* relief trip in 1903 and with *Nimrod* on Shackleton's 1907–09 expedition.[14]

The *Terra Nova* carried an ambitious team. Although the South Pole was high on the list of priorities, Scott was also determined to undertake a big scientific programme that would add academic status to the venture. Edgar's officers, apart from Scott and Lieutenant Evans were: Henry Robertson Bowers, a Lieutenant in the Royal Indian Marines, a man whose beaky nose quickly earned him the nickname 'Birdie'. He was short, 5ft 4in, stocky and full of energy – 'the hardiest traveller that ever undertook a polar journey'. Lieutenant Wilfred Montague Bruce, Royal Naval Reserve and Kathleen Scott's brother, travelled to Vladivostok to meet Cecil Meares, the man appointed to choose the sledge dogs and give Meares assistance in getting the dogs and the ponies, (which Meares also selected), from Russia and across land and sea to join up with *Terra Nova*. Scott was determined to get the best use possible from skis on this expedition, so Tryggve Gran, a Sub-Lieutenant in the Norwegian Navy, was appointed as ski expert. The First Officer was Victor Campbell, 'The Mate' often 'The Wicked Mate'. Stories about him were many; Gran said he never liked being on watch with Campbell because he (Campbell) turned him into a drumstick (a domestic).[15] Laurence Titus Oates, a Captain in the Inniskilling Dragoons, was in charge of the ponies. He was destined for Antarctic heroism and contributed £1,000 to Scott's coffers. The Commander was Harry Pennell (Pennylope). He was the navigator and was also in charge of magnetic work. He was considered one of the most competent members of the expedition. Finally there was Lieutenant Rennick, who looked after the hydrographical work and deep-sea sounding.

The scientific complement was the biggest ever to travel to Antarctica. Dr Wilson's protégé, Apsley Cherry-Garrard, an immensley wealthy young man who had given £1,000 to the expedition and who was later to write *The Worst Journey in the World*, was appointed Assistant Zoologist. Many other members of the scientific staff would go on to international fame: Raymond Priestley and Australians Thomas Griffith Taylor and Frank

Debenham were the geologists and Canadian Charles Wright the physicist. George Simpson was the meteorologist who was to make pivotal observations and conclusions on wind and weather conditions of Antarctica. Dennis Lillie and Edward Nelson were biologists and there were two surgeons, Edward Atkinson and George Levick.

Herbert Ponting was the famous 'Camera Artist' who photographed the crew, including Edgar. His photographs and film, which were to prove invaluable for advertising and providing funds for the expedition, remain prized collectable items to this day. The motor expert was Bernard Day. He had had experience with the motors used on Shackleton's expedition.

Thirty-three of the company were to be on shore duties[16] and Edgar was in this group. Edgar's letter to his mother in the early part of the voyage said that he was well, that he had seen Sarah and two of her sisters in Cardiff, but that other cousins had not turned up. He asked his mother to write to him in Cape Town. He sent his love to his aunts and uncles 'and anyone that enquires'. He was her 'Ever loving Son'.[17]

On board, the men, in cramped accommodation and working conditions, getting to know each other slowly. They worked at the bilge pumps (in spite of all efforts Terra Nova leaked and the men had to spend about half an hour each watch pumping out seawater). Her rolling was enough to make some of the men seasick. Edgar did not start off well with his temporary Captain, Lieutenant Teddy Evans. He had apparently spotted an error over the ordering of some ski bindings, a subject he had good experience in, and he reported this error to Scott. Teddy Evans, who had made the order, was not pleased, particularly when Edgar was put in charge of the ski equipment rather than himself.

'Crossing the line' was on 15 July and Edgar was now experienced at the ritual. He was Neptune. The show began on the 14th, when Neptune's messenger, Triton, arrived to announce that Neptune and his Queen, Amphitrite, would be visiting the ship. Resplendent in his royal robes Edgar appeared, supported by Queen Amphitrite, the strapping Petty Officer Frank Browning. Their followers were the doctor (Seaman James Paton), a barber (Bosun Alfred Cheetham), a barrister (another Petty Officer, George Abbott), all ably helped by Captain Oates and Lieutenant Atkinson as bears. Edgar's friend, Tom Crean, and Petty Officer Thomas Williamson were the policemen.

The Clerk (Abbott), read Neptune's address to the Ship's company, which showed Edgar's quick wit. After welcoming his audience to Father

Neptune's domain and stating that unwilling initiates would be attended to by Neptune's stalwart policemen, the clerk went on to wish the expedition every success. But he commented on the ship's bad leak (perhaps due to cargo shifting so often, or perhaps the tuneless singing of Shanties at the pumps?) and said that it was tough that the stiff breezes he had sent, had veered round so that they travelled straight up the hawse pipes (the area on the ship's bow that the cables go through), causing the sails to have to be furled in the middle watch (the watch between midnight to 4 a.m.). He asked if the ship was towing a sea anchor or whether the rudder was athwartships (lying across) and checking progress, because the ship moved so remarkably slowly. He presumed, 'she would go a long way in a long time'.[18]

The actual initiation, which followed Edgar's advice that the 'Main Brace' should be spliced (drink should be issued), was predictably violent. The doctor inevitably 'prescribed' a pill, a gobstopper of soap and tallow, washed down by a mixture of vinegar and cayenne to every initiate. This was followed by lathering from a bucket of whitewash and another of soot, a shave with a 3ft wooden razor and then the drop into the bath 12ft below. The first to go (Nelson) pulled the 'barber' into the bath with him. Others tried to fight Neptune's assistants in spite of the warning they had been given and most were overcome by the 'police' Crean and Williamson. But Gran (Norwegian, so perhaps unfairly included) chucked the 'doctor' over his shoulder into the bath and was 'lathered very gingerly after that'.[19] The captain decorated Father Neptune with the Grand Cross of the Victorian Order. The Main Brace was promptly spliced with port wine (drinks all round). A concert followed, but to some of the disappointed crewmen the atmosphere was still 'somewhat dry';[20] they wanted more in the alcoholic line.

Following *Discovery*'s trail, *Terra Nova* called on South Trinidad, one of the fabled Treasure Islands,[21] great rocks and corals, many sharks swimming around and with one accessible shore. Edgar recorded the birds again: Terns, Petrels, Gannets. The stretch down to South Africa was helped by strong westerly winds, which allowed *Terra Nova* to fly along under full sail and arrive on 15 August, (though still fifteen days overdue), in the Naval Base of Simon's Bay. She had travelled over 7,000 miles. In South Africa good will abounded, the locals were as hospitable as ever. The ship was repainted in the dockyard. Other ships sent gifts of bread, eggs, and fresh meat. Edgar had reason to be proud of *Terra Nova* when she left Simon's Bay after eighteen days with Scott now in command. He wrote to his mother cheerfully, saying that the plans were for them to leave for the ice in December and saying he had received a letter from his brother, Charlie, 'quite a spasm for him wasn't it?' Again he signed himself her 'ever-loving son' and he sent his regards to all the relations.

Illustrating a perennial worry of all expeditions, Stoker Lashly reported problems with his teeth. He asked Dr Atkinson to pull some out and, in a way that makes the modern reader blanch, Drs Atkinson and Wilson attacked the problem. They had six goes at the first tooth, a tooth that remained as tightly in its socket when they gave up as when they started. Then they pulled out three others, breaking two during the process. Afterwards Lashly wanted them to have another go at the first.[22]

As they sailed onto Melbourne, the voyage was characterised by the usual delights and discomforts of seaboard life: *Terra Nova* rolled vigorously, sometimes the lee rail was well under water and the sea flooded along the starboard side and into the laboratory and sleeping quarters. By 2 October, the wind had fallen. The crew postulated that they were travelling in front of a storm system that was moving at about 150 miles a day. They hypothesised that if they had been in a sailing ship without steam, the cyclone would have caught them and they would have been in continually bad weather. The fact that *Terra Nova* had auxiliary steam meant that they could keep ahead of the storm. They speculated that this could explain the reports of particularly bad weather encountered by sailing ships on that latitude.[23] Lieutenant Evans wrote that he and Scott had definitely selected Edgar to be one of the seaman selected for the shore party (with three Irish companions: Robert Forde, Pat Keohane and Tom Crean).[24]

On 12 October Melbourne was reached. A telegram was waiting for Scott, one that outraged the loyal Edgar. The telegram read: 'Beg leave to inform you, *Fram* [Amundsen's ship] proceeding Antarctic. Amundsen.' The race to the Pole was about to begin though the British did not at first appreciate this; their initial reaction was muted, they did not think that Amundsen would go to the same part of Antarctica as themselves. Roald Amundsen, (1872–1928), the famous Norwegian explorer, had left Norway with the avowed intent of travelling to the Arctic basin and the North Pole. But this was a ruse and he kept the truth from everyone except his brother. Amundsen needed a coup and his South Pole ambitions were hatched when two American explorers, Frederick Cook and Robert Peary, both claimed independently to have reached the North Pole. Geologist Raymond Priestley later remembered Amundsen's conquest of the South Pole as 'the greatest geographical impertinence that history records'[25] (Priestley's opinion was that Amundsen's expedition was to make money). If Scott had known earlier that there would be rivalry in the Antarctic he might well have modified his plans which were not based on speed, but he only fully appreciated the competition risks months later when Amundsens's ship was found by chance, just miles along the Barrier from Scott's base. By contrast, Amundsen, fully aware of Scott's plans, knew that swift progress was essential for the Norwegians to get to the Pole first.

The British expedition plans continued. The Australian Government contributed £2,500 to the expedition. Marconi, the radio pioneer, offered wireless assistance (refused, because the equipment was too bulky),[26] and on 28 October, *Terra Nova* sailed on to another warm welcome at Lyttelton, the port of Christchurch, New Zealand, nine years after Edgar's visit on *Discovery*.

Terra Nova was in New Zealand for a month. Her persistent leak was attacked again and reduced to a degree that the hand pump could control it in two daily sessions of a quarter of an hour. The stores were unpacked and repacked with 'Birdie' Bowers in capable charge. Each item was marked with a red or green band depending on whether it was designated for Scott's Main Party or an Eastern Party that, it was planned, would investigate the land east of the Barrier. The men practised assembling the prefabricated huts. Their living space on the main deck was horribly over-crowded, but Edgar, as the men's spokesman, requested that their comfort should not be considered. He said that because there was such a need to squeeze in extra supplies, 'they were prepared to pig it anyhow'.[27] The ponies and dogs were quarantined on Quail Island before being taken on board. The New Zealand press was enthusiastic, writing that 'Our American cousins have discovered one of the Poles and the record of British exploration will be fittingly crowned if the expedition succeeds in planting the Union Jack on the other'.[28]

The sailors enjoyed Christchurch; some of them enjoyed themselves in the traditional naval way; drink and women. On this occasion Edgar definitely disgraced himself by going on a drinking spree. Before the ship departed for Port Chalmers for coaling on 26 November, and after the Bishop of Christchurch had blessed the ship, Edgar, drunk, fell into the harbour whilst getting on board. Although Scott seemed to have taken the Cardiff episode in a matter-of-fact way, this second episode was different. The expedition had been disgraced publicly. He dismissed Edgar.

Why did Edgar do it? He may simply have wanted the satisfaction of a last, good and prolonged, drinking bout. It may equally have been a guilt reaction. New Zealand was his last link with civilization to be followed by irrevocable separation from his dependent wife and family. He may well have wanted to blot out these and other disagreeable thoughts. Either way dismissal would have been a disaster. He had come off the naval payroll to join *Terra Nova*, so the loss of expeditionary pay would have been a big financial blow for his family. Probably the financial loss would have not been permanent. Edgar was still officially on the naval list and it is likely that after such an episode, he would have faced disciplinary action in Portsmouth and probably disrated. But he would have been on reduced naval pay and the shame to his family would have been considerable

When he was sober Edgar went to Scott, who was still in Lyttelton, to apologise and to ask Scott to reconsider his decision. After initial resistance Scott relented and the two men travelled in the same express train to Port Chalmers, Edgar acting as if nothing had happened.[29] Scott's decision annoyed Lieutenant Evans. Teddy, who was still unhappy about Edgar's promotion to ski master.[30] Teddy also thought that the reinstatement was bad for discipline. But Scott's loyalty and affection for Edgar was genuine. Edgar was a member of the Guarantee Party. They had covered miles of Antarctic wasteland together and gone through conditions that Lieutenant Evans could only imagine; Edgar had been tried and trusted in the worst Antarctic circumstances. Scott did not want to lose his talisman.

Terra Nova left Lyttelton on 29 November. There was the usual excited send off; special trains were put on so that people could watch the departure – all the ships in the harbour were decorated. Cherry-Garrard wrote there was 'a general hullabaloo'.[31] The ship was dangerously overloaded, her deck like a floating farmyard: there were nineteen ponies, all swaying continuously as the ship lifted up and down (Scott has specified that he wanted white ponies only because on Shackleton's expedition, the dark ponies had died before white ones), thirty-three dogs (presented by schools from all over the country, which barked and snarled and strained at their chains), two cats, two rabbits, a pigeon, squirrels and a guinea pig. In addition the deck groaned with 'thirty tons of coal, 2,500 gallons of petrol, some tons of pony fodder and petroleum'. *Terra Nova* also carried '162 frozen sheep and three bullocks'.[32]

In addition there were three caterpillar-track motor sledges. These were potentially a huge innovation in Antarctica. Shackleton had taken a motorcar on the 1907 expedition and thought that motorised transport was feasible in Antarctica.[33] Scott went further; he was the first to pioneer motor sledges in Polar conditions, a possible development that worried Amundsen. There were innumerable sacks of coal and stacks of petrol cases. Mutton from the New Zealand farmers found a place in the icehouse along with three carcasses of beef and boxes of sweetbreads and kidneys.

The seas through which they passed to reach the pack ice are amongst the stormiest in the world. Dante wrote that those who have committed carnal sin are tossed about ceaselessly by the most furious winds in the second circle of Hell, and this is how it appeared to one of the officers as *Terra Nova* pitched and plunged about in a force 10 gale for thirty-six hours.[34] Edgar understood, all too well, the implications for the overloaded ship. As the waves broke with increasing fury over the deck, the ponies began to fall over, the coal loosened petrol cases and the chained dogs were thrown to and fro by each successive wave.

The hatches were battened down, but by 4 December the ship had slowly filled with water. The crew tried unsuccessfully to stop the mountainous waves that washed all over the deck by pouring oil overboard. Coal sacks became battering rams and loosened the petrol drums (150 gallons were lost).[35] The ship's violent tossing opened the deck seams and allowed coal dust to pour into the bilges (the part of the ship below water level where the sides curve towards the keel) and, in spite of the clean up, the dust mixed with blubber from *Terra Nova*'s previous occupation as a whaler. Geologist Priestly wrote later that, in addition to the blubber, one of the sailors must have spilt a barrel of oil in the mainhold which also got mixed with the coal and formed into coal balls 'about the size of composition cricket-balls and these had blocked the pipes leading from the pump'.[36] Lashly worked for hours, unsuccessfully, to try to clear the pipes. The boiler fires had to be closed down; if water got into contact with the boilerplates the boiler would buckle and become useless for further steaming. The engine driven pump was shut down. The ship was at the mercy of the sea as the men worked on furiously, clinging to the rails and up to their waists in water. Officers, scientists and men formed a chain gang and bailed for their lives for twenty-four hours, as the wind raged up to 72mph. Though the men knew that they were dependent on each ship's plank staying firm, they still sang sea shanties (that helped the rhythm of heavy bucket passing) that could be heard above the roar of the waves. When allowed a rest period, Edgar threw himself into his hammock and slept, oblivious of the pitching and rolling of the tortured ship.

Finally the engineers managed to cut a hole in the bulkhead,[37] so that Lieutenants Evans and Bowers could crawl to the hand pumps and pull out those lumps of oily coal dust. Often working under water, the two finally managed to get the hand pumps working. At last the storm subsided, the water level gradually receded, the fires were relit and the ship pumped dry. It had been a near miss. Two ponies and one dog died, tons of coal had been lost overboard along with 100 gallons of petrol.

The ship reached the pack ice, ominously further north than expected, on 9 December. Although Scott had thought that *Terra Nova* was large enough to make an attempt at getting through the pack early,[38] and though she could and did butt away at the heavy ice, she had nothing of the power of modern icebreakers and eventually took a month to get through. Sometimes progress was limited to one knot at full power, so to conserve coal the fire was put out. But every day spent pushing through ice had an effect on the timetable, 'Truly getting into our winter quarters is no light task; at first the gales and heavy seas and now this continuous fight with the pack ice.'[39] By 23 December the coal supply was down to 300 tons.[40] The 25 December, in the pack, was altogether too Christmassy for Scott, but the day was celebrated with a church service, Christmas hymns and lusty singing. The Men had mutton for the celebration lunch (they thought that penguin was not good enough for Christmas),[41] plus beer and whisky. Crean's rabbit gave birth to seventeen babies.

Finally, on 30 December, *Terra Nova* escaped from the ice pack. Victoria Land in all its mysterious, pristine, majestic beauty could be seen about 60 miles ahead. Mount Sabine and the Admiralty Range looked glorious. The high snow peaks were lit by the sun and looked as if they lay over the clouds, like a layer of white satin. On New Year's Day the watch sighted Mount Erebus. Scott headed for his intended base camp, Cape Crozier, but found it impossible to land because of a heavy northerly swell, so *Terra Nova* steamed directly to the Skuary, a rocky cape just north of the ice edge, renamed Cape Evans in honour of Lieutenant Teddy Evans, Scott's second in command. The base was 12 geological miles north of Hut Point,[42] meaning that later on in the expedition the men would have an additional 12 miles to sledge. Ice anchors were let down and unloading began.

The first task was to build the accommodation in which the men would spend the winter. The ship was moored 1.5 miles from the landing place and all the stores had to be ferried by sledge across the pack ice. In the disembarkation one of the motor sledges disappeared through the ice. These expensive experiments had cost £1,000 each; the loss was equivalent to Edgar's wages for thirty years.

Edgar worked tirelessly; he helped unload the ship, build the hut, 10ft above sea level,[43] check the sledges and assist Dr Wilson in the bloody occupation of killing and preparing seal carcasses for the larder. Scott thought he was impressively competent. He had no doubt that the (non-motorised) sledges that Edgar had fitted would work well. The hut was triple-walled and heavily insulated, with seaweed quilting on the roof. It was divided by a wall of packing cases, with scientists and officers on one side, men on the other. The arrangement has been criticised, with detractors saying that the division demonstrated Scott's over reliance on naval hierarchy and his discomfort in being with men of a different social class. This view can be challenged. Scott had already shown on the *Discovery* expedition how he could exist easily with the seamen; in fact one of his attractive characteristics was that he was comfortable with all classes. But what of the sailors? Their whole upbringing and education had schooled them against social integration. Their cultural connections and framework were different. They would have found enforced intimacy with the officers and scientists an unwelcome constraint on their behaviour. They needed a safety valve, a separate unit to let off steam. This was shown later; when Edgar was on a sortie with three officers, he never swore in front of them. But when they returned to base he reverted to his normal vocabulary. When Debenham heard him through the partition he said; 'that sounds like Taff but it can't be – he never talked like that with us'.[44] Edgar would not have wanted to be curbing his tongue full-time.

He wrote to his mother on 3 January 1911. Headed '"*Terra Nova*" Cape Crozier, Victoria Land', he mentioned the bad weather and the pack ice, but only in passing. He was certainly no moaner. He said he expected to be in Antarctica for about fifteen months. He stamped the letter with an Antarctic stamp, marked 'Victoria Land', a unique curiosity, he thought. He asked his mother to keep it. He mentioned his wife; she probably had a job getting the children back to school. He sent his love to all.

They had brought a farmyard with them, but now it was even bigger. In addition to the ponies, dogs, rabbits and cats, Skua gulls nested and fought over seals and squawking penguins.[45] They all wondered where *Fram* was.

Probably Meares was the only one to voice the horrid suggestion that if Amundsen was on the ice near them, he could go straight for the Pole.[46]

After a week's hard sledging and the cargo over the ice, the equipment and supplies were well stored at Cape Evans. Scott planned a series of sorties before the winter: a depot-laying party in preparation for the attempt on the Pole the following year and two other expeditions – an Eastern Party that would carry out scientific and surveying work in King Edward VII Land and a Western Party which would carry out a similar mission in South Victoria Land. Edgar was a member of the second party. Scott's depot-laying party was to have far-reaching effects; there was near disaster as some members avoided death by a hair's breadth, and of the eight fittest ponies that had been taken on the trip five died, a misfortune that Scott was ultimately to claim contributed to the deaths of the Polar Party.[47]

The plans were in action.

Notes

1 The oak panelled room where the dinner took place remains today and a seven-course dinner is recreated accurately and enjoyably by the Captain Scott Society of Cardiff on the 13 June every year.

2 Richards, S., *Letter to Mr Pound* relating his discussion with Sarah Owen (Evans) about Edgar getting tight. 18/06/1965, Swansea Museum, Box 210, PO Edgar Evans.

3 *The Cambrian* 17/06/1910.

4 Copy of letter from Stanley Richards dated 18/06/1965 concerning his conversation with Edgar's niece, Sarah Owen who recalled Edgar's condition after the reception. Royal Institution Swansea.

5 Richards, S., *Letter to Mr Pound* relating to Edgar's drunken episode, 10/06/1965, Swansea Museum, Box 210, PO Edgar Evans.

6 Ibid.

7 Gwynn, S., *Captain Scott*, The Golden Hind Series, London, 1930, p. 204.

8 Ibid., p. 165.

9 *Western Mail*, 12/02/1913.

10 Bowers, H.R., *Letter to Edith Bowers 07//06/1910*, SPRI, MS 1505: D.

11 Gregor, G., *Swansea's Antarctic Explorer, Edgar Evans, 1876–1912*, Swansea City Council, 1995, p. 33.

12 *The South Wales Times*, ?/06/1910. Newspaper Clipping, SPRI.

13 Ibid.

14 Having served on *Morning* and *Nimrod*, Cheetham continued his Antarctic service when he went with Shackleton on *Endurance*, (1914–1916). He was drowned when his ship was torpedoed in 1918.

15 Cherry-Garrard, A., *Diary No. 1* SPRI MS 559/18/1–4: BJ, 10/09/1910.

16 Ed. Jones, M., *Robert Falcon Scott, Journals*, Oxford University Press, Oxford 2005, p. 5.

17 Evans, Edward, *Letter to Lois Evans 21/06/1910*, Swansea Museum.

18 Abbott, G.P., *Journal 01/06/1910–17/10/1911*. SPRI, MS 1754/1D.

19 Cherry-Garrard, A., *Diary No. 1* SPRI MS 559/18/1–4: BJ, 15/07/1910.

20 Abbott, G.P., *Journal 01/06/1910–17/10/1911*. SPRI, MS 1754/1D.

21 Cherry-Garrard, A., *Diary No. 1* SPRI MS 559/18/1–4: BJ, 26/07/1910.

22 Ibid., 30/08/1910.

23 Ibid., 10/10/1910.

24 Evans, Edward, *Letter to Daniel Radcliffe*, SPRI, MS 1013/2/3.

25 Priestley, R., Lecture; *The Antarctic Past and Present*, SPRI, MS 1097/15:D.

26 Cherry-Garrard, A., *Diary No. 1* SPRI MS 559/18/1-4:BJ, 26/07/1910.

27 Ed. Jones, M., *Robert Falcon Scott Journals*, Oxford University Press, Oxford 2005, p. 10.

28 New Zealand *Evening Post*. 10/06/1911.

29 Gregor, G., *Swansea's Antarctic Hero Edgar Evans, 1876–1912*, Swansea City Council. Swansea. 1995, p. 37.

30 Richards, S., *Letter to Reginald Pound*, 14/06/1965. Edgar Evans Swansea Museum Box 210.

31 Cherry-Garrard, A., *Diary No. 1* SPRI MS 559/18/1-4:BJ, 29/11/1910.

32 Evans, Edward. *Letter to Daniel Radcliffe*, SPRI, MS 1013/2/6.

33 SPRI, Unknown newspaper clipping, 02/1907. Shackleton was described as FRGS, FRAS and Silver Medallist of the Royal Geographical Society.

34 Cherry-Garrard, A., *The Worst Journey in the World*, Picador, London, 2001, p. 49.

35 Evans, Edward. *Letter to Daniel Radcliffe*, SPRI, MS 1013/2/6.

36 Priestly, R., *The Polar Expedition As A Psychological Study*, SPRI, MS 1097/16.

37 A division that creates watertight compartments in the hull of a ship, so that leaking in one compartment will not flood the whole ship.

38 Unknown newspaper clipping, 28/08/1910, SPRI.

39 Scott R.F., *Scott's Last Expedition Vol. 1*, John Murray, London 1935, p. 29.

40 Cherry-Garrard, A., *Diary No. 1* SPRI MS 559/18/1-4:BJ, 23/12/1910.

41 Ibid. 25/12/1910.

42 Hut Point could not be reached, as McMurdo was iced up.

43 Evans Edward, *Letter to Daniel Radcliffe*, SPRI MS 1013/2/4.

44 Debenham, F., *Letter to Stanley Richards*, 25/05/1962 Swansea Museum, box 210 PO Edgar Evans (Red File).

45 Cherry-Garrard, A., *Diary No. 1* SPRI MS 559/18/1-4:BJ 10/01/1910.

46 Ibid., 10/01/1911.

47 Scott, R.F., *Scott's Last Expedition, Vol. 1*, John Murray. London 1935 p. 472.

12

The First Western Party

The 1911 autumn sledging trip: 27 January to 15 March. Edgar, with scientists Griffith Taylor, Charles Wright and Frank Debenham, spent over six weeks exploring and studying the geology of the Dry Valleys, the Ferrar Glacier, the Koettlitz Glacier and the Taylor Glacier.

The Dry Valleys in Victoria Land are one of the few areas in Antarctica where geologists can easily study the rocks because the valleys are perennially free from ice and snow. Scott, Edgar and Lashly were the first to discover these oases and briefly explored them, on their way back from their Western Journey of 1903. The 1911 expedition was to examine them in more detail.

Edgar returned to the area as sledge master and cook of the Western Party. He was particularly suited for the expedition; he had more experience of Antarctic sledging than practically anyone and the three scientists were tyros; they knew they were lucky to have him. Taylor wrote later that Edgar was 'at ease with the officers',[1] good in emergencies, unfailingly cheerful, amusing and he kept everyone's spirits up. He was a compulsive, funny, storyteller: he told them how at home he trimmed ducks' bills so that fowls could get a fair amount of food.[2] He kept the scientists 'in stitches' with stories about his school; stories, which Debenham thought unexpectedly, were as good as *Stalky and Co.* (a popular book by Kipling about a badly run boarding school). He told them about the *Discovery* expedition. Once, when he, Dr Koettlitz and Lieutenant Armitage had killed a seal and he was called in for supper, he asked where the sweetbreads were.[3] The officers told him they had eaten them; an acquired taste they said, he would not have liked them. When it was his turn to cook, he fried and ate the remaining sweetbreads. When Koettlitz and Armitage enquired where they were he replied, respectfully, that he had eaten them; 'What?' 'Yes, I acquired the taste for them in the night, sir.'[4]

Later in the expedition he announced his prospective method of proposing to a girl: 'Kin you keep yourself and help me a bit too? If so, then *you're* the "pizened critter" for me.' 'If she doesn't "bite" then you're better off without her, if she does then you're richer instead of poorer.'[5] He offered to teach the others a one-handed clove hitch and bet them the price of a dinner that they would not be able to do it after he had demonstrated it six times. He exaggerated when he told his companions that he had run away to join the navy at the age of 13. He said that he had been very sorry for it for two years, but had gradually grown to like the service.

He was a keen reader and his conversation was full of literary allusions. On this expedition the team carried volumes of Browning, Tennyson, a dictionary and novels as well as scientific volumes. Edgar had *The Red Magazine* (a monthly publication) and a thriller by William Le Queux.[6] He liked thrillers. He did not like Kipling whose stories about the navy were, in his opinion, much too concentrated. He extolled the writings of his favourite author Alexandre 'Dummass'. The scientists could not understand whom he meant until he described the plot of *The Three Musketeers*.[7]

His practical skills were invaluable. He taught his companions how to sledge and camp; how to put up and take down the tent, how to cook for four men in that tent (ice melted in the stove quicker than snow and so used less fuel), 'the hiss of the primus stove was a particularly welcome sound',[8] and how to cobble ski boots (sewing from inside the boot with a sewing awl, a curved implement that could be manoeuvred inside the boot). He could advise them on the first signs of frostbite or scurvy. He was always ready to do the hardest jobs and, importantly, he was tactful and respectful with his advice; he gave the tips without making the novices feel inferior.[9] But he was always ready to give his opinion; when they argued about their scientific finds he would break in with the most 'fearful and wonderful suggestions'.[10]

After Edgar had died, Taylor remembered with affection the Canary Island hat (a large floppy creation) that he had worn on sunny days,[11] 'but it soon turned into the official balaclava'.[12] He remembered also the bets that he lost trying to do the one-handed clove hitch. Debenham clearly liked him. In the accounts there is no sense of a class barrier; instead there is a sense that Edgar had qualities that the more educated men admired.

Terra Nova carried both the Western and Eastern Parties to their drop off point. The Western Party was left at Butter Point, across McMurdo Sound, about 30 miles from their base. There were cheers and goodbyes from the whole ship's company as the ship sailed out of sight.

Australian Griffith Taylor was the principal geologist; he was to investigate the effects of wind, water and ice on the land. His fellow Australian, Frank Debenham, also a geologist, was to help by collecting specimens. Charles Wright was the 'iceologist', the physicist/glaciologist, who was to examine and photograph ice crystals. The men set out with two sledges, a 12ft and a 9ft, but were able to leave one at a depot, so pulled just one sledge for much of the time.

Their aim was to make a geological exploration of the region between the Dry Valleys and the Koettlitz Glacier, to find how the land had been affected by glacier movement, wind, frost and water. Taylor, particularly, wanted to ascertain how their findings compared with observations in warmer climates. Their orders were to climb the Ferrar Glacier to the junction with the Dry Valley Glacier, to go down the glacier and investigate the Dry Valleys, then to make a geological exploration of the Koettlitz Glacier, returning via Hut Point (Scott's base of 1902), to Cape Evans. Scott suggested that when they had investigated the Dry Valleys they could move east to get to the Koettlitz either by climbing up that feared 'Descent Pass' that Edgar had navigated with such difficulty in 1902, or, if this proved impossible, return to the sea ice and progress to the east around Butter Point. In the event, the expedition developed the geological discoveries made in *Discovery* days, made maps of the Lower Ferrar and Dry Valleys and then went on to the Taylor Glacier (named for Griffith Taylor after the expedition), exploring the lower part of that valley. Edgar gave the name 'Wales Glacier' to one of its tributaries.[13] They returned via the Koettlitz Glacier and made detailed maps of its tributary valleys.

The point about this expedition was that its primary focus was scientific. The team could take any time they wanted to examine features of interest.

The expedition was tough; no dogs could be spared so they man–hauled throughout. Debenham wrote later; 'we got into one or two tight spots on the journey but when we did, he (Edgar) never showed any alarm and usually made a joke in the middle of what looked like being a very risky job'.[14] His main problem throughout the expedition was his nose, which regularly got frostbitten. When his sledge-mates told him the trouble was flaring again, he talked about the offending member as if it was a difficult dependent, not directly connected to him and he told his 'old Blossom' off severely. Later in the expedition he also got a frostbitten ear when unbelievably, he was just wearing a tam-o'-shanter (no ear protection). He admitted that the problem was pure carelessness on his part.

They left the drop off point on 27 February taking provisions for eight weeks. They went off at a cracking pace, not even saying goodbye to those friends who remained on the ship. Taylor had geological hammers, note-books, binoculars and specimen bags hanging out of every pocket. Edgar was cook for the first week, Debenham, cook's mate, to take over after a week. The pots were aluminium, a good conductor of heat or cold. They had to be careful not to touch the pots with their bare fingers or their skin would stick to the surface. Each man hauled about 270lbs.[15] On their first tramp they noted unusual features for Antarctica – extensive patches of moss.[16] By the end of the first day's sledging they were in a wonderful position; they could look up the Ferrar Glacier, where straight lines of dark hills ran upwards on each side of the ice, the mountains behind showed clearly against the western sky. When they looked back they could see the ship, now a tiny speck on the horizon, their last link with (relative) civilisation for two months. When Edgar cooked their first meal they could hardly manage the pemmican, which is often far too rich for the beginning of a sortie. The temperature was 13°F.[17]

On the lower part of the glacier they found, surprisingly, Emperor penguins in their moult phase. By 1911 it was known that the Emperors breed in Antarctica, also that they went through a moulting phase of two or three weeks before they returned to the sea, but it was not known previously that these lordly birds chose the Ferrar Glacier as one of their moulting spots.[18] Throughout the moult the Emperors go without food; their old feathers would get waterlogged if they went into the sea and Edgar watched the birds as they wandered around, old patches of feathers hanging from them unattractively, as they bad-temperedly batted each other with their flippers.

Hauling was heavy work; the scientists were in a 'somewhat flabby condition'[19] and Taylor in his account of the journey gives credit to Edgar for his 'mighty strength' and his care of the sledging equipment.[20] After three days, they were well advanced on the glacier, the sledging became 'damnable' as they pulled through snow of up to 10in deep.[21] By 31 January they camped below Cathedral Rocks, near where the Ferrar Glacier divides into two. Cathedral Rocks were known to Edgar, but new to the scientists who decided that they were well named. They thought that the high ridges and sharply cut ends looked like the transepts of a cathedral;[22] they could also see Descent Pass that Edgar had navigated in 1902. It looked formidable.

From their vantage point they could still look back on Ross Island with Mount Erebus still smoking and the sea. The glacier stretched above. Edgar wrote in his journal about how impressed he was with the rugged surroundings. In early February they descended the same steep glacier leading to the Dry Valleys that Edgar had gone down in 1902. But the 1911 expedition went further beyond the glacier and deeper into the valley than they had done in 1902; the men spent a week studying the geology of the valley which is 25 miles long and 4 miles wide, encased by mountains of over 5,000ft and completely free of ice and snow at a latitude of over 77°S. It was a remarkable and beautiful spot. Thaw streams ran down the glacier, and Edgar wrote that he 'did not expect to see scenery like this'.[23] Taylor studied the glacial landscape[24] and Edgar became interested in collecting rock samples and later fossils in the moraine rocks (Taylor offered him cash if he found any).[25]

The Dry Valleys deserve their name insofar as there is no snow, but there is plenty of water, due to the thaws. After Scott, Edgar and Seaman Lashly had discovered the upper part of the Dry Valleys in 1903 the scientists of 1911 were understandably keen to add useful knowledge about these phenomena. We now know that the dry valleys are a row of valleys in Victoria Land named because of their low humidity and lack of snow and ice cover. The floors of the valleys are covered by grey, loose gravelly material. They were formed when katabatic winds,[26] reaching 200mph, swept through, evaporating any moisture in their path. Scott originally named the valley 'Death Valley', because there was nothing obviously alive there, but in fact bacteria proliferate in the summer melt water and provide nutrients for the soil. The Americans in their preparation for the

Mars probe used the area, as the conditions are the nearest earth equivalent to that planet.

The valley's lack of snow meant that they could not use their sledge and they set off for a few days exploration with a tent, sleeping bags and dry provisions; Edgar carried his sleeping bag, the tent, the tent poles and his provisions slung over his shoulder. This was not a problem for him. The others made do, carrying their sleeping bags, collecting bags, camera and biscuits.[27] Importantly, at least from Edgar's point of view, they did not take the cooker. The meals were all cold, 'make-believe' meals.[28] Each day they had ten biscuits, a stick of chocolate, 2oz cheese and 1.5oz butter.[29] Edgar felt the lack of a hot meal keenly and he believed that food could only be of benefit when it was warm; a diet of cheese, biscuits and chocolate was simply not enough. His journal over these days is full of complaints about the unsatisfactory nature of his rations. One day he complained he only had biscuits, butter and icy water for one meal, not even cheese and chocolate. Sucking ice or snow did not help. Their thirst was only quenched for a few minutes. They thought that the biscuits were similar to porridge in that their comforting effect wore off in a short time leaving a horrid vacuum; in addition, Debenham wrote, they were so hard that they sometimes had to be broken up with a hammer.[30] But he thought the scenery was lovely.

The glacier they had descended ended in a drainage lake two miles long surrounded by mountains. The lake was partially frozen; its edge was covered with four inches of smooth, clear ice – ideal for skating. A rock bar, a 'reigel', projected into it giving the lake an hourglass appearance. Taylor named the 'reigel' and the lake after his friend Professor Bonney of Cambridge. At the far side of Lake Bonney, reached with much slipping and sliding, was an area that Edgar instantly dubbed 'the football fields'. It was full of holes filled up with gravel and sand, obviously the sort of football field he was used to. This was where Scott, Edgar and Lashly had turned back in 1903, after this everything was new. Edgar wrote that now, he had had the satisfaction of seeing the whole of it.[31] They found about twenty seal skeletons and wondered how they came to be there. Edgar was amazed that they had managed to climb so far up and thought that they had probably died of starvation, because having got up, they could not get down. The alternative theory, that they had come up purposely to die, did not appeal. The men explored south till they were almost back to the coast again. When Taylor and Edgar climbed a reigel near the end of the valley they could see the sea, just about 13 miles away[32] and they travelled further south towards the water, climbing over moraine heaps.[33]

Edgar described the lower part of the valley; 'the more one sees of this place the more one is impressed with the rugged scenery, there are mountains all around with glaciers coming down the sides of them, then the valley is extremely interesting from a geological point of view there are six inland lakes, of course at present they are frozen over but in summer they are not –they are made from the thaw of the glaciers and melting of snow, some are quite two miles square and there is any quantity of rocks of all descriptions … The last time I was here I only came a third of the way through the Dry Valley now I have the satisfaction of seeing the whole if it'.[34]

After four days the end was in sight and about time too; 'my belly fairly rattles. We hope to get back to Glacier Camp tomorrow, a feed of Pemmican will be very welcome or anything hot in fact. Four days of dry biscuits is enough for a while.'[35] He complained that it was the first time that a sledging party had tried to go without hot food in the Antarctic. The venture into the Dry Valleys had been a new departure; explorers did not usually separate themselves from their sledges for more than a few hours.

By 10 February, they were below Cathedral Rocks again. They could congratulate themselves. They had found a treasure trove of geological and biological specimens in the Dry Valleys. Some of the fossils that Edgar collected contained primitive flora and microorganisms. It was very cold and they celebrated their return to hot food eagerly. They ate, a lot, double hoosh and double cocoa, at last liquid food. This was followed predictably by stomach-ache. Edgar's solution was a 'massage with an ice axe' or 'an operation for appendicitis with the same'.[36]

On 11 February, Edgar and Taylor, roped together, went, as instructed by Scott, to explore the possibilities of the Descent Pass, 7 miles away. If they could have negotiated it they would have been saved the journey back to the coast. The going was very heavy. They got into a maze of crevasses. As they progressed there was a noise like an earthquake as they stepped on a crust of snow, this was followed by a peculiar shudder, lasting for seconds. They found that their axes went far too easily through the ice. Suddenly they found they had sunk up to their thighs in the snow. The surface started caving in. They were on the edge of a 'profound' crevasse and retreated cautiously.[37] They thought that they could never have got their sledge over the gaping void and prudently decided to go down to Butter Point and along the coast to the Koettlitz Glacier.

They were soon back from where they started, at the base of the Ferrar, at the junction of glacier and sea ice, though the rapid descent was accompanied by 'plenty of cusses'[38] as they fell on the ice and ridges. At the base they could still see their old sledge tracks. The interesting discussions continued: for example, did they get enough sugar? Edgar thought they did not. He wrote that they discussed several things but 'did not settle them'.[39] One of these queries was that he did not think that New Harbour was at the mouth of the Dry Valley. He opined that this was not what he had seen from the mouth of the Dry Valleys the week before. Wright supported his argument. Debenham bet him he was wrong.[40] Edgar was incorrect.

At the base of the glacier the sea ice was on the move. It had gone out 8 miles in the two weeks they had been in the mountains. Killer whales circled in the sea, below cracks in the ice that got bigger as the men looked at them. Debenham wrote that Edgar normally kept his diary with 'much pain and tribulation', but on 13 February he was excited to write about the sea ice moving. It was clear that it would not withstand any weight. They retreated to the fast ice close to the land and then started climbing towards the mountains again. The aim was to get to the Blue Glacier in a couple of days and then onto the Koettlitz Glacier. Progress was slow as they pulled through snow up to their knees on a steep upward slope. Taylor wondered if anyone had ever adopted a worse route with a laden sledge.[41] They could only make strides of a few inches and could not get a good pull on the traces. They fell repeatedly and the sledges capsized, altogether an exhausting business. Edgar delivered his strongest curse in the presence of officers: 'May the curse of the seven blind beggars of Egypt be upon you.'[42] This was delivered with emphasis at every halt. Their breath froze as soon as it reached the air. They had icicles hanging onto their moustaches and beards that made them look like walruses.

They did 5 miles in eight hours, climbing 600ft up the long snow slope that runs along the coast from Butter Point to the Blue Glacier. Their footgear gave them trouble. It took much tugging, shoving and chafing to get their feet into boots that were as stiff as iron, then having to do them up with frozen fingers.[43] The nails in the soles transmitted the cold into the boots, and Debenham wrote that sometimes they had to hit them with a geological hammer to get them into shape, especially if snow had got in and frozen. Edgar wore puttees to guard against this and found them remarkably successful. Debenham thought that the worst part of the ordeal was when the boot actually thawed; he said that then there was a pitched battle between the owner of the boot and the boot itself as to which gave in to the others temperature. He wrote that he had never guessed that cold feet could give such excruciating pain.[44]

Between 17 and 25 February they struggled through truly terrible surfaces up the middle of the 'desiccated [Koettlitz] glacier, now weathered into pie-crusts, bastions and pinnacles of every conceivable shape'.[45] They reached the north side of the glacier and explored the moraines, hanging valleys and 'ice slabs' in the foothills of Mount Hooker. There was a lake with seals swimming in it. A stream flowed from this lake; over 20 miles long it reached the sea near the Blue Glacier. They named the stream 'Alph', from Coleridge's poem *Kubla Khan* in which a sacred river runs in a pure stream into the Mediterranean Sea:

> Where Alph, the sacred river ran
> Through caverns measureless to man,
> Down to a sunless sea.

There are repeated comments about card games: 24 February, the two Australians (Debenham and Taylor) versus Canada and Wales (Wright and Edgar). Australia lost handsomely. In March, Edgar won a dinner from Debenham and Wright. He admitted he had lost, at least once, to Taylor (when they were safely back Edgar lost a game of cribbage to Taylor 'to the astonishment of the seamen').[46]

The return began on 2 March. Travelling via the north-west side of the Koettlitz, they found, for a change, that the ice was smooth and comparatively easy and assumed they were on the frozen surface of the Alph. This was confirmed when one day water suddenly rose up through the snow flooding the floor of the tent. It seemed that tidal water had come surging into the Alph. On the 9th Edgar wrote that it was the first time he had spent his birthday sledging. He wrote that pulling one of the sledges that day was 'a bugger'; they pulled hard enough to 'break the heart of the sledge, never mind the party pulling'.[47] To celebrate he had two cups of tea and an extra biscuit.

The Western Party reached Hut Point on 14 March, laden with sacks of geological and fossil samples. They had made maps of the Lower Ferrar and Taylor Glacier and explored the lower part of the Dry Valleys for the first time. They had added many new features to the map and named them.[48] Scott wrote that the party 'gave Edgar a very high character'.[49]

So Edgar ended another exciting and productive Antarctic exploration.

Notes

1 Taylor, G., *Letter to Stanley Richard*, 11/06/1962, Swansea Museum, Box 210, (Edgar Evans).
2 Ibid.
3 The pancreas or thymus of a calf, lamb, or other young animal soaked, fried and eaten as food. They were considered a delicacy.
4 Debenham, F., *Journal*, 19/01/1911–08/03/1911 MS 279/2: BJp.
5 Ibid., p. 78.
6 William Le Queux, 02/17/1864–13/10/1927. An Anglo-French journalist and writer who wrote 150 novels dealing with international intrigue, also books warning of Britain's vulnerability to European invasion before the First World War.
7 Taylor, G., *Journeyman Taylor, The Education of a Scientist*, Robert Hale, London, 1958, p. 99.
8 Speak, P., *DEB, A Biography of Frank Debenham*, Polar Publishing, Guildford England, 2008, p. 31.
9 Debenham, F., *Journal*, 19/01/1911–08/03/1911 MS 279/2: BJ p. 40.
10 Debenham, F., *Letter to Stanley Richard*, 25/05/1962, Swansea Museum, Box 210 (Edgar Evans).
11 Taylor, G., *Letter to Stanley Richard*, 11/06/1962, Swansea Museum, Box 210 (Edgar Evans).
12 Ibid.
13 Ibid.
14 Debenham, F., *Letter to Stanley Richard*, 25/05/1962, Swansea Museum, Box 210 (Edgar Evans).
15 Debenham, F., *Journal*, 19/01/1911–08/03/1911 MS 279/2: BJ p. 40.
16 Taylor, G., *Journeyman Taylor, The Education of a Scientist*, Robert Hale, London, 1958, p. 98.
17 Evans, E., *Journal, 27/01/1911–12/05/1911*, SPRI, MS 1487: BJ, 27/01/1911.
18 Debenham, F., *Journal*, 19/01/1911–08/03/1911 MS 279/2: BJ p. 45.
19 Ibid., p. 46.
20 Taylor, G., *Journeyman Taylor, The Education of a Scientist*, Robert Hale, London, 1958, p. 98.
21 Debenham, F., *Journal*, 19/01/1911–08/03/1911 MS 279/2: BJ, p. 48.
22 Ibid., p. 49.
23 Ibid., 04/02/1911.
24 Taylor, G. , *Journeyman Taylor, The Education of a Scientist*, Robert Hale, London, 1958, p. 98.
25 Debenham, F., *Journal*, 19/01/1911–08/03/1911 MS 279/2: BJp, p. 56.

26 Derived from the Greek 'going down'. They occur when cold dense winds are pulled down by the force of gravity.

27 Debenham, F., *Journal*, 19/01/1911–08/03/1911 MS 279/2: BJp, p. 60.

28 Evans, E., *Journal 27/01/1911–12/03/1911*, SPRI, MS 1487: BJ, 03/02/1911.

29 Debenham, F., *Journal*, 19/01/1911–08/03/1911 MS 279/2: BJp, p. 57.

30 Ibid., p. 64.

31 Evans, E., *Journal 27/01/1911–12/03/1911*, SPRI, MS 1487: BJ, 06/02/1911.

32 Ibid., 05/02/1911.

33 Debenham, F., *Journal*, 19/01/1911–08/03/1911 SPRI, MS 279/2: BJp, p. 61.

34 Evans, E., *Journal 27/01/1911–12/03/1911*, SPRI, MS 1487: BJ, 06/02/1911.

35 Ibid., 06/02/1911.

36 Debenham, F., *Journal*, 19/01/1911–08/03/1911 MS 279/2: BJp, p. 70.

37 Taylor, G., *Journeyman Taylor, The Education of a Scientist*, Robert Hale, London, 1958, p. 100.

38 Evans, E., *Journal 27/01/1911–12/03/1911*, SPRI MS 1487: BJ, 12/02/1911.

39 Ibid., 12/02/1911.

40 Debenham, F., *Journal*, 19/01/1911–08/03/1911 MS 279/2: BJp, p. 77.

41 Taylor, G., *Journeyman Taylor, The Education of a Scientist*, Robert Hale, London, 1958, p. 100.

42 Debenham, F., *Journal*, 19/01/1911–08/03/1911 MS 279/2: BJp, p. 79.

43 Ibid., p. 78.

44 Ibid., p. 78.

45 Taylor, G., *Journeyman Taylor, The Education of a Scientist*, Robert Hale, London, 1958, p. 100.

46 Taylor, G., *Letter to Stanley Richard*, 11/06/1962, Swansea Museum, Box 210, (Edgar Evans).

47 Evans, E., *Journal 27/01/1911–12/03/1911*, SPRI MS 1487;BJ, 09/03/1911.

48 The naming was difficult to agree on. Years later Debenham wrote that Edgar's suggestions had been too naval and too mess-deck. He (Debenham) decided against female names, but when he named a glacier the Kitticarrara Glacier, this was resented by Edgar who opined that the rule against female names was being broken.

49 Ed. Jones, M., *Robert Falcon Scott Journals*, Oxford University Press, Oxford, 2005, p. 146.

13

The Winter Months, 1911

Although they had reached Hut Point (*Discovery's* headquarters) they were still some 15 miles south of Cape Evans. The home base could not be reached until the sea ice had frozen over sufficiently for safe transport. Hut Point was already crowded; Scott and his party, having returned from laying depots on the Barrier, had been in the hut for two weeks, and the scientific party increased the cramped community to sixteen. There was ominous news for Taylor's party. After *Terra Nova* had deposited Edgar's group, she had carried the Eastern Party to the far end of the Barrier. Unable to get ashore on King Edward VII Land, she steamed back along the Barrier and into a bay, the Bay of Whales, some 60 miles closer to the Pole than the English base. Here, the crew were astounded to find a ship. It was Amundsen's *Fram*. She was carrying just nine men but over 100 dogs (Amundsen magnanimously offered some dogs to Scott). There was now absolutely no doubt that the Norwegian was single-minded in his determination to get to the Pole first. Lieutenant Evans wrote that he hoped that the 'best man may win'.[1]

In the face of this unexpected challenge Scott decided that he would not change his plans; the scientific aims of the expedition could not be sacrificed in order to win a race. But the Pole remained a priority, both in terms of national pride and because the achievement would be sure to attract funds to help the expedition's big financial outlay. Edgar thought Amundsen's change of plan deceitful; he knew, none better, of Scott's months of careful planning and was angry and indignant. The scientists were upset too. But they all understood that in Amundsen they faced formidable competition. He was experienced both in Arctic travel, having navigated through the North-West Passage, and he had been on an expedition to the Antarctic (though not to its interior) in 1897. His display of dog driving was formidable when the British met him in the Bay of Whales. But Amundsen, too, had his worries. He was worried about Scott's motor sledges. He feared they could rob him of success.

The sixteen men were in Hut Point for a month waiting for the sea to freeze. Evenings, lit by the dim glow of candles and blubber lamps, were spent in long discussions.[2] The hut had a central room, 'Villa Virtue',[3] where Dr Wilson, Cherry-Garrard, Lieutenant Bowers, Captain Oates and the dog handler, Meares, slept. The other officers, including Scott, slept in shared accommodation around the hut with the men.[4] Hardly a class-conscious division. Seals were killed and the food supplemented by the remains of Shackleton's 1908 visit; his biscuits were thought to be particularly good, especially when they were toasted and smeared with blubber. Debenham was a cook and had a particular talent for making chapatis.

They left Hut Point on 11 April as a large party. Edgar was with Scott, Lieutenant Evans, 'Birdie' Bowers, Taylor, Wright, Debenham, Petty Officer Crean and the Norwegian ski expert, Gran. They took enough food for twenty-four hours. The aim was to keep on land initially and then to go over the sea-ice to Cape Evans. When the group stopped for lunch Edgar and Taylor prospected the ice to make sure it was safe to cross (Taylor had previously fallen through a weak patch). Eventually they all attempted to reach Cape Evans in a night's march. The journey was difficult; they were caught by a blizzard (when they finished their food) and it eventually took them two days to make the journey to Cape Evans. They arrived, ravenous and exhausted, on 13 April.

On 23 April the sun disappeared. There were a few excitements over the winter months: a bitch had six puppies and killed them all.[5] The men played football on the ice when there was still enough light. Edgar was always Captain Oates' first choice for his team: 'Go on Taff, break them up', 'Right-o, sir'. Dr Atkinson left the hut and got lost; his hand got badly frostbitten. Edgar was in charge of a search party and, always in the forefront of activities, was photographed by Ponting bandaging Atkinson's hand.

There were also lectures. The Men attended the first few, but a lecture on parasitology was too much and Edgar did not attend any after this, so missing Dr Atkinson's lecture on scurvy (which Atkinson interestingly thought was catching and in which he reiterated the theory that the disease was caused by bacterial acid poisoning and correctly stated that eating fresh vegetables was a way to halt it). Edgar also missed Scott's suggestion for building igloos on the Southern Attempt, a suggestion turned down because of the two hours' labour that would be needed after a day's hauling.

Midwinter was celebrated with the hut decorated with flags, an enormous cake, an extravagant meal and alcohol. Edgar, according to Scott, enjoyed himself by 'imparting confidences in heavy whispers'.[6]

Photographer Ponting wrote that Edgar was the dominant personality of the mess-deck over the winter months. Ponting said that Edgar's previous Polar experience, his build, his stentorian voice and manner of using it, all compelled 'the respect due to one who would have been conspicuous in any company'. Ponting thought that Edgar was one of Scott's towers of strength; he had heard Scott telling Edgar that he did not know what the expedition would do without him on more than one occasion.[7]

The focus of the winter was preparation for the Pole attempt. A first at the Pole would add a huge kudos to the expedition; failure would diminish its achievements. Scott's plans were explained. The sledges were overhauled and Edgar worked hard on them. The dogs and the ponies needed attention; the dogs, in particular, were a source of irritation. As well as providing interest and amusement, they repeatedly escaped their traces and rushed off after seals and penguins, or got their tongues stuck to frozen tins, a problem only remedied by catching the dog and warming the tin.

Scott was worried about ski boots and bindings. He knew that the 2lb boots could chafe the men's Achilles tendons. Edgar's practical skills resolved the problem (one which had concerned Amundsen for years). He made a ski shoe with a double sole of sealskin, stiffened with wood, into which the men could fit their soft fur finnesko. The shoe was held in place by a strap and the modification was stronger, allowing more flexibility than the standard boot. He sewed the boots with waxed thread.[8]

The finnesko/shoe combination weighed less than a ski boot[9] and was an undoubted success.

Anticipation for the Pole attempt was increasing.

Notes

1   Evans, Edward. *Letter to Daniel Radcliffe*, SPRI, MS1013/2/4.
2   Ibid., p. 102.
3   Taylor, G., *Journeyman Taylor, The Education of a Scientist*, Robert Hale, London, 1958, p.101.
4   Ibid., p. 101.
5   Cherry-Garrard, A., *Journal*, MS 559/18/1–4; BJ Vol. 2, 19/08/1911.
6   Ibid., p. 232.
7   Ponting, H.G., *The Great White South*, Duckworth, London, 1932, p. 162.
8   Personal communication. September 2010, Jean Scholar, granddaughter of PO Fred Parsons.
9   Ed. Jones, M., *Robert Falcon Scott's Last Expedition*, Oxford University Press, Oxford, 2005, p. 239.

14

The Polar Assault

Scott took Edgar on one sortie before the assault on the Pole. Along with Edgar, scientist George Simpson and 'Birdie' Bowers, he set out to check the rate of flow of the Ferrar Glacier by recording how far ice stakes, positioned seven months previously, had moved. This was the first observation on the movements of a coastal glacier and they found that the stakes had moved variable distances; between 24 and 32ft. They thought that the Ferrar Glacier was 'lively'. The group were away for thirteen days, on the last day they covered 21 miles, man-hauling into the teeth of a freezing headwind. They 'captured many frostbites'.[1] Edgar was 'a treasure'.[2]

Edgar had been well briefed on Scott's plans for the Polar Assault. There were to be three stages – the Barrier, the Beardmore Glacier and the Plateau.[3] It was planned to get across the Barrier with motorised sledges (which, he hoped might significantly improve progress over the Barrier by comparison with Shackleton), ten horses and the dogs. Scott thought that the ponies would be reliable for the Barrier stage, after which they were to be killed.[4] He calculated that each pony could pull 550lbs (perhaps more), between them a total of 5,500lbs. The dogs were to return to base when they had pulled their loads over the Barrier. Scott did not think that animals would be able to survive the Beardmore Glacier's fearsome conditions and crevasses.[5] Here he was influenced by Shackleton, who had consulted Armitage, his colleague on *Discovery*, who had been second-in-command on the Jackson Harmsworth Expedition of 1894–97. Jackson had recommended Russian ponies for Polar exploration[6] and Shackleton had become critical of dogs.[7] Scott himself had seen one dog team disappear down a crevasse in February 1911 and he knew that Shackleton's last pony had fallen into an endless abyss on the Beardmore on the 1908 Pole attempt. The British position was that if the plateau was as bad as Shackleton described, no beast could stand the trials of getting onto it, but that 'man could do what beasts would not'.[8]

Scott's plans were made before he had any idea that Amundsen's presence would make the lack of dogs crucial, but he determined to stick to the plans. He did take dogs, but only thirty-four, compared to Amundsen, who took over a hundred. But by this stage he was realistic about his chances; he had heard how well the Norwegian team controlled their dogs, he knew he would have to start later than his rival because ponies suffered so badly in Antarctic conditions and he wrote that if Amundsen achieved the Pole it would be before the British, because he (Amundsen) could travel fast with dogs and was certain to start early. Scott warned that the British venture might be belittled and he wrote: 'After all it's the work that counts not the applause that follows.'[9] But he worried also that Amundsen would get the news back first in 1912.[10]

Scott wrote to Edgar's wife Lois just before the team departed. He said that Edgar had told him a great deal about her and that he could imagine that she and the children wanted to see him come home. He assured Lois that Edgar was very well, very strong and in good condition. He knew the family would be disappointed, but he thought that it was likely that Edgar would stay in the South for an extra year. If so, he asked Lois to remember that Edgar was certain to be in the best of health and that it would be all the better when he did come home. Scott wrote that he hoped that Edgar would get a good billet on his return, which would make it unnecessary for him to leave her again. 'He is such an old friend of mine that no one deserves so well all I can do for him.' She must not be anxious or worried.[11] [12]

The attempt was critically dependent on dates. Scott recorded that the distance was 1,530 geographical miles; if they could keep up with Shackleton's daily distances they would return near the end of March, in the early part of winter when temperatures would be very low. In

Antarctica there is a 'Coreless Winter'; temperatures drop immediately at the end of summer and remain low till October (lower for longer than the Arctic). Meteorologist George Simpson estimated that the temperatures at the last stage of the Barrier journey would be around -20°F, very challenging, after a long plateau trek, but endurable.[13] In the event, at the end of their Barrier journey, the British were to suffer temperatures that were up to -20°F – colder than the typical horrors.[14]

Edgar was full of optimism at the start; he thought that the motor sledges had real potential. When he watched the four men, Lieutenant Teddy Evans, Stoker Lashly, Engineer Bernard Day and the Steward Frederick Hooper, set off on 24 October with the caterpillar-track sledges he was enthusiastic: 'Lord, Sir, I reckon if them things can go like that you wouldn't want nothing else.'[15] The motor sledges pulled at about 1 mile per hour,[16] but did not get far; the caterpillar tracks were reasonably successful but the cylinders got too hot, whilst wind on the carburettors made them too cold; one motor failed after 14 miles, the other after 50. Their loads were repacked, 740lbs onto a 10ft sledge, which the four men pulled furiously to a pre-arranged rendezvous. The extra physical work of hauling would take its toll and affect Lieutenant Evans and Lashly later on the attempt at the Pole.

On the same day (1 November) that the tractors were abandoned the pony caravan set out. There were ten pony leaders in three groups, Edgar was one of them, leading Snatcher, and when the cavalcade halted he shared a tent with Scott, Oates and Dr Wilson.[17] As the team got ready to set out Scott again praised Edgar, writing: 'Edgar Evans has proved a useful member of our party; he looks after the sledges and sledge equipment with a care of management and a fertility of resource which is truly astonishing – on "track" he is just as sound and hard as ever and has an inexhaustible supply of anecdotes.'[18] Edgar's 'fitness to travel' was self-evident; any suggestion that he was below par seems misplaced. The dog teams with two dog-drivers, Cecil Meares and Dmitri Gerof, had left earlier and when the ponies set out, Edgar's Snatcher romped away, leading the party.[19]

Ponting filmed the pony parties' departure. The weakest went first, followed by the stronger. Some ponies struggled from the start and wide gaps opened between them. They were still in their summer coats and got seriously chilled as they plodded over the featureless, monotonous white surface; the teams saw no sign of land for days, sky and snow merging into a white pall.

After five days they were delayed by a blizzard. The ponies suffered particularly badly. Scott had organised for snow walls to be built to protect them from wind and snow, but the fine snow still got in their eyes, noses, ears and under their coats, where it turned to ice. Rugs were little help as they quickly became soaked.[20] The ponies' progress was in marked contrast to the dogs, which pulled their loads with little difficulty – their nictitating membranes protecting their eyes from the snow.[21] [22] The teams built depots and snow cairns at roughly 70 mile intervals. Each was provisioned with enough fuel and food (buried deeply to prevent fat in the pemmican from deteriorating) for a week, so that the returning parties would be well supplied. Five depots were built on the Barrier: Corner Camp, Bluff, One Ton, Mid, and Southern Depots.

One Ton Camp was reached on 15 November. Scott had left provisions there earlier in the year and the ponies' loads were lightened by leaving bundles of seal meat for food supplies for the return journey. The party covered about 13 geographical miles a day, but the snow surface was awful. Scott thought that a worse set of conditions for the ponies could not be imagined as their hooves sank deep into the snow; snow-shoes were not worn regularly, and Scott wrote that he wished the animals would wear them.[23] On 21 November they caught up with Lieutenant Evans' motor party and camped together. This motor party foursome, having man-hauled, were fit but already ominously hungry.[24] It was becoming clear that rations that satisfied men leading ponies (or men sitting on dog sledges), were not enough for those actually pulling the sledges. Hunger was to bedevil man-hauling parties. After a few days on a sortie, men began to feel an overwhelming craving for food that was only eased for a few hours by a meal. Days were occupied with thoughts of food and nights were plagued by food dreams; when they woke the craving was almost unbearable, and every hair-covered morsel was 'watched over with the eager solicitude of a dog for a bone'.[25]

Scott followed Shackleton's daily progress chart. He reasoned that if he could keep going at a pace equal to, or even ahead of Shackleton, he would have a chance of success. The ponies were all to be killed at, or before, the Beardmore Glacier and the meat used to feed both dogs and men. The dogs would return from the Beardmore and after the pony slaughter, the men would start to man-haul. Dog handler Meares eyed the ponies with anticipation, and when Oates shot the first pony (Jehu), on the night of 23 November, Jehu made glorious feeds for four days for twenty dogs.[26]

Over the next eleven days four more ponies (but not Edgar's Snatcher) were killed. The pony handlers watched Meares suspiciously. They were fond and protective of their charges; they also knew that the longer their particular pony survived, the less time they would have to man-haul. One pony 'cut up well' and the man-hauling team enjoyed a nice piece of undercut[27] (the meat was boiled and added to the pemmican). After a delay due to poor conditions the teams pushed on and reached their second depot, Lower Depot.

The first two of Scott's planned returnees, Hooper and Day (from the motor party), turned back on 24 November. As the fourteen remaining men continued slowly south, they began to see mountains fringing the Barrier in the distance. They progressed in three groups according to speed: man-haulers, ponies, dogs, with Scott always comparing his progress to Shackleton's. But his advance was slower: visibility was poor and they were soon several days behind schedule. By comparison, Amundsen's men either skied beside the sledges or rode on them, covering over 20 miles a day.

When, on 29 November, the mists rolled away, the surface continued to be bad and the ponies' hooves sank deeply into the snow. But on that day, in glorious sunshine, they passed the 82° 21S 'furthest south landmark' of Scott's, Shackleton's and Wilson's 1903 expedition. The huge twin-peaks of Mount Markham, discovered by that party, could be seen in the distance. They could congratulate themselves that in contrast to the fifty-eight days it had taken the three to get there in 1903, the 1911 party reached it in twenty-nine.

In 1908, Shackleton had found a route from the Barrier onto the plateau via the Beardmore Glacier and Scott aimed at this tributary, the Gateway. This path, leading onto the main glacier, avoided the most awful of the pressure ridges that piled up at the glacier/Barrier junction. But as the teams approached the Gateway a gale struck and snow piled in drifts, burying the sledges. The men steered by compass in 'simply horrible conditions'.[28] Bowers mused about Amundsen; if Amundsen had not had any problems, he should have reached the Pole. But Bowers' opinion was that the Norwegian was a sneaking ruffian: 'Old England may be a long way off, but we will do our best for her honour down here at the limit of our globe.'[29]

Any hope of immediate British progress was lost when, on 5 December, the gale developed into a howling, white, thick, blizzard, which raged 'such as one might expect to be driven at us by all the powers of darkness'[30] and which trapped the men at the bottom of the Beardmore for four days. The peculiar feature of this blizzard was that it was warm, making things even more unpleasant. Streams of water ran down the door flap and into the tent. The men lay in sopping sleeping bags. The temperature was 27°F.

> The snow is melting and everything's afloat
> If this goes on much longer we shall have to turn the tent upside
> down and use it as a boat

They could not see as far as the next tent, let alone the nearby mountains. No one understood what it meant: was it exceptional local circumstances? Scott wrote that no foresight could have prepared for this state of affairs.[31] Because of the unanticipated halt, Scott had to break into summit rations, the more generous allowance meant for glacier work: 16oz biscuit (made by Huntley and Palmer), 12oz pemmican, 2oz butter, 0.57oz cocoa, 3oz sugar and 0.86oz tea per day (no oatmeal, which would be too difficult to cook).[32]

The delay was serious. It was to make them late on the glacier, late at the Pole and late in the season on the return journey. This was to expose them on their return from the Pole to the lowest Barrier temperatures recorded for over seventy years.[33]

Those ponies that remained were in a pitiable state; Edgar had to dig Snatcher out of his snowy covering every few hours. But they had to keep the ponies going somehow; they were needed for that last haul onto the glacier as the loads were too heavy for the men to pull. At last the weather improved a little and on 9 December the team started out again. The ponies, stiff from days in the blizzard, floundered on. Sometimes they could only pull for a few yards. Edgar had to flog Snatcher to keep him going. The dogs followed with the remainder of the load. When the ponies had finally got their loads onto the glacier they were shot; in a way it was a relief not to see them suffer any more, but Edgar reluctantly led Snatcher to his execution and the men called the camp, 'Shambles Camp'. By now Amundsen was on the plateau.

The expedition made three depots on the Beardmore Glacier: Lower, Mid and Upper. At the Lower Depot, Meares turned back with his dogs on 11 December. He took letters from all the men; Edgar sent messages to his family.[34] The dogs had performed well but there was no more food for them and Scott, still believing that the glacier would be too tough for them, wanted to preserve them in good condition in case they were needed for a possible attempt the following year. Twelve men were now left to man-haul up the awesome 120 mile, crevasse-ridden glacier as it rose from Barrier level to over 9,000ft. They hauled about 200lbs each. Bowers wrote that 'he had never pulled so hard, or so nearly crushed my inside into my backbone by the everlasting jerking with all my strength on the canvas band round my unfortunate tummy'.[35] Edgar was the same.

He pulled with Scott, Edward Wilson and Titus Oates. It could take them eleven jerks to get the 800lb sledges started and then the men had to strain every muscle and fibre to keep the thing moving onwards and upwards. They had to relay on the soft snow of the lower slopes, taking half the load and then going back for the remainder, so doubling the distance covered. As they pulled their legs were buried up to calf level, the sledges were covered in snow and if a sledge stopped, they had to jerk again on their harnesses (often up to fifteen times) to get it going again. Their breath fogged their goggles and snow blindness caused agonies. They stumbled over and into crevasses; the sledges had to be continually turned over to scrape frozen snow off the runners. The surface changed to shiny blue ice with an irregular surface resembling a series of combs. The men ate the pony meat which they thought was beneficial, but they were in fact already suffering from serious malnutrition. Each day their body fat, essential for insulation against the cold, diminished and they were noticeably thinner. Just as important was the loss of muscle bulk which meant pulling became more exhausting. Although they were taking in about 4,500 calories they needed over 7,000 calories to man-haul up the glacier[36] so they were already in negative balance. In addition, their diet contained no vitamin C and virtually no other vitamins.

On 14 December, Dr Wilson wrote that his team, with Scott, Edgar and Oates, were the strongest pullers, although the weights they were pulling were the same as the other two teams. They experimented by changing sledges; Edgar's team still pulled the best.[37] This must have influenced Scott when he made his final decision on the men to haul to the Pole.

On that day, as the British teams struggled up the glacier, Amundsen and his four companions reached the Pole.

By 17 December the going was better. The British advanced 11 miles, climbing up a series of pressure ridges and tobogganing as fast as possible down the other side. On the 18th they made over 12 miles and on the 19th over 14. They were nearly 6,000ft above the Barrier. They all wore the crampons, and the ski shoes that Edgar had made during the winter which were a great success. Scott was delighted and Edgar very pleased. Scott wrote that the team owed Edgar much.[38]

By 21 December they had found a good place for the Upper Glacier Depot at 85°S, over 6,000ft above the Barrier and close to the steep slope that ascends to the plateau. The march that followed was long and hot, over blue rugged ice with crevasses everywhere. Scott managed to get the party through the crevasses but it took a huge amount of energy to pull the sledges up the steep slopes and to stop them overrunning on downward slopes. But Edgar thought the glaciers and mountains were stupendous. As they pulled, Scott watched the individual performances of the men, and on 21 December, at 85°3', he decided on the Support Party that was to be sent home. This left just eight men to pull two sledges: Scott, Edward Wilson, Edgar and Titus Oates were in one team, 'Birdie' Bowers, Stoker Lashly, PO Crean and Lieutenant Teddy Evans in the other. Scott forced a fast pace, marching for over nine hours, and he wrote of the delightful feeling of security he experienced when they finally reached the summit proper on 23 December. Though the surface was covered with sastrugi, the horizon levelled off in every direction and it was a wonderful feeling to have reached a horizontal surface at last. There was a vast silence around them, only broken by the sounds of the sledges. The teams made three depots on the plateau: Three Degrees, One and a Half Degrees and Last Depot.

But the strain was telling on all the men and must have been particularly bad for Lashly and Lieutenant Evans who, in addition to man-hauling up the Beardmore, had pulled their loaded sledge for 400 miles across almost the whole length of the Barrier. Dehydration was a problem that affected them all. At this altitude (where the oxygen level was lower) to cope with their extreme exertion they had to hyperventilate and needed about 6L of fluid (over 10 pints) each day;[39] they were actually taking 6 pints per day. Even the indomitable Bowers wrote on the 23rd that he was getting exhausted and all his muscles 'have had their turn at being stiffened up'.[40] Christmas Day was made memorable when, perhaps because of their fatigue, Lieutenant Evans' team nearly came to grief. Lashly fell into a deep crevasse and nearly pulled the rest of his crew in with him. Although Scott wrote that even the fall had not disturbed Lashly's equanimity, his (Lashly's) comments were considered afterwards to be unsuitable to record. He was hauled out with difficulty. It was his 44th birthday.

Edgar loved his food, especially a good, hot meal and he appreciated the celebration Christmas food; four courses: pemmican, horse meat flavoured with onion and curry powder and thickened with biscuit, then a sweet arrowroot cocoa and biscuit hoosh, plum pudding, followed by cocoa with raisins. Finally a dessert of caramels and ginger[41] enhanced the general sense of well-being.

The men hoped that the worst was over – it was not.

On the last day of the year Edgar had an accident that did much to imperil the whole expedition. Scott had decided to strip down the 12ft sledges, remove the worn runners, put on fresh 10ft runners and so convert the sledges into lighter ones. Edgar, Crean and Lashly did the work in sub-zero temperatures, a task that took them till 11 p.m. Scott wrote (again) that Edgar was the most valuable asset to the party and that to build a sledge under those conditions was a fact worth special record.[42] But Edgar cut his hand, it was probably not a big cut and he hid the injury. Certainly Lashly does not mention the incident in his diary. Edgar may have thought that the cut was not serious; in any event he wanted desperately to be in the Pole Party. If his *Discovery* explorations had brought him fame, how much more would a 'First to the Pole' achieve? He may well have planned to run a pub in South Wales when he left the navy. It was an occupation he was familiar with. His father-in-law had been the long-established licensee of the Ship Inn in Middleton. His wife had been brought up in the pub and Edgar, with his practical mind, his out-going personality and his new fund of Antarctic stories, would have been a natural as a publican. A first to the Pole would have guarenteed the pub's success.

By 30 December, the expedition finally caught up with the dates in Shackleton's journal. Two important things happened on 31 December: Scott laid the first Polar cache, Three Degree Depot, and he also took the remarkable decision to order the 'other' team, Lieutenants Evans and Bowers, Crean and Lashly, to leave their skis, sticks, ropes and axes at the Depot, possibly to save the 80lbs of weight. This is a decision that has been much criticised, as it was eventually to leave 'Birdie' Bowers to march 300 miles to the Pole and back. But for now the four men plodded through the snow whilst their companions continued with skis and sticks for a further three days until the final decision was made. Up to this point it was assumed that Scott had planned for four men to go to the Pole, and probably for days he had decided in favour of his own team of Wilson, Oates and Edgar. But on 3 January, 170 miles from the Pole, he went to Lieutenant Evans, Lashly, Crean and Bowers' tent and announced that he was sure he could reach the Pole if they would give one man up and make the homeward journey shorthanded. Evans said that 'of course we consented'[43] and 'Birdie' joined Scott's team. In the event the three who returned were to have huge problems; Lieutenant Evans suffered terribly from scurvy and eventually had to be left with Lashly, whilst Crean made an amazingly brave solo journey to get help for his leader.[44] But on that final day of 1911, supplies were redistributed; 'Birdie' transferred his share of the food and, uncomplainingly, trudged to and from the Pole. But it meant that extra time and fuel had to be spent cooking meals for five, a point that Scott had not considered.

On 8 January Scott reiterated his praise of Edgar saying that it was only at that time that he realised how much was due to Edgar, commenting on the indispensable ski shoes and crampons – the product of Edgar's manufacture, design and good workmanship. Edgar was also responsible for every sledge fitting, tent, sleeping bag and harness. Scott said there had not been a single expression of dissatisfaction relating to any of them.[45]

Scott, Bowers, Edgar, Wilson and Oates journeyed on, man-hauling on difficult surfaces with minimum temperatures averaging -23°F. They had a month's supply of food for the five men to get to the Pole and back to the last depot. Scott and Wilson pulled in front, Oates and Edgar behind; Bowers, on foot, was between the four. Although the pulling was fearsome they were buoyed up because they thought they were ahead of the Norwegians; on 9 January 1912 they passed Shackleton's furthest southernmost point and since they assumed that Amundsen would get onto the Plateau via the Beardmore Glacier and they could see no signs of dogs or sledges, they thought that they were in the lead; 'All is new ahead'.[46] But every mile was at a tremendous cost. Scott wrote on 12 January 'With the surface as it is one gets horribly sick of the monotony and can easily imagine oneself getting played out … It is going to be a close thing'.[47] They started to descend to the Pole and made their final depot on 15 January. There was sunshine at last, not a cloud in the sky. 'Only twenty-seven miles from the Pole. We *ought* to do it now.'[48]

But on 16 January 'the worst has happened or nearly the worst'.[49] Bowers' sharp eyes detected what he thought was a cairn.[50] Half an hour later he made out a black speck, which clearly was not snow. As the five marched towards it, the speck became a black flag fluttering in the wind. They had been beaten. Nearby were sledge tracks and ski tracks and many dog prints in the snow, underlining one of the reasons for Amundsen's success. The disappointment was intense and Scott wrote that they had 'many (bitter) thoughts' and 'much discussion'.[51] The prize had been snatched from them, but at least one of the party was glad that they had got there by good British man-haulage.[52] Edgar's thoughts are not recorded. The five thought that they had been beaten by two or three weeks and now they had to face the return home. Scott wondered if they had the strength. Bowers wrote to his mother that they were all fit and well and should, with luck, catch the ship in time for the news. He thought that he could not have better companions and that five was a pleasant little crowd when he was so far from home. To his sister, however, 'Birdie' admitted that they were losing strength and that he felt very weary at the end of a long busy march.[53]

On the 17th, they marched in the coldest conditions that Wilson could ever remember.[54] There was a force five gale and 54° of frost. They had, in fact, endured colder temperatures, but now loss of their body fat cruelly reduced their resistance to cold. They made their own exact British calculation for the Pole (about half a mile from Amundsen's flag)[55] and 'Birdie' wrote to his mother from 'the apex of the earth'.[56] The conditions were so awful that after five hours on the march, Edgar's hands (in spite of double woollen and fur mitts) were so cold that the team stopped and treated themselves to a good 'week-end' lunch with pieces of chocolate. Edgar smoked a cigarette brought by Wilson, a queer taste after weeks without tobacco.

At the point that the British judged to be the Pole, they flew the Queen Mother's (Queen Alexandra) Union Jack and their own flags and took photos. In these images the men are so engulfed by clothes that it is difficult to comment on their appearance, but Edgar's nose looks white, his face sunken. In the afternoon they passed the Norwegian's most southerly camp 'Polheim' and found a small tent with equipment and a letter for Scott to forward to the Norwegian King Haakon. Then they started north. 'Well we have turned our back now on the goal of our ambition with sore feelings and must face our 800 miles of solid dragging – and goodbye to most of our day-dreams!'[57] On the day the British reached the Pole, Amundsen and his companions were only a week away from their quarters in the Bay of Whales having done the journey in ninety-nine days. They had taken fifty-two dogs and killed twenty-four of them in comparison to Scott's lack of dogs on the Plateau.[58]

In the weeks between the Norwegian and British arrival at the Pole the Antarctic winter had begun. The temperature was already dropping below zero. The wind blew from the south, whistling around the tent at night.[59] Their successful return depended both on speed and their ability to pick up their food cairns, and both these were to cause problems. The return was doomed – all five men were to die.

They had to begin by pulling up a rise. The Pole is lower than the highest part of the plateau, which had to be climbed before the descent to the Beardmore Glacier. The return journey began well;[60] wind from the south allowed them to use their floor cloth as a makeshift sail to help with the sledge, but as the wind strengthened, the snow blew in drifts and this made it difficult to pick up the tracks from their outward journey and they sometimes had to unharness and search for the tracks. Poor visibility made picking up the cairns difficult too. Edgar's fingertips were badly blistered and the snow surface became like sand. Sledge hauling was exhausting and appallingly monotonous. On 20 January Oates recorded that one of his toes had turned black.

Edgar was deteriorating too. As well as the problems that beset them all – malnutrition, loss of body fat and muscle (as the heaviest man in the party he was the most affected by the deficiency in calories), dehydration, lack of vitamins, low body temperature and problems with altitude – he suffered from specific problems; his cut hand (the injury on 31 December) and a postulated brain injury that was caused, it is suggested, by relatively minor falls into crevasses.[61]

His hand trauma is well recorded. On 7 January, well before the Pole and seven days after the initial injury, the cut had 'a lot of pus in it'.[62] Scott commented on the same day that the cut was nasty and secondary to sledge making.[63] On 17 January, as the British team searched for their exact South Pole position, Wilson recorded that they stopped and camped for lunch because of Edgar's cold hands (Oates and Bowers, as well as Edgar, had bad frostbite of their noses and cheeks too).[64] On the 23rd Scott wrote that Edgar was far from well; 'There is no doubt that (Edgar) Evans is a good deal run down, his fingers are badly blistered and his nose is rather seriously congested with frequent frostbites. He is very much annoyed with himself which is not a good sign.'[65] On the 25th, Edgar's fingers and nose were in a bad state (and Oates was suffering from a very cold foot). On 28 January, as they pulled north in the biting wind, Wilson commented again on Edgar's badly blistered fingertips.[66] By the end of the month, when they were still 600 miles from base, Edgar's nails were falling off, the fingers were raw and oozing;[67] it was agonising for Edgar to remove his mitts and gloves. Scott wrote that Edgar's hands were really bad and to his (Scott's) surprise, he was showing signs of losing heart.[68] To this, Scott added that he was disappointed in Edgar.

Wilson dressed Edgar's fingers every day with an antiseptic solution, melting snow with a spirit lamp. Although the fingers were still 'quite sweet' (not apparently infected) on 4 February, by the following day they were suppurating and his nose was 'bad and rotten looking'.[69] Wilson wrote that Edgar was feeling the cold a lot and always getting frostbitten. He was visibly thinner.

Edgar's 'head injury' is not recorded as a major event. On 4 February, Wilson wrote that Scott and Edgar had fallen in a crevasse to their waists[70]; Scott wrote that it was the second fall for Edgar.[71]

The return was a race between the season, the conditions, the men's fitness and their food supplies. By 31 January they reached Three Degree depot, the last depot on the plateau, 180 miles from the Pole. They picked up Bowers' skis, a week's food supply and a note from Lieutenant Evans before progressing north, where the Beardmore, with its chaos of crevasses, awaited them. They reached the rim of the plateau on 4 February. Not only did Edgar fall into a glacier that day, but Scott described him as becoming rather dull and incapable.[72] From the rim of the plateau they could see those rocks, which were the upper markers of the Beardmore Glacier. It was a relief to see rocky outcrops after days and days of featureless whiteness. The party's initial progress down the glacier was adequate, but after three days spent threading their way through crevasse fields to finally reach the Upper Glacier Depot, Edgar deteriorated significantly. Daily distances were halved. He was now incapable of helping with the camp work and was holding the party up. His hands were festering, his nose looked awful, he became withdrawn and unlike himself, and was feeling the cold terribly (in spite of the fact that they were now taking extra food, seven days rations in six days).[73] Oates, too, was deteriorating, his toes were black and his nose and cheeks were 'dead yellow'.[74]

In spite of these anxieties Wilson took some time on 7 February to collect rock and fossil specimens. On the 8th, they spent half a day collecting more. Wilson was a passionate investigator. The Polar expedition gave a unique opportunity for study of the Beardmore Glacier and collection from this fascinating area had always been part of the scientific programme. Also Scott may have thought that to give Edgar (and Oates) a rest would be beneficial. In the event, the specimens that were collected were later found to have embedded fern-like fossil leaves and stems of Glosopteris, a plant that flourishes in warm temperate climates. These would give incontestable proof of profound changes in the earth's climate and show that Antarctica had once formed part of a great, warm, southern continent.

On 11 February, in hazy and distorting light, they got lost in a maze of ridges, getting more and more despondent. Food became the dominant anxiety. Could they find the next depot? Breakfast was one biscuit, then they had a single meal left. To their exquisite relief they stumbled on their depot, but, because they were not covering the necessary daily distances to get them safely to the next depot, they had to reduce their rations making three meals of pemmican stretch to four. When they left the mid-glacier depot on 13 February they had only enough food for just over three days. On the 14th, Scott wrote that Edgar showed them a huge blister on his foot; this delayed the march whilst his crampons were adjusted. Scott felt that Edgar was getting worse continually. His slowness added to the overwhelming anxieties about food, now reduced to an evening meal of biscuit with a thin hoosh of pemmican. By 15 February they were approximately 18 miles from the Lower Glacier Depot.

Edgar collapsed on 16 February. He was giddy and could not even walk beside the sledge. The party camped, but by this time they had only enough food for a day, so no further delay could be considered. The 17 February started without a premonition of its eventual tragic outcome, although by now Edgar was a shambling caricature of his former self. His foot worked out of his ski shoe (the shoe that he had manufactured) and he stayed behind to readjust the shoe. The remainder of the party went on, but when they saw he was not coming behind them, they stopped and cooked a meal. When still he did not arrive, they went back to look for him and found he had collapsed again, his clothes were dishevelled and he was crawling over the snow. He talked slowly and said, when asked what had happened, that he did not know, but he thought he must have fainted. When he tried to walk, he collapsed again. Oates stayed with him whilst Wilson, Scott and Bowers went back for the sledge. He lapsed into unconsciousness and died two hours after reaching the tent. His companions made a prayer over his body, covered it and left it to be engulfed by snow. At the time of his death he had been 109 days on a diet low in all vitamins and wholly lacking in vitamin C. He died three weeks before news of Amundsen's victory was blazoned around the world.

His companions obviously went over the events. But this was no time for prolonged reflection; they were in a stark struggle for survival themselves. They decided, however, that he had begun to get weak before the

Pole and that the downward path was caused by his fingers, his falls and his loss of confidence in himself.

They left the foot of the glacier on 19 February. Bowers' diary finished on the 25th, Wilson's, with no warning, on the 27th. At the Southern Barrier depot there was a shortage of oil.[75] In the Middle Barrier depot, oil was short again. On 16 or 17 March (Scott had lost track of dates), Scott said that Oates had announced that he could not continue. He had gangrene (needing treatment by amputation), his leg was unbearably painful, his hands were frostbitten and he could not feed himself. Months before, at Cape Evans, Oates had said that it would be a sick man's duty to eliminate himself. Now he held out until he could see that there was no possibility of surviving, and then he ended his life by crawling out of the tent to die on the snow in the freezing temperatures. Wilson had a supply of opium and morphine and Scott had ordered him to hand these out. Whether Oates could have taken the tablets before crawling out of the tent is debatable, his hands were so bad that Wilson was feeding him. It seems reasonable to surmise, however, that if he had come to his decision earlier, the remaining three might have been able to progress faster.

Scott, Wilson and Bowers made their final camp 11 miles south of One Ton Depot. There they perished slowly. On 18 November 1912, eight months later, a search party found the tent along with their bodies and graphic accounts of their doomed return.

Notes

1 Ed. Jones, M., *Robert Falcon Scott Journals*, Oxford University Press, 2005, p. 287.
2 Ibid., p. 287.
3 Scott, R.F., *Preliminary lecture on Southern Journey*, 1911, SPRI, MS 1453/28: D.
4 Scott, R.F., *Preliminary lecture on Southern Journey*, 1911, SPRI, MS 1453/28: D.
5 *Scott's Last Expedition The Journals*, Carroll and Graff, New York, 1996, p. 196.
6 Riffenburg, B., *Nimrod*, Bloomsbury, London, 2004, p. 120.
7 Fisher, M & J., *Shackleton and the Antarctic*, Houghton Mifflin Company, Boston, 1958, p. 107.
8 Bowers, H., *Journals Relating to the British Antarctic Expedition, 1910–1912* MS 1505/3/5/9; BJ.
9 Ed. Jones, M., *Robert Falcon Scott, Journals*, Oxford University Press, Oxford, p. 302.
10 Wilson, E.A., *Letter to Mr and Mrs Reginald Smith*, SPRI, MS.599/142/9/D.
11 *Evening Post*, Vol. LXXXV, Issue 38, 14/02/1913.

12 *South Wales Daily Post,* 13/02/1913.

13 Soloman, S., *The Coldest March,* Yale University Press, London, 2001, p. 165.

14 Ibid., p. 192.

15 *Scott's Last Expedition The Journals,* Carroll and Graff, New York, 1996, p.323.

16 Cherry-Garrard, A. *Diary,* SPRI, MS 559/4; BJ, 24/10/1911.

17 Ed. King, H.G.R., *Diary of the Terra Nova Expedition to the Antarctic,* Blandford Press, London, 1972, p. 183.

18 Ed. Jones, M., *Robert Falcon Scott Journals.* Oxford University Press, Oxford, 2005, p. 303.

19 Ibid., p. 312.

20 Bowers, H., *Journals relating to the British Antarctic Expedition 1910–1912,* SPRI, MS 1505/3/5/9; BJ.

21 A transparent protective layer under the eyelid that can cover the eye surface, protecting and moistening it.

22 Although both dogs and ponies have nictitating membranes the exposed corneal surface is much bigger in the pony than the dog. The membrane has no blood supply and the cold sustained for long periods of movement may have resulted in corneal damage more easily in the ponies. Personal communication, Professor Peter Bedford, 2011.

23 Ed. Jones, M., *Robert Falcon Scott Journals,* Oxford University Press, 2005, p. 334.

24 Cherry-Garrard, A., *Diary 03/11/1911–28/01/1912.* SPRI, MS 559/5: BJ.

25 Priestley, R., Lecture, *The Psychology of Exploration,* SPRI, MS 1097/16/1; D.

26 Ed. King, H.G.R., *Diary of the Terra Nova Expedition to the Antarctic,* Blandford Press, London, 1972, p. 206.

27 Ellis, A.R., *Under Scott's Command Lashly's Antarctic Diaries,* Victor Gollancz, London, 1969, p. 126.

28 Bowers, H., *Journals relating to the British Antarctic Expedition 1910–1912,* SPRI, MS 1505/3/5/9; BJ.

29 Ibid.

30 Seaver, G., *'Birdie' Bowers of the Antarctic,* John Murray, London, 1947, p. 239.

31 Ed. Jones, M. *Scott's Last Expedition The Journals,* Carroll and Graff, New York, 1996, p. 339.

32 Bowers, H., *Journals relating to the British Antarctic expedition, 1910–1912,* SPRI, MS 1505/3/5/9; BJ.

33 Soloman, S., *The Coldest March,* Yale University Press, London, 2001, p. 293.

34 The letters were not preserved.

35 Bowers, H., *Journals relating to the British Antarctic Expedition, 1911,* SPRI MS 1505/3/5/9; BJ.

36 Fiennes, R., *Captain Scott,* Hodder and Stoughton, London, 2003, p. 285.

37 Ed. King, H.G.R., *Diary of the Terra Nova Expedition to the Antarctic,* Blandford Press, London, 1972, p. 217.

38 Soloman, S., *The Coldest March,* Yale University Press, New Haven and London, 2001, p. 190.

39 Personal communication, Dr Edward Coats, 2010. (From the Omega Challenge Race to the pole 2009.)

40 Seaver, G., *'Birdie' Bowers of the Antarctic*, John Murray, London, 1947, p. 245.

41 Ellis, A.R., *Under Scott's Command: Lashly's Antarctic Diaries*, Victor Gollancz, London, 1969, p. 132.

42 Ed. Jones, M. *Scott's Last Expedition: The Journals*, Carroll and Graff, New York, 1996, p. 363.

43 *Daily Mirror*, 22/05/1913.

44 Lieutenant Evans returned to England with the relief ship.

45 Ed. Jones, M. *Scott's Last Expedition: The Journals*, Carroll and Graff, New York, 1996, p. 369.

46 Ibid., p. 370.

47 Ibid., p. 373.

48 Ibid., p. 374.

49 Ibid., p. 375.

50 Ibid., p. 376.

51 Ibid., *Appendix 111, 'Significant changes to Scott's original Base and Sledging Journals'*, p. 470.

52 Bowers, H., *Journals relating to the British Antarctic Expedition, 1910–12*, SPRI MS 1505/3/5/9: BJ.

53 Ibid.

54 Ed. King, H.G.R., *Diary of the Terra Nova Expedition to the Antarctic*, Blandford Press, London, 1972, p. 232.

55 *Daily Mirror*, 23/05/1913, (Commander Evans' Lecture in the Albert Hall).

56 Bowers, H., *Journals relating to the British Antarctic Expedition, 1911*, SPRI MS 1505/3/5/9.

57 Ibid., p. 378.

58 At Cape Evans, some skeletons of Scott's dogs remain with collars and chains still attached.

59 Bowers, H., *Journals relating to the British Antarctic Expedition, 1911*, SPRI MS 1505/3/5/9.

60 Evening Post, Vol. XXXV Issue 38 14/02/1913.

61 Ed. Jones, M., *Scott's Last Expedition: The Journals*, Carroll and Graff, New York, 1996, p. 397.

62 Ed. King, H.G.R., *Diary of the Terra Nova Expedition to the Antarctic*, Blandford Press, London, 1972, p. 230.

63 Ed. Jones, M., *Scott's Last Expedition: The Journals*, Carroll and Graff, New York, 1996, p. 368.

64 Ibid., p. 376.

65 Ibid., p. 383.

66 Ed. King, H.G.R., *Diary of the Terra Nova Expedition to the Antarctic*, Blandford Press, London, 1972, p. 238.

67 Ibid., p. 289.

68 Ed. Jones, M., *Scott's Last Expedition The Journals*, Carroll and Graff, New York, 1996, p. 387.

69 Ed. King, H.G.R., *Diary of the Terra Nova Expedition to the Antarctic*, Blandford Press, London, 1972, p. 240.

70 Ibid, p. 239.

71 Ed. Jones, M., *Scott's Last Expedition : The Journals*, Carroll and Graff, New York, 1996, p. 389.

72 Ibid., p. 390.

73 Ed. King, H.G.R., *Diary of the Terra Nova Expedition to the Antarctic*, Blandford Press, London, 1972, p. 239.

74 Ibid., p. 240.

75 The paraffin had leaked out because of inadequate seals on the tins that had allowed evaporation.

15

The Aftermath

The news was cabled to Britain on 11 February 1913 and the reality of the disaster flew immediately around the world. Amongst the many letters and messages that had been found in the tent was Scott's 'Message to the Public', which (though this may not have been Scott's intention) forcibly focussed attention on Edgar's deterioration as a most significant contribution to the failure and death of the whole party. Over the next months in some quarters, Edgar was to be stigmatised as being the primary cause of the tragedy, not only being the first to die, but also as the only member of the party who was not of officer status.

Scott wrote that 'the advance party would have returned to the glacier in fine form and with a surplus of food, but for the astonishing failure of the man whom we had least expected to fail. Edgar Evans was thought the strongest man of the party'.[1] After this Edgar became labelled as the 'Strong Man', with the implication that physical strength was his only asset, an implication often made by those with no knowledge of his contributions to Scott's expeditions. When the official report was telegraphed to London, two paragraphs from Scott's sledging journals were quoted in full; one relating to Edgar's death, the other, Scott's account of Titus Oates' death. The contrast in the modes of death, the self-sacrificing Captain and the Petty Officer (who held them up before he finally died a natural death), was gripping.

Some of the early reports that made him the scapegoat were refuted; the early rumour that the fate of the Southern Party was sealed when Edgar's four companions had to drag him hundreds of miles on a sledge was denied,[2] and Lieutenant Teddy Evans stated that reports that Edgar had gone mad were cruel, scandalous and without foundation.[3] However, his four companions, notably Oates, who also seriously slowed the party's progress, were hailed as heroes.

Three days after the official report, one and a half million children in elementary schools throughout the country gathered to hear 'The Immortal Story of Captain Scott's Expedition'. The 'Message' and Scott's account of Oates' death were quoted in full.[4] The scene was set. Many Edwardians saw a tenuous relationship between physical strength, mental capacity and social status,[5] and there are photographs and descriptions of Edgar as the 'strong man' which emphasised how mere strength did not necessarily imply a good character. Self-control and self-discipline were viewed as the epitome of masculinity, particularly for the middle or upper classes. It was the core of the heroic character and Edgar appeared to have lost control of his rational thought. He definitely did not represent the heroic ideal. *The Times Weekly Edition* quoted a report from Christchurch, New Zealand, that said 'It would seem from what escaped some of the survivors that (Edgar) Evans lost his reason for the time, being under the great stress of fatigue and privation and was incapable of obeying orders, or assisting his hard pushed companions in the weary work of pulling the sledge. Indeed it became necessary in the end to lay him on it.'[6] Edgar, the 'strong man', failed first and contributed significantly to the fate of his companions. Throughout February 1913, newspapers projected the view that Edgar had had serious psychological problems.

Remarkably, none of the articles suggests a physical cause for Edgar's deterioration. Class and education were promoted as the important issues. Edgar's demise was hastened by his relative lack of education. He was not a gentleman and, therefore, apparently less able to withstand the strain of the return. The *Daily Express*' front-page article on 12 February 1913 quoted an 'eminent mental specialist' who stated that it was the uneducated man who would feel 'the mental strain and the dreary monotonous life amid eternal snows' more acutely than the educated man.

The specialist wrote that:

> … experiments have proved that the brain is only kept active and healthy by the stimulus it is constantly receiving from the senses. The limitless white of the still snows would provide little stimulus for the eye to transmit. The deadly silence would deprive the ear of work. The monotony of the food would prevent the brain receiving the stimulus of a new taste. To an educated man this strain would be bad enough but he would be able to stimulate his brain with his store of learning … The absence of such a stimulus in an uneducated man such as presumably Seaman Evans would have been, might have been succeeded by a kind of self-mesmerism followed by mania and the delusion that he was being kept from food and home, both close at hand.[7]

In short, Edgar's education had not given him the psychological reserve to cope with the conditions, though it seems implausible nowadays that a knowledge of Virgil was considered helpful to a man battling against Antarctica's furies. Edgar's behaviour was contrasted unfavourably with the heroism of Oates and his comrades Scott, Wilson and Lieutenant Bowers.

Historian Professor Max Jones states that the extent of the criticism should not be exaggerated and that most commentators did not single out Edgar particularly as the cause of the disaster.[8] This may be so, but the effect of the articles that were published must have been devastating to his wife, children and relatives in South Wales who were faced with the intimation, made by clever, educated men, that Edgar a seaman, had not only caused the death of the man he sincerely admired, but other important members of the 'gentleman class'. His oldest child, Norman, would have had taunts at school; his father had let the side down. The family's hero had been demoted to anti-hero status.

His children must have been devastated when they saw the Player's cigarette card series. Player's produced small coloured cards to go in their cigarette packets, a collection avidly collected by children. In the series on Polar exploration the first four are: Captain Scott, Commander Evans, Captain Oates and Dr Wilson. Number six is Lieutenant Bowers, but number five – 'Taking Sea Temperatures' – was presumably the proposed illustration of Edgar, deliberately omitted. Other cards in this British series include a sledge party crossing a crevasse, sledge flags, Adélie penguins, the victorious Amundsen and his compatriot, Oscar Wisting, at the South Pole. Edgar's omission is marked and extraordinary.

Like English Gentlemen: To Peter Scott from the Author of Where's Master? (by J.E. Hodder-Williams) was a children's book published in 1913. One can only hope that neither Edgar's children nor their friends read it: 'There were four men with the hero at the South Pole and their names are worth remembering, One was Petty Officer Edgar Evans, a great big brawny seaman who had been with him for many years.'[9] The book recounts how they reached the Pole and started their return, 'but Evans, the man of mighty muscles, seemed to have lost his strength. He was always a little behind the others, found it harder than they to pull himself out of the snow drifts ... He stopped dead "I'm done", said he[10] ... But they were English gentlemen these four, the hero and Dr Wilson and Captain Oates and Lieutenant Bowers and so, such a thing as leaving Evans behind never came into their heads.'[11] The diatribe continues: 'they counted the cost. They were willing to pay the price. Even if the price was to be their own lives ... they were English gentlemen'.[12] In contrast to Edgar, when Oates failed, his whole thought was for his comrades to save themselves. He knew, when the time came, 'how English Gentlemen die'.[13]

H.D. Rawnsley wrote a Sonnet Sequence dedicated to the Antarctic Heroes. The Seventh Sonnet, dedicated to Edgar, contains the lines:

Ah, well for him he died, nor ever knew
How his o'er wearied stumbling forward drew
Death's snare about his friends to hold them fast[14]

The insidious damage was done. The feeling that Edgar had somehow failed because of his class persisted for years. The scientist and explorer Brian Roberts[15] wrote in the 1930s: 'Science is no inspiration to those who have only done manual labour ... This was surely the explanation of Seaman Evans' unaccountable breakdown when Scott's party realised they were not first at the Pole. The others knew that the true value of their journey had not been lost but to him it must have seemed that all their effort had been in vain.'[16]

It took years for Edgar to regain his rightful status as one of the Antarctic heroes. Gary Gregor, the librarian at Swansea Museum, wrote the first biography of his life as late as 1995.

Notes

1 Arranged Huxley, L., *Scott's Last Expedition Vol. 1*, Smith Elder, London, 1913, p. 605.
2 Pictures Past, The National Library of New Zealand, Evening Post, Vol. LXXXV, Issue 40, 17/02/1913, p. 7.
3 *Daily Mail*, 15/02/1913.
4 Ed. Cubitt, G.; Warren, A., *The King Upon His Knees* (Chap. 6 by Jones, M.) Manchester University Press, 200, p. 110.
5 Jones, M., *The Last Great Quest*, Oxford University Press, Oxford, 2003, p. 111.
6 *Times Weekly Edition*, 21/02/1913.
7 *Daily Express* 12/02/1913, No. 4009.
8 Jones, M., *The Last Great Quest*, Oxford University Press, Oxford, 2003, p. 112.
9 Hodder-Williams, J.E., *Like English Gentlemen To Peter Scott*, Hodder and Stoughton, London, [1913], p. 31.
10 Ibid., p. 37.
11 Ibid., p 41.
12 Ibid., p. 43
13 Ibid., p 48.
14 Rawnsley, H.D., *To the Heroes of the Antarctic, A Sonnet Sequence* British Review April 1913 80–84.
15 Brian Birley Roberts 1912–1978. Member of British Graham Land Expedition 1934–37. Researched into cold climate clothing. Involved in drafting Antarctic Treaty of 1959.
16 Brian Roberts, Personal Journals 1934–37 Vol. 1 British Graham Land Expedition Vol. 1 01/12/1934–09/12/1935, p. 168.

Why Did Edgar Die First?

Amundsen wrote later that the main reason for the final tragedy was that the British had endured the terrific strain of man-hauling, whereas the Norwegians 'had dogs all the way to the Pole and all the way back to our base'.[1] He said he never pulled anything at all.[2] He was probably right in his conclusion insofar that if Scott had actually managed to get dogs on the plateau and kept them healthy, the dogs would have been able to pull the enfeebled travellers across the plateau and down to the Barrier, saving the explorers precious calories and time by allowing the injured to ride on the sledges. Certainly by the time the explorers died their bodies had been ravaged by a multiplicity of problems that were interdependent in contributing to their deaths. Conditions such as vitamin deficiency, malnutrition, dehydration and hypothermia all combined inextricably to accelerate the downward spiral, and Edgar, the heaviest man in the party, suffered the most. In addition, he and Captain Oates stand out with specific problems. Oates had an old war wound and gangrene. Edgar suffered from a cut hand that festered and needed constant attention; he had a fall that could have caused an intracerebral bleed and, as the only non-officer, he could have suffered from a feeling of cultural isolation.

Malnutrition plagued the whole party; they were unaware of this but records of dreams of delicacies that vanished, food-shops that were shut and obsessive ruminations about food are commonplace. Edgar and his companions had been man-hauling since early December 1911. The summit rations of approximately 4,571 kcal per man per day had been started in those bleak days at the base of the Beardmore Glacier. These rations consisted of 1,054 kcal of protein, 1,953 kcal of fat and 1,564 kcal of carbohydrate.[3] Amundsen's assault team's calorie intake was similar, but the two expeditions had totally different calorific demands. The British were man-hauling whilst the Norwegians travelled on sledges pulled by the dogs, or on skis without loads. Recent studies have shown that Scott's men would have used over 7,000 calories per day for the exhausting occupation of man-hauling.[4] So although the diet contained the correct percentage of carbohydrate according to modern information,[5] the total intake was too low. Taken from 7 December 1911, until Edgar died on 17 February 1912 (seventy-two days), each member of the team had built up a staggering calorie shortfall of approximately 175,000 calories. To fully comprehend what this deficit means, an average man eats 2,500 calories a day when performing his daily activities, so it is easy to see how this astounding calorie deficit, approximately equal to a single man's intake for seventy days in normal life, would have affected the explorers.

When Sir Ranulph Fiennes and Dr Mike Stroud man-hauled across the Antarctic for sixty-eight days (fewer days than Edgar), they each lost 44lbs in weight.[6] But, in addition, Edgar was the biggest man of the party. An individual's food requirements depends on his weight as well as his physical activity and Edgar's resting and hauling metabolic rate would have been higher than his companions; he would have needed a greater calorie intake to support his size. His rate of weight loss must have been considerably faster than his companions, and Scott wrote, 'we are pretty thin, especially Evans (he meant Edgar), but none of us are feeling worked out'.[7] As Edgar lost weight he lost his insulating body fat.[8] He would have lost muscle also,[9] and this would have made man-hauling increasingly challenging. Cherry-Garrard wrote that Edgar must have had 'a most terrible time'. He went on, 'I think it is clear from the diaries that he had suffered very greatly without complaint. At home he would have been nursed in bed; here he must march'.[10]

Intertwined with malnutrition is hypothermia. This is defined as a core body temperature of below 35°C or 95°F. The men were often pulling into the wind and sometimes into snow – a dangerous combination. The cold and his sweat reduced the insulation properties of Edgar's clothes to practically nothing.[11] His temperature dropped, he shuddered in the wind and the only time he would have been reasonably comfortable was when he was actually pulling the sledge.[12] The cold struck as soon as he stopped. Shivering and shuddering increases heat production,[13] but as the concomitant disadvantage of increasing calorie requirements and the deadly combination of malnutrition, exhaustion, insufficient insulation and insufficient fluids decreased his ability to maintain body heat. Dr Wilson wrote that Edgar was 'feeling the cold a lot always getting frost bitten'.[14] He had always had this tendency. It has been shown that a previous cold injury is a significant risk factor for frostbite,[15] and this was the case with Edgar. As his body temperature fell he would fumble with accustomed tasks, he may have become forgetful[16] and he may have felt sick. As his struggle continued he was increasingly at risk of irregular heart rhythms.[17]

On the high elevation of the Antarctic Plateau, there is a lower atmospheric pressure than at sea level. This means there is less oxygen to breathe as the air is 'thinner'. To maintain a sufficient level of oxygen in the blood, the explorers had to breathe rapidly. Each breath contains water vapour, as can be seen even at land level, when breath exhaled on cold dry days 'steams', and these droplets, which freeze instantly, are sometimes called 'the shower of life'. The explorers had to overbreathe constantly and, as a result, lost significant water vapour. The fluid lost in their breathing contributed to their dehydration.

In addition to the sweat and water vapour lost when they were man hauling, the problems continued when they got into their sleeping bags. When Edgar toggled down to rest in his bag, he knew he had no hope of an undisturbed sleep until the moisture from his breath and the perspiration from his clothes (which added to the icy layer already coating up the inside of the bag to a degree that it took over half an hour to wriggle into), warmed to something approaching body temperature.[18] Until then the men shivered (and probably cursed) until something approaching comfort overtook them.

On 17 December Scott wrote that the team got thirsty and chipped up ice on the march as well as drinking 'a great deal' of water at the halts.[19] In fact 'they were always thirsty'.[20] In 1911, the importance of keeping well hydrated was not understood and the men drank about 6 pints (3,400ml) of fluid each day[21] (mugs of tea at breakfast, lunch and dinner, plus fluid in the pemmican). This is completely inadequate. It is now known that enough fluid should be taken to keep the urine fairly dilute (i.e. a pale colour) and flowing freely. When, in 2009, the British team man-hauled across the Plateau to the Pole in the Omega 3 race (at about the same time of year as Scott, though ninety-seven years later), they covered more ground on a daily basis but drank between 6–8L, per day, virtually double Scott's intake. They drank 4–5L when they were pulling and the remainder in the tent. On this intake their urine was darker when they drank 6L, pale when they drank 8.[22] In Antarctica the atmosphere is dry and sweat evaporates quickly from the skin, and in 1911 the men may not have actually realised that they were sweating, though they would probably have had headaches and felt short-tempered. Edgar may have been conscious of his heart racing. But even if the team had been aware of the need for the increased fluid intake, this would have been difficult to manage logistically. Enough fuel to heat ice or snow was a cause for concern on the return from the Pole when the fuel (paraffin) was found to have evaporated from the tins,[23] and dehydration was to be a crucial factor in their fate.

Of the general problems endured by all the party altitude sickness is an unlikely cause of Edgar's death. He had been on the Plateau for weeks and had acclimatised to the altitude during his exhausting climb up the Beardmore Glacier. Although people are sent back to sea level from the Plateau every year,[24] the problem most frequently arises in those who have not had the time to acclimatise and nowadays the majority who work in the Antarctic have arrived by plane. Edgar and the remainder of the team had had time to acclimatise.

Vitamin deficiency unites the party's general problems with a specific problem in Edgar's case. Vitamin C deficiency has been suggested as the primary cause of Edgar's death on 17 February.[25] This is unlikely, although the explorers had been on a diet deficient in vitamin C (on the Barrier, the Beardmore Glacier and the Plateau) for more than fifteen weeks. Summit rations also contained less of the other vitamins than the Barrier rations[26] and had insufficient folic acid and vitamin B12. But clearly Edgar did not have overt scurvy; Dr Wilson, a careful reporter and not afraid to chart the men's medical problems, makes no mention of scurvy, a condition he was all too familiar with. However, Edgar must have had sub-clinical vitamin C deficiency, a condition that can exist without any clinical signs of scurvy whatsoever. We now know a good deal about scurvy, its causation and its signs. It is known that when a person previously saturated with vitamin C goes on a diet without fruit or vegetables, signs of scurvy do not appear for about sixteen weeks, after which time skin dryness and thickening occurs, followed by small petichiae – small purplish skin spots due to the release of a tiny amount of blood from very small blood vessels, the capillaries. Problems with the healing of cuts come later. However, blood levels of vitamin C reach low levels well before clinical signs develop.[27]

Edgar always hated eating seal meat and its offal (which contains the vitamin), so his blood levels are very likely to have been low. But since he had no clinical signs of early scurvy, it is less likely that the fall into a crevasse up to his waist on 4 February would have caused a significant intracerebral bleed secondary to vitamin C deficiency. Scott would have been most unlikely to have allowed time to be spent looking for specimens on 8 February, however important this was for their scientific programme, if he had thought that Edgar was on an irreversible downward course. On 13 February, Edgar was able to cooperate in looking for a depot and raised hopes with the shout of 'depot ahead', (although his 'depot' was, in fact, just a shadow).[28] He had no obvious localised weakness on one side of the body (which commonly happens in an intracerebral bleed) and there is no record of headaches. He was able to get into his skis and start in the traces on the day that he died, no doubt attempting to keep up till the end. The problems that were reported: 'no power to assist with camping work'[29] and 'giving us serious anxiety'[30] can equally well be ascribed to a number of conditions. His difficulty with his boots was caused, not by paralysis, but because of frostbitten hands. Scott's comment that Edgar was 'becoming rather dull and incapable'[31] were made on the very day that Edgar had his fall, suggesting (as Scott had written previously), a problem that had been going on for far longer than a few hours.

Other factors that could have contributed to Edgar's deterioration are: psychological problems and infection. Could the whole deterioration be secondary to psychological troubles? Dr Wilson recorded in his diary that he wrote for his family that Edgar's collapse was 'much to do with the fact that he had never been sick in his life and is now helpless with his hands frost-bitten'.[32] But psychological problems are an unlikely suggestion. Edgar was an intelligent extrovert. He had good social skills and could talk equally well to officers and non-officers.[33][34] Although the concept of 'depression' did not exist in 1910, there are no positive clues to suggest this diagnosis, which is characteristically a recurrent condition.

Edgar's behaviour before and between expeditions carries absolutely no hint of a 'personality wobble'. He had good family links and bonds to sustain him. He wanted to return to Antarctica and volunteered to do so. He contributed well until the final few weeks and on the day he died he was alert enough to ask for some string to tie up his boots. He may have been low, but his symptoms do not suggest serious, incapacitating depression. Debenham interpreted Edgar's low mood as being due to the fact that he (Edgar) thought that he had let Scott down, firstly by cutting his hand and then by delaying the party, i.e. that his psyche was responding to external factors, rather than being the primary cause of his problems. This was a comment supported by Scott's writing on 30 January, that Edgar had not been cheerful since the accident. If Edgar's plans for opening a pub in South Wales[35] were dashed by him not getting to the South Pole first (and there is no obvious reason why they should have been; his friend PO Tom Crean ran a successful public house in Ireland until his death in 1938),[36] Edgar's resilient, steely, gregarious mind would have readily turned to other enterprises. He was not a man to suffer from cultural isolation. He was too confident of himself.

Infection may well have contributed to Edgar's death. Bacteria can exist in Antarctica's sub-zero temperatures.[37] One such bacterium is Staphylococcus aureus, a bacterium commonly carried in the nose[38] and sleeping bags,[39] and the likely cause of Edgar's hand infection. Abscess formation typically occurs seven days after a wound becoming infected, as happened to Edgar. By February, his frostbitten fingers were suppurating and his nose was very bad (almost as bad as his fingers) and rotten looking. Infection would have increased his resting metabolic rate, so exacerbating his calorie requirements and further increasing his weight loss. A possible scenario is nasal carriage of staphylococci resulting in a wound infection in his hand and, following this, invasion of the blood stream, probably repeated.[40] There need not have been any signs in the arm – the bacterium could have silently gained ascendancy and the final picture can be interpreted as low blood pressure and collapse related to infection.

Another infection that had been put forward as the cause of Edgar's death is anthrax: a bacterial infection particularly found in animals (in this case the ponies), that can be transmitted to humans.[41] Typically, when anthrax affects the skin, an ulcer develops surrounded by fluid-filled blisters. It seems a less likely diagnosis here. It was Edgar's fingers and nails that persistently gave the greatest trouble. Anthrax was a condition that

Dr Wilson would certainly have been familiar with from his training in St George's Hospital and he would have recorded his findings, particularly the characteristic black, necrotic (dead) tissue at the point where infection had started. Furthermore, pus is not a feature of anthrax and pus was a marked feature in Edgar's case. Also, no other members of the expedition, who had also been in close contact with the animals, showed evidence of the disease. Interestingly when floors in the Base were renovated recently and examined for anthrax, none was identified.[42]

Roland Huntford writes that Edgar had been 'exposed to the risk of venereal disease',[43] despite providing no supporting evidence. Whatever disease is implied by this statement, it would not have contributed to Edgar's death. The legal definition of venereal disease includes syphilis, gonorrhoea and chancroid (which can be ignored in this account).[44] The genital ulcers of primary syphilis would have been noted on Edgar's medical examination, as would a rash related to secondary syphilis. In addition, none of the symptoms described in Edgar's case suggest the long-term complications of syphilis as a contributing factor to his death. However, it is impossible to disprove (or prove) whether Edgar had the post-acute phase of gonorrhoea. This could have caused discomfort in passing urine but would not interfere with his ability to man-haul and would have had no effect on his final days.

An intriguing suggestion was made by a Welsh television company that Scott, pushed beyond his limits by Edgar's incapacities and convinced that the team would do better without him, shot Edgar as he lay confused and helpless on the snow.[45] This can be dismissed. Guns were not taken onto the plateau (every consideration was given to weight). When his companions found Edgar crawling around on the snow, Scott went back with Wilson and Bowers to get the sledge, leaving Oates with Edgar. Wilson, deeply religious and conscious of the sanctity of life, could never have written his untroubled farewell letters to his wife, family and friends, if there had been any suggestion of murder.

An interesting condition called paradoxical undressing could have affected Edgar in his last few hours. This forms a part of many hypothermic deaths. The term 'paradoxical' is used because the victim's temperature is already too low to sustain life, but as hypothermia tightens its insidious grip, the victim begins taking off his clothes. Scott wrote that Edgar's clothes were disarranged, his hands uncovered and frostbitten.[46] The cause of paradoxical undressing, which even today causes police to assume some victims of hypothermia have been assaulted, is not clear. A possible explanation is that the hypothalamus, that part of the brain that regulates body temperature, finally fails and releases its control of the small blood vessels in the skin, allowing them to dilate so that the victim suddenly feels hot and throws his clothes off. This condition clearly was not the cause of Edgar's downward spiral, but may have contributed to his demise.

When all these diverse medical conditions have been considered, it has to be asked if Edgar should have included in the Pole Party in the first place. The answer must be that he was a natural choice. Scott considered that he was strong, fit, a good companion and a representative of the lower deck. Of the other two lower deck representatives Lashly and Crean, Chief Stoker Lashly had already man-hauled the 400 miles from Corner Camp and was in no fit state for a gruelling further advance, so the choice was between Edgar and Crean. The choice in favour of Edgar was probably because Edgar was already a member of Scott's sledge team, a team that had proved how well it could pull. Scott had no reason to doubt Edgar's fitness so there was no reason to change the team's membership.[47] Debenham wrote later supporting the choice of Edgar and saying that he 'did not think for a minute that "Taff" was chosen as the last of the five men'. Debenham thought that Scott had intended to take Edgar from the first, as the 'most skilful sledge master and rigger, the strongest man and unendingly cheerful'. Debenham understood the significance of Edgar's cut hand mentioned in Scott's diary and he (Debenham) wrote that after Edgar had cut his hand he was no longer cheerful, but he interpreted Edgar's slowing down as being firstly, 'because he thought he had let his Captain down by having the accident and secondly, later, because he knew he was delaying the party'.[48] Debenham added that he 'thought that Scott added Oates as the last of the five as a reward for his management of the ponies and because he wanted the Army to be represented'.[49] He wrote that if one could talk of an 'odd man out', it would be Oates; he was not an accomplished sledger and he had a leg wound from the Boer War. This was a comment supported by a note in Cherry-Garrard's journals in which he writes that Drs Atkinson and Wilson had discussed the final choice and agreed that Oates was very 'done up'. Dr Atkinson had said that he did not think that Oates wanted to go.[50] Debenham reiterated that Edgar always got on well with officers (with the exception of Lieutenant Evans), and that he personally thought that his subsequent death was related to the cut hand.[51] In Edgar, Scott chose a tried and true companion, an experienced and intelligent sledger, a cheerful, good-natured man. When it came to the return, any other man would have suffered comparably. Edgar's unique problems, his larger size and his hand infection, could not have been anticipated.

When Edgar was clearly failing should his companions have given him the morphine tablets that Dr Wilson carried and allowed him to die painlessly before abandoning him to the snowy wastes? Although his death released them from this appalling ethical dilemma, two of those companions, at least, would not have left him if he had become incapable. The moral issue of what to do if one of them failed had obviously been discussed: Dr Wilson would never abandon a comrade. His whole life had been governed by a love of God and a desire to serve others. He had no fear of death. He would have stayed with Edgar; his creed, the essential condition that bound all dangerous enterprises, was that men must stand by each other in distress, even beyond the bounds of reason. Bowers, too, was deeply religious; to abandon Edgar would have been unthinkable. Furthermore, although Edgar was slowing their progress hugely, they did not consider that he was actually dying.

In relation to the remainder of the doomed party, after Edgar's death Scott said that the delays the party had suffered on the return had greatly weakened them by firstly making inroads into their surplus provisions and, secondarily, by making them later in the season than had been planned. This delay meant that the snow surface resembled sand – impossible to pull over. This well-known phenomenon is due to the fact that when the temperature falls to 30° below zero, sledges cease to glide. The low temperature of between -30 and -40° does much to explain the slowness of the British party on the Barrier. With a distance between depots of 70 miles and only enough food and fuel in each depot to cover that distance, the party had to average over 9 miles per day. For a week, however, the best march on the Barrier approximated 9 miles and, in the later stages, progress deteriorated to as low as 3. Their failure to maintain the required speed was undoubtedly due to Oates' breakdown, which became a tax on the party's energies. When they met persistent winds and frequent blizzards, they must have known that the outlook was hopeless. The *Times Weekly Edition* wrote, however, that they 'never relinquished their gallant struggle and fought on to the bitter end'.[52]

Edgar did not fail because he had not got to the Pole first. No one, neither his companions on that fateful journey nor the newspaper articles afterwards, seem to have grasped the basic fact that he was ill. The effects of the insufficient calories affected Edgar greatly as the largest and strongest of the party and his extra needs were exacerbated by his hand infection. These problems accelerated on the return journey, causing weakness and a greater susceptibility to the cold. The deterioration was so gradual that it was not understood by his companions, but in the light of modern understanding of body physiology it is possible to say that the collapse was due to a failure of the survival measures to maintain core body temperature and that his acquired infection is likely to be a pivotal cause of his premature demise. He probably had no idea what was happening in the toxic, confused state of his last few hours as he played out a twentieth-century Greek tragedy in which nature and malevolent fate combined to defeat him. But, to the last, he tried to obey and support Scott.

Notes

1 *The Cambrian*, 01/02/1913.
2 Pound, R., *Evans of the Broke*, Oxford University Press, Oxford, 1963, p. 119.
3 Rogers, A.F., *The Death of Chief Petty Officer Evans*, The Practitioner, Vol. 212, 1974, p. 576. Butter in the diet gave over half the vitamin A and Carotene requirements for work at 4,500 kcal per day, plus a little vitamin D. Milk powder in the biscuits provided insufficient quantities of thiamine, nicotinic acid, riboflavin, folic acid and vitamin B complex. There was no vitamin C.
4 Fiennes, R., *Captain Scott*, Hodder and Stoughton, London, 2003, p. 283.
5 Stroud, M., *Nutrition Across Antarctica*, BNF Nutrition Bulletin, 19, 1994, p. 150.
6 Fiennes, R., *Captain Scott*, Hodder and Stoughton, London, 2003, p. 285.
7 Scott, R.F., *Scott's Last Expedition vol 1*, Murray, London, 1935, p. 434.
8 Ward, M.P.; Milledge, J.S.; West, J.B., *High Altitude Medicine and Physiology*, Arnold, London, 2000, p. 171.
9 Ibid., p. 168.
10 Cherry-Garrard, A., *The Worst Journey in the World*, Picador, London, 1994, p. 544.
11 Ward, M.P., Milledge, J.S. West, J.B. *High Altitude Medicine and Physiology*, Arnold, London, 2000, p. 296.
12 Priestley, R.E., *The Psychology of Polar Exploration*, SPRI, MS 1097/16/1; D.
13 Ward, M.P.; Milledge, J.S.; West, J.B., *High Altitude Medicine and Physiology*, Arnold, London, 2000, p. 296.
14 Ed. King, H.G.R., *Edward Wilson, Diary of the Terra Nova Expedition to the Antarctic*, Blandford Press, London, 1972, p. 240.
15 Cattermole, T.J., *The epidemiology of cold injury in Antarctica*, Aviation & Space Environmental Medicine, 1999, Alexandria, Virginia, USA. p. 135–140.

16 Ward, M.P.; Milledge, J.S. ; West, J.B., *High Altitude Medicine and Physiology*, Arnold, London, 2000, p. 297.

17 Ibid., p. 298.

18 Priestley, R.E., *The Psychology of Polar Exploration*, MS 1097/16/1; D.

19 Scott, R.F., *Scott's Last Expedition vol 1*, Murray, London, 1935, p. 396.

20 Ibid., p. 397.

21 Bowers, H., Miscellaneous stores list (compiled with Robert Falcon Scott British Antarctic Expedition 1910–1913), SPRI, MS 1453/30; D.

22 Personal communication, Dr Edward Coats, member of the British team, 2010.

23 This evaporation was due to insufficient seals on the tins.

24 Fiennes, R., *Captain Scott*, Hodder and Stoughton, London, 2003, p. 322.

25 Rogers, A.F. *The Death of Chief Petty Officer Evans* The Practitioner Vol. 212, 1974, p. 580.

26 Ibid., p. 576. The rations contained little Thiamine, Riboflavine, Pyridoxine.

27 Crandon, J.H.; Lund, C.C.; Dill, D.B., *Experimental Human Scurvy*, New England Journal of Medicine, 1940, vol. 233, p. 353–369.

28 Scott, R.F. *Scott's Last Expedition vol 1*, Murray, London, 1935, p. 444.

29 Ibid., p.444.

30 Ibid., p. 445.

31 Ibid., p. 437.

32 Ed. King, H.G.R., *Edward Wilson, Diary of the Terra Nova Expedition to the Antarctic*, Blandford Press, London 1972, p. 243.

33 Taylor, G., *Letter to Stanley Richard*, 11/06/1962, Swansea Museum, Box 210, (Edgar Evans).

34 Debenham, F., *Journal*, 19/01/1911–08/03/1911 MS 279/2: BJp, p. 54.

35 Soloman, S., *The Coldest March*, Yale University Press, New Haven and London, 2001, p. 283.

36 Smith, M., *An Unsung Hero, The Remarkable Story of Tom Crean*, Headline Book Publishing, 2001, p. 309.

37 Hadley, M.D., *Nasal carriage of staphylococci in an Antarctic Community*. The Staphylococci, Proceedings of the Alexander Ogston Centennial Conference, Aberdeen University Press, 1981, p. 241–253.

38 Ibid., p. 239.

39 Ibid., p. 245.

40 Personal communication, Professor T.H. Pennington, University of Aberdeen, 2006.

41 Falckh, R.C.F., *The Death of Chief Petty Officer Evans*, Polar Record, 1987, 23 (145) p. 397.

42 Personal Communication, Robert Headland, Emeritus Associate, SPRI.

43 Huntford, R., *Scott & Amundsen*, Hodder and Stoughton, London, 1979, p. 328.

44 Chancroid is a sexually transmitted disease that causes a ragged ulcer at the site of the infection and is treated with antibiotics.

45 Davies, J., *The Last Journey*, Drama-documentary by Cardiff television and film company, Fflie. HTV Wales 31/07/2002, previously screened on Welsh TV company S4C, as *Y Daith Olaf.*

46 Scott, R.F., *Scott's Last Expedition vol 1*, Murray, London, 1935, p. 446.

47 Crean came to the fore when on the return journey to base camp, Lieutenant Evans became dangerously ill with scurvy. Crean undertook an amazing 18 hour solo walk to Hut Point. He and Lashly were awarded the Albert medal for saving Lieutenant Evans' life.

48 Debenham, F., Letter to Stanley Richards 25/05/1962, Swansea Museum, Box 201, Edgar Evans Red File.

49 Ibid.

50 Cherry-Garrard, A., *Diary*, SPRI, MS 559/4; BJ,.Vol 3 19/02/11–11/10/11 24/10/1911.

51 Debenham, F., Letter to Stanley Richards 25/05/1962, Swansea Museum, Box 201, Edgar Evans Red File.

52 *Times Weekly Edition*, 21/02/1913.

Epilogue

Terra Nova (carrying the Cardiff flag)[1] reached Cape Evans on 18 January 1913. The ship had been thoroughly cleaned and a celebratory meal prepared for the five who, it was assumed, had reached the Pole and come back safely. Their letters were in individual pillowcases with each man's name printed on it; *Terra Nova* carried supplies of chocolate, cigars and champagne – festive luxuries for all the men who had been marooned in Antarctica for months.

Teddy Evans had recovered from his scurvy. He had been promoted to Commander while he was in England and now he returned with the *Terra Nova*. He shouted across the water through a megaphone, 'Are you all well?'[2] The ominous pause that greeted his enquiry spoke volumes. The silence was followed eventually by Lieutenant Campbell's reply, 'the Southern Party reached the South Pole on January 18th last year, but were all lost on the return journey – we have their records'.[3] The news of the heroes' deaths was greeted with silent shock, flags were lowered to half mast, celebrations shelved and the letters re-stored, for return to those wives, mothers, family and friends who had written with such eager anticipation.

A 9ft cross was erected on Observation Hill, the hill that overlooked Hut Point, Edgar's home on the *Discovery* days. The cross recorded the names of the dead men and the final line of Tennyson's poem *Ulysses*, a tribute chosen by Cherry-Garrard:

To strive, to seek, to find and not to yield.

When *Terra Nova* reached New Zealand, press contracts required her to lay out to sea for twenty-four hours after the sad news had been cabled to Britain (on 11 February) and the next of kin informed. It was 12 February 1913 when she eventually entered Lyttelton harbour, her white ensign flying at half-mast. Here the crew found 'the Empire – almost the civilised world – in mourning. It was as though they had lost great friends'.⁴

At home, Lois heard the news on 11 February. She was in Gower. When the expedition funds had become seriously depleted after a year in Antarctica, volunteers in the crew, including Edgar, had offered to forgo their pay for twelve months. The decision had had a domino effect on the dependents and Lois and her children had moved back to Gower to live with her parents. She was on the beach with her youngest son, Ralph, when the telegram arrived. It was from New Zealand, sent by Commander Teddy Evans and forwarded from Portsmouth. It read simply: 'Members wish to express deepest sympathy in your sad loss.'⁵

The older children heard rumours of the disaster at school, but the full extent of their loss was only clarified when a journalist from the *South Wales Daily Post* arrived to interview Lois. The reporter, describing her condescendingly as 'quite a superior and refined little woman', wrote that she had said: ⁶

I received a bundle of letters last May, which had been brought to New Zealand by Commander Evans when he left the party.⁷ They were about fifty in number and covered the period of a whole year. The last one which though undated appeared either to have been written in December 1911 or January of last year was written in pencil. It stated that he was only 150 miles from the Pole and that the party were in good health and very confident of success. Since then I have heard nothing until this morning.⁸

From the first she stoically supported her man: she told the press, 'I have this consolation; my husband died bravely and it seems he did not have to undergo such suffering as the other members of the party went through.'[9] Her widowed mother-in-law, Mrs Sarah Evans, also rallied to the cause: 'I was always proud of my boy and am prouder than ever to know that he died a hero's death.'[10] But just a few days later a reporter from the *South Wales Daily Post* found Mrs Evans distressed at the rumour that it was 'through Edgar that the other members of the party had lost their lives'; Mrs Evans said, 'I'm worried because I feel that if he hadn't broken down they – Captain Scott and the rest of them – would have been alive to-day.' She went on, 'I can't help thinking about it all the time ever since I read about them being – forced to wait for him … Perhaps it would have been better if they had left him behind.'[11]

The reporter wrote that despite all efforts, the 'worthy old dame refused to be comforted'.[12]

A local memorial service was speedily arranged on Sunday 16 February in St Mary's church, Rhossili. Following this, mention was made in the *Gower Church Magazine* of that damaging phrase in Captain Scott's last message about, the 'strong man of the party - the man whom we had least expected to fail'. But the *Gower Church Magazine* went on: 'A thrill of sympathy was felt all over the world on receiving the tragic news of the death of the five heroes on their return journey after the discovery of the South Pole. Rich and poor have sent messages of heartfelt sympathy with those who have been stricken with grief and have suffered such a loss.'[13]

Memorial Services were held for Edgar in Cardiff and in chapels and churches throughout Gower. In Swansea's Albert Hall, prayers were offered for the bereaved of Gower,[14] and Lois did have valued support from many sources; Commander Teddy Evans had suffered his own bereavement when his wife, Hilda, died from peritonitis on the return from New Zealand. He had moved on from the days of his antagonism to Edgar and clearly empathised with Lois to whom he wrote a gracious and consoling letter:

Dear Mrs Evans,
I am writing to sympathise with you on your terrible bereavement.
Your husband died a gallant death on the return march from the Pole after faithfully serving his leader, Capt. Scott, through a most trying time
He lost his life for the honour of his country, and the British Navy will be proud of having possessed such a brave man. His 'grit' will for ever be an example to the lower deck, his ability was remarkable and I wish to convey to you from the whole expedition our sorrow.

I also write to tell you of the admiration we felt for your dead husband.
I shall soon be in England, and I will see that you and yours will never want.
If you are in immediate need write at once to:

Mr Wilkinson Green

Secretary to Sir Edgar Speyer, Bart,

7 Lothbury, London EC,

I cannot tell you how sorry I am for you.

Believe me,

Your sincere friend

Edward G.R. Evans

Commander R.N.[15]

This generous and supportive letter must have been a talisman to Lois that she could treasure. A letter from one of her husband's officers to cherish, words that would sustain and guard her and the children against all slights. Teddy Evans was as good as his word. He travelled to meet Lois to hand over Edgar's pocket book (sealed with two government seals and only to be opened by her). Yet another Evans, this time the Acting Secretary of the British Antarctic Expedition Committee, visited her and guaranteed that she and her children would receive enough money to cover their needs, until the relief fund, organised by his committee was in actual operation.

Lois said afterwards that, in relation to finance, she was pleased with the arrangements made for her future. The Admiralty had announced that the two naval representatives on the expedition, Scott and Edgar, would be treated as if they had been killed in action, so Lois received Admiralty and government pensions of approximately £91 p.a. and a lump sum of £96. The Admiralty pension included money for her children (2 shillings per week for each child until the boys were 14 and Muriel was 16),[16] though Lois had to prove her children were still alive each year before receiving the government pension.[17] Additionally she received income of £1,250 from a trust fund raised by voluntary subscription. International as well as national organisations had contributed to the fund; it was said that the widows and orphans were wards not only of England but of the Empire.[18] As well as these monies she had Edgar's British Antarctic Expedition salary of £44 per year.

All this was a relief to Lois; the total she received was a very significant figure to her, far more than a Petty Officer's salary and probably a larger sum than she had ever dreamed of (though the monies precluded her taking up an offer from the London Orphanage Asylum, to board and lodge and educate one of her children until the age of 15). The sum was, in fact, considerably less than the money allocated to Scott's widow Kathleen, who received a lump sum of £2,676, Admiralty and government pensions of £325 p.a. and the income from a combined trust fund of £12,000 in addition to Scott's British Antarctic Expedition salary and income from books and articles.[19] But the settlements granted to Lois, relatively modest as they were, gave her independence and dignity.

There were some national tributes: The Royal Humane Society's tribute of 11 February recorded 'its deepest sympathy and condolence to the relatives of Seaman (Petty Officer) Edgar Evans R.N'.[20] The British Schools and University Club of New York sent Lois a three-page address in careful calligraphy (saying that 'overcome in the Polar desert, they died for the honour of England').[21] *The Scotsman* of 17 February 1913 wrote that Edgar had been a splendid seaman and his Commander's faithful sledge comrade in the memorable inland expeditions. The *Daily Express* started a fund by selling Scott Memorial Booklets (6d for twelve).

Lois was not present at the memorial service in St Paul's cathedral, on 14 February, which was reported in *The Times* as a 'National Homage to the Dead'.[22] The mourners were led by King George and attended by representatives of the Scott, Oates, Bowers and Wilson families, but not Lois. It is not clear if she was invited. If so, perhaps she simply had not got the funds, or the inclination to travel to London so soon after receiving the news that she was a widow. It was a big occasion; attending were government ministers, Ambassadors and 'ministers of foreign states', national services, scientific societies and 'representatives of official life'. The *Dead March* from *Saul* was introduced by a roll of drums and was one of the most moving parts of the ceremony, which concluded with the National Anthem.[23] The Cathedral was full; an estimated 10,000 people were unable to get in. But Lois was pleased when, after the ceremony, Frank and Eliza Evans, the parents of Commander Evans, wrote to her saying that it was only the Will of Providence that had taken one Evans instead of another. 'We trust that you, your children and your husband's mother will in time recover from the effects of the terrible misfortune which has fallen upon you.'[24]

On 26 July King George V, with Prince Louis of Battenberg in attendance (a Lord Commissioner of the Admiralty), received the widows of those who had lost their lives in the expedition at an investiture in

Buckingham Palace. During the private ceremony the King presented the wives with the medals and clasps that had been awarded to their late husbands in an event that must have been overwhelming for Lois. These Polar Medals were octagonal and hung on ribbons on which engraved clasps were suspended, each clasp recording the dates of the expedition that the recipient had been on. Edgar had been awarded his Polar Medal and Clasp after the *Discovery* expedition, so Lois was presented with his 'Antarctic 1910–1913' clasp by the King in recognition of her husband's role.[25]

King George then went on to decorate surviving members of the expedition with their Antarctic Medals and Clasps (plus additional Albert Medals[26] to PO Crean and Chief Stoker William Lashly for their bravery in saving the life of Commander Evans). 'Birdie' Bowers' medal was then presented to his mother and Commander Evans accepted Oates' medal on behalf of the family.[27] There was a problem, however, over Edgar's actual 1902–04 medal; Lois had sold it,[28] presumably when she was in financial difficulties in the later years of the *Terra Nova* expedition. Subsequently a duplicate medal was made and given Lois in 1914.[29] Robert Swan carried this medal and the clasps to the South Pole on his 1984–86 expedition that followed Scott's 1911 route.[30]

In contrast to the other explorers, Edgar's death was not followed by an outpouring of Welsh (or British) patriotic grief. This can be explained in several ways. Firstly, those national newspapers which had expressed their reservations about Edgar's role, that he had 'let the side down', that his companions, by staying with him had imperilled their own lives,[31] had resulted in unease and, consequently, a reluctance to bang the nationalistic drum with too much fervour. If it was true that Edgar had been the weak link that brought the party down, especially if he had not faced death with the dignity of Captain Oates, then this was an outcome that could not be eulogised. Secondly, there was local suspicion that Edgar had neglected his family.[32] But Edgar had never meant to ignore his family. When he signed on he was due to retire from the Navy after a few years and he hoped that the years in Antarctica would actually secure their future. The expedition's finances were well out of his sphere. Other crew members left their wives and children. To criticise him for leaving Lois and the children in need is being wise after the event. Importantly, his family never doubted this; his father-in law and his wife praised him as a good father, son and husband. The third reason for reserve was the nationally deeply engrained Edwardian prejudices concerning rank and education.

There were a few attempts to raise support for a memorial in Wales. The Swansea newspaper *The Cambrian* called for there to be '… at Swansea or in Gower some permanent memorial to the honour of Petty Officer Evans, who thus links this locality with one of the most heroic exploits of the British race'.[33] The *South Wales Daily Post* reported the mayor of Swansea as saying, 'this is an occasion when the whole country will take the matter up. But there is also a local aspect and in movements of this kind Swansea has never been behind'.[34] But virtually nothing happened. Calls for a permanent memorial in South Wales fell on deaf ears. No specific memorial for Edgar appeared in Cardiff or Swansea, though a clock tower in the shape of a lighthouse, with the names of the Polar Party above the door, was presented to Cardiff city and sited by the lake in a city park.

The only memorial erected in the early years was put up in 1914, by Edgar's loyal, determined, widow.

The *Gower Church Magazine* reads:

A beautiful memorial tablet has been erected in Rhossili Church to the memory of the late Mr Edgar Evans Chief Petty Officer, who accompanied Captain Scott to the utmost point of the South Pole, and who perished on the return journey, to be much lamented by his widow and widowed mother, both at the time the news reached them residing at Rhossili Parish.[35]

The tablet is inscribed:

To the Glory of God
In the memory of
EDGAR EVANS[36]

The Rector, who had married Lois and Edgar nearly ten years earlier, told the congregation that Edgar would go down in history as 'one who was deemed worthy to be chosen among the few last out of the band of heroes to accompany Captain Scott to the South Pole'.[37] The Reverend Lewis Hughes said that Scott had valued Edgar as 'the strong man of the party, one with a wonderful head, equal to any emergency and brave in the face of difficulty'.[38] He added (optimistically) that Edgar would never be 'forgotten by his country or fade from its annals' and that the expedition had 're-taught a world growing more luxurious and effeminate, the glory of a soldier's endurance and capacity for stern duty'. He concluded (including Edgar in his comments, in spite of the pejorative comments concerning Edgar's education) that the 'expedition encouraged the possession of scientific courage to the last'.[39]

Edgar would not have cast himself in the heroic mould. He was a sailor who had made the most of his opportunities. Like many people he probably hoped to benefit from the remarkably successful ventures to which he had contributed. But Antarctica had become a fascination to him. Personal gain had not been the main motive for him taking part in sorties that had so significantly increased knowledge about the unknown continent for the benefit of Britain and the world. But equally, he did nothing to deserve the comments about his 'astonishing failure', which cast a long shadow. Mud sticks and Edgar was temporarily, if lightly, airbrushed out of the record of the Antarctic heroes. He was not mentioned in the 1920 or 1933 *Who's Who* of Wales. He is still not in the *Dictionary of Eminent Welshmen* or the *Dictionary of Welsh Biography*. Indeed, national recognition took years.

Even after the Second World War, appreciation came in small, slow steps. In 1948, Lois, by now the only wife remaining of the Polar Party, was an honoured guest at the premiere of the Royal Command film *Scott of the Antarctic* with her sons, Ralph and Norman. Edgar was played by the acclaimed actor, James Robertson Justice. The film gave belated recognition to Edgar's contribution to Scott's expeditions.

In 1954, Sarah Evans (the niece who had gone to wave goodbye to Edgar in Cardiff in 1910) recorded her reminiscences which were the basis of an article, *Edgar Evans: A Gower Hero*[40] written by Dr Gwent Jones, a founder member of the Gower Society. Later, a piece appeared in the *South Wales Evening Post*.[41] This reignited the enthusiasm of the curator of Swansea Museum, Mr Stanley Richards, who canvassed vigorously for greater recognition, at least in Wales, of Edgar's contributions. Mr Richards wrote about Edgar as *The Martyred Hero of Antarctica*, and mounted a vigorous crusade on Edgar's behalf. Specifically he campaigned for a local memorial in Swansea.

Major recognition came initially from outside Wales. In 1964 HMS *Excellent*, the Royal Naval Gunnery School at Whale Island, Portsmouth, built a new accommodation block for the petty officers; the building was named 'The Edgar Evans Building'. It had a plaque that commemorated Edgar and displayed a pair of original skis used during the expedition. This was an important piece of Naval social history; the building was the first to be named for a Petty Officer (rather than a famous admiral) and showed that, fifty years after his death, Edgar's contribution was being recognised – at least by the Navy. Members of Edgar's family attended the opening and the Second Sea Lord; Sir Royston Wright, spoke of Edgar's strength of character, devotion, loyalty and bravery.[42] The buildings were replaced in 2009 by a bigger, better accommodation block with a conference room and ballroom, but which retained Edgar's name. Opened by The Princess Royal in the presence of Edgar's grandson, John, and his great-grandson, Joshua, the buildings were named after two naval war heroes: Chief Gunner Israel Harding VC,[43] [44] Sergeant Norman Fitch VC[45] and Edgar. The plaque and skis remain in a prominent position.

In 1974, Dr A.F. Rogers, an Antarctic veteran, produced an article on Edgar's death in *The Practitioner*.[46] The article was of extreme importance because it was the first to consider in an objective manner, *medical* causes that could have contributed to Edgar's death. But critical assessments of Edgar's perceived disadvantages[47] and the inference he was not wholly loyal to Scott,[48] belittled his reputation in spite of other objective articles, which considered his medical problems.[49] [50]

Finally, in 1994, Swansea Council hosted a Civic Ceremony with Edgar's daughter Muriel, aged 87, as guest of honour. Camera artist Herbert Ponting's film of the *Terra Nova* expedition was shown and the Lord Lieutenant of West Glamorgan presented a bust of Edgar to the city. Here at last was the recognition that Edgar deserved. Sir Michael Llewellyn, the Lord Lieutenant, described Edgar as a very courageous man and the Lord Mayor of Swansea, reminding his audience that Edgar had his roots firmly in south-west Gower and suggesting that perhaps his recognition had been 'much too long in coming'.[51] Gary Gregor's appreciation of *Swansea's Antarctic Explorer*[52] was published in 1995.

Appreciation continued outside Wales. Books such as *Captain Scott* by Ranulph Fiennes,[53] *Antarctic Destinies* by Stephanie Barczewski,[54] and *A First Rate Tragedy* by Diana Preston[55] gave an unbiased assessment of Edgar's contribution. New Zealand survey expeditions preserved his name by naming two geographical features in the Ross Dependency after him: the Evans Piedmont Glacier, a low coastal ice sheet off Victoria Land named in the 1950s by a New Zealand survey party and the Evans Névé, named by a New Zealand geological survey in the 1960s.

Edgar's status and character is now being re-established after years of disparagement. Reappraisal of Scott's expedition, in relationship to current scientific knowledge, has produced physical reasons for his untimely death.

Those perceived defects, Edgar's rank and relative lack of education (factors completely beyond his control), are now understood to have played an insignificant role. Any doctor today, giving as his first diagnosis that Edgar's deterioration was due primarily to non-physical causes, could reasonably be accused of negligence. The implication that the lack of rational thought reflects inferiority and that rational thought is evidence of man at his highest level (and can protect a man by supplying him with greater reserves in adversity), is surely wrong. To suggest that Edgar could have avoided death, or faced it with greater composure, grit and courage if he had had a better education, is fanciful. The consolations of education and philosophy can only go so far. Any man facing death is more likely, if he can think at all, to be thinking of his immediate necessities, rather than of Virgil or other thinkers' philosophies.

In relation to the contrasting ways that Edgar and Captain Oates met their deaths, the situations are completely different. Oates was credited with meeting death in a magnificent, gentlemanly way because he remained in control of himself. He was able to articulate his last thoughts for his mother and his regiment, whilst Edgar was not able to make decisions or leave messages. But the reason that Oates remained in control of his actions was that, in contrast to Edgar, he was fully conscious throughout, only too horribly aware of his agonising gangrenous foot (which it is reasonable to assume obliterated the comforting solaces of philosophy or education). Although Oates may have wished for the relief of diminished consciousness, he remained, perforce, fully cognisant. He was able to make a decision, therefore, on when he thought that all hope for recovery or survival was finished and when his condition was materially damaging his companion's chances. Then, he ended his life for the benefit of his comrades. If Edgar had been aware of what was happening to him, he might well have done the same, but in his toxic and confused state he had no control over the way he died.

Edgar is now mentioned in the *Oxford Companion to the Literature of Wales*[56] and the *Oxford Dictionary of National Biography*.[57] He fully deserves his heroic place in Antarctic history: for his contributions to the *Discovery* expedition when with Scott and Lashly, he was in the first group to travel on the plateau and, on their return, to make the striking geographical discoveries of the Dry Valleys in the Western Mountains; for his contributions to the *Terra Nova* expedition, his expertise and practicality as sledging expert, his willingness to impart this knowledge to his colleagues, his humour and his self-control, right up until the last days of the final Polar Assault.

Scott appreciated his numerous gifts and Edgar reciprocated with a loyalty that endured despite the divisions of class, rank and education. He died as he had lived – doing his best.

Notes

1 *Western Mail*, 13/02/1913.
2 *Nottingham Guardian*, 13/02/1913.
3 Pound, R., *Evans of the Broke*, Oxford University Press, Oxford, 1963, p. 123.
4 Cherry-Garrard, A., *The Worst Journey in the World*, Picador, London, 2001, p. 593.
5 *Morning Post*, 12/02/1913.
6 *Morning Post*, 12/02/1913.
7 Lieutenant Teddy Evans suffered very badly, almost fatally, from scurvy when he led the final Supporting Party back from the plateau in 1912. He returned to England on the *Terra Nova*.
8 All these letters appear to have been destroyed.
9 *Morning Post*, 12/02/1913.
10 *South Wales Daily Post*, 12/02/1913.
11 *Cambrian*, 21/02/1913.
12 Ibid.
13 *Gower Church Magazine*, 17/02/1913.
14 Gregor, G.C., *Swansea's Antarctic Explorer: Edgar Evans 1876–1912*, Swansea City Council, 1995, p. 73.
15 *South Wales Daily Post*, 13/02/1913.
16 Jones, M., *The Last Great Quest*, Oxford University Press, Oxford, 2003, p. 108.
17 Ibid., p.107.
18 *Times*, 19/02/1913.
19 Jones, M., *The Last Great Quest*, Oxford University Press, Oxford, 2003, p. 108.
20 Sotheby's catalogue, SPRI 07/10/1984.
21 Ibid.
22 *Times*, Saturday, 15 February 1913, p. 8, issue 40136; Col A.
23 *Western Mail*, 15/02/1913.
24 *Cambrian*, 21/02/1913.
25 Ibid.
26 The Albert Medal was first issued in 1866 and discontinued in 1971. Originally issued for saving life at sea, it was extended in 1877 to cover saving life on land.
27 *Times*, Monday 28 July 1913, p. 9, Issue 40275, Col A. Court Circular.
28 Personal communication, John Evans, Edgar's grandson, 2010.

29 Yelverton, D., *Antarctic Unveiled*, University Press of Colorado, Boulder, Appendix 8.

30 Mear, R.; Swan, R., *In the Footsteps of Scott*, Jonathan Cape, London, 1987. p. 142.

31 *Times*, 06/11/1913.

32 Gregor, G., *Swansea's Antarctic Explorer Edgar Evans 1876–1912*, Swansea City Council, Swansea, 1995, p. 82.

33 *Cambrian*, 14/02/1913.

34 *South Wales Daily Post*, 14/02/1913.

35 *Gower Church Magazine*, March 1914.

36 There were two mistakes on this commemorative tablet. The words 'to seek, to strive, to find and not to yield' were written on it rather than, 'to strive, to seek, to find' and in the relief above the tablet the explorers were depicted with one ski-stick (as had been used in *Discovery* days) rather than two.

37 *Gower Church Magazine*, March 1914.

38 Ibid.

39 Ibid.

40 Jones, G., *Edgar Evans: A Gower Hero*, Gower, 1954, vol. vii.

41 *South Wales Evening Post*, 05/02/1954.

42 *Portsmouth Evening News*, 18/12/1964.

43 Victoria Cross. This is the highest military decoration. It is awarded for valour in the face of the enemy to members of the armed forces of the Commonwealth countries.

44 Israel Harding, 1833–1917. Victoria Cross awarded for Harding's bravery in defusing a live shell that landed on HMS *Alexandra* in Alexandria in 1882. His action saved many lives.

45 Norman Finch 1890–1966. Victoria Cross awarded for his defence of HMS *Vindictive* at Zeebrugge in 1918, when, severely wounded, he continued to defend the ship against enemy fire, firing from an exposed position and saving many lives.

46 Rogers, A.F., *The Death of Chief Petty Officer Evans*, The Practitioner, *212*, 1974.

47 Huntford, R., *Scott and Amundsen*, Hodder and Stoughton, London 1979, p. 522.

48 Ibid., p. 520.

49 Falckh, R.C.F., *The Death Of Chief Petty Officer Evans*, Polar Record, 1987, 23(145).

50 Williams, I., *Edward Wilson, medical aspects of his life and career*, Polar Record, 2008, *44* (228).

51 Gregor, G., *Swansea's Antarctic Explorer Edgar Evans 1876–1912*, Swansea City Council, Swansea, 1995, p. 82.

52 Ibid.

53 Fiennes, R., *Captain Scott*, Hodder and Stoughton, London, 2003.

54 Barczewski, S., *Antarctic Destinies*, Hambledon Continuum, London, 2007.

55 Preston, D., *A First Rate Tragedy*, Constable, London, 1997.

56 Ed. Stephens, M., *Oxford Companion to the Literature Of Wales*, Oxford University Press, 1986, p. 187.

57 *Oxford Dictionary of National Biography*, Oxford University Press, 2004, p. 680–681.

Index

Other titles published by The History Press

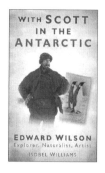

With Scott in the Antarctic: Edward Wilson: Explorer, Naturalist, Artist

ISOBEL WILLIAMS £13.49

Edward Wilson (1872–1912) accompanied Robert Falcon Scott on both his celebrated Antarctic voyages: the *Discovery* expedition of 1901–4 and the *Terra Nova* expedition of 1910–13. Wilson and his four companions died on the return journey. This biography, the first full account of the Antarctic hero, traces his life from childhood to his tragic death.

978-0-7524-5246-3

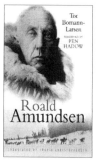

Roald Amundsen

TOR BOMANN-LARSEN, TRANSLATED BY INGRID CHRISTOPHERSEN £14.99

Roald Amundsen was the first person to reach the South Pole and December 2011 marks the centenary of this achievement. The only full biography of the Polar explorer to be published in English, this work uncovers his life, using accounts from his diaries and his own books. It explores the drama, humour, and adventure of his life, and reveals the character of a man who was prepared to do anything to reach his goal.

978-0-7509-4344-4

James Fitzjames: the Mystery Man of the Franklin Expedition

WILLIAM BATTERSBY £18.00

James Fitzjames was a hero of the early nineteenth-century Royal Navy. When he joined the Franklin Expedition at the age of 32 he thought he would make his name. But instead the expedition completely disappeared and he never returned. Its fate is one of history's great unsolved mysteries, as were the origins and background of James Fitzjames – until now. A fascinating biography drawn on personal letters and journals, most never published before.

978-0-7524-5512-9

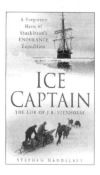

Ice Captain: a Forgotten Hero of Shackleton's Endurance Expedition: the Life of J.R. Stenhouse

STEPHEN HADDELSEY £18.00

Much has been written on Antarctic explorer Ernest Shackleton, but this is the story of the Endurance Expedition's other hero, J.R. Stenhouse (1887–1941), who, as captain of the SS Aurora, freed the ship from pack ice and rescued the survivors of the Ross Sea shore party. He was later appointed to command Captain Scott's *Discovery*.

978-0-7509-4348-2

Visit our website and discover thousands of other History Press books.

www.thehistorypress.co.uk

8836332R00116

Printed in Great Britain
by Amazon.co.uk, Ltd.,
Marston Gate.